*f*P

THE
NEW
MARKET
LEADERS

---

*Who's Winning and How
in the Battle for Customers*

Fred Wiersema

THE FREE PRESS

New York London Toronto Sydney Singapore

*f*P

THE FREE PRESS
A Division of Simon & Schuster, Inc.
1230 Avenue of the Americas
New York, NY 10020

Book design by Susan Hood

Manufactured in the United States of America

1   3   5   7   9   10   8   6   4   2

Library of Congress Cataloging-in-Publication Data
is available.

ISBN 0-7432-0465-4

to Catherine and Annelise,
my supreme loves

Contents

The New Market Leaders

CHAPTER 1

Meet the New Market Leaders

The idea for this book originated during a World Economic Forum summit meeting in 1996. Over lunch, I joined a number of U.S. and European executives in an animated discussion about the emerging Internet economy. In the United States, some of the Europeans noted, managers appear fascinated by colorful stories about upstarts, whereas in Europe they show a bias for hard data and solid track records. "Tell me," one person asked, "when you watch all the hype about the Web and these New Economy players, how do you size up their true influence and potential?" With no satisfactory answer, it occurred to me that we needed a fresh way to look at companies' performance and market strategies, and one that would apply to both conventional and new businesses.

Consider: When *Fortune* magazine surveyed more than ten thousand executives, directors, and securities analysts to compile its 1999 list of most-admired companies, Caterpillar Inc. led the industrial and farm equipment suppliers, and Merrill Lynch & Co., Inc., the securities firms.

The question is, did *Fortune*'s list really identify the role models for the New Economy? Did it pick out those companies that strongly influence how the marketplace is evolving in this era of unprecedented competition? These questions assume critical importance as managers try to cope with today's challenges.

When I designed my own list of the top 100 new market leaders that same year, Caterpillar and Merrill Lynch were not on it. And that was only the beginning of where the lists differed.

My list included then (as it still does) Yahoo! Inc., QUALCOMM Inc., Amazon.com, Inc., Amgen Inc., Solectron Corporation, Infinity Broadcasting Corporation, and Carnival Corporation. These highfliers and others whose names you recognize instantly—because their appeal to customers and performances in the stock market over the past several years have been nothing short of phenomenal—were not even mentioned on *Fortune*'s 1999 roll of honor. A year later, *Fortune* still had not recognized them.

How can that be? To start, I cast a much broader net to find the most influential companies. Unlike my friends at *Fortune*, I didn't restrict my list to the ten largest corporations in each industry, which rules out up-and-coming companies. And I gave much greater weight to the one success factor that I consider absolutely critical in the New Economy: an organization's ability to attract valuable customers, both now and in the future. This is vital because today's most serious business challenge doesn't involve implementing new management techniques, raising capital, or any of the familiar bugaboos of recent decades. Today's most serious business challenge, as we shall see, is a scarcity of customers.

It seems that times are changing faster and becoming more uncertain with each turbulent day, and questions are emerging from everywhere: How will the Internet affect brick-and-mortar retailing? Will today's upstarts become tomorrow's dominant players? Should we simply improve our current practices, or do we need to revolutionize the ways we operate?

Broadly speaking, there are three ways that companies deal with such questions, none of which is perfect.

- First, market-leading companies such as Microsoft Corporation and Sony Corporation take the future in their own hands by creating it, thus setting a standard for others to follow. Still, in spite of their tremendous success in shaping demand, these firms have setbacks when the marketplace doesn't follow their lead, as Sony did when its Betamax VCR format succumbed to VHS.

- Second, companies may anticipate the future by understanding the trends and undercurrents at the root of change—technological, demographic, or social trends—and then figuring out how these affect their businesses. For example, Royal Dutch/Shell is famous for its long-term-scenario planning. Finland's Nokia Corporation and Japan's NTT DoCoMo, Inc., are well known for anticipating their customers' explosive demand for cellular services. This approach suffers, however, when it comes to the kind of abrupt, revolutionary change represented by the Internet.

- Third, companies may simply try to learn from others at the forefront of change. Cisco Systems, Inc., has a knack for spotting new ventures that are developing breakthrough technologies, and then acquiring those companies. To quench its thirst for knowledge, the General Electric Company sends teams of people around the world to learn from innovative companies such as Cisco.

This book endorses all three approaches, with an emphasis on the third—learning from successful companies. Also, it offers a new logic to identify both promising up-and-comers that are transforming the way business is done and veteran companies

3

whose experience and time-tested practices continue to exert inordinate influence in the marketplace. Eclipsing the others are the one hundred new market leaders, a collection of businesses that are stellar by almost any standard.

In this group, we find a hundred companies that, in the six years ending in May 2000, increased their sales, on average, *three times* faster than their peers. (In comparison, the hundred most-admired corporations on *Fortune's* list grew a little more than twice as fast as their peers.) In addition, we find a hundred enterprises whose investors earned an average annual return of *48 percent* since 1994. This surpassed not only *Fortune's* hundred most-admired corporations (which returned on average 29 percent per year) but all major stock market indices, including the hot Nasdaq, which went up 32 percent per year in the same time period, and the more staid Dow Jones Industrials, which returned 20 percent. In fact, the top 100 market leaders' return was more than three times higher than the return on the average stock in the 5,009 companies that I have been tracking. Those stocks returned an average of just 14 percent per year. (Mind you, we are talking about five extraordinary years.)

What these companies share, beyond their outstanding performance, is an awareness of today's most crucial challenge: the scarcity of customers. Customer scarcity should not be construed to mean that there aren't an enormous number of customers or that they aren't buying enough. In fact, never in history have there been more customers whose collective buying power has been more formidable. The problem is that the typical company, battling increasingly voracious competitors for customers' shortening attention, does not see or feel this awesome buying power, because, paradoxically, supply and demand get out of synch when markets undergo the kind of turbulence they are undergoing today.

Surging productivity has created such an abundance of products and services that customers—at least those in the industrialized world—can barely keep up with them all. At the same time, customers have unmet needs. It's like when everyone brings a covered dish to a neighborhood picnic and you end up with far too much food but no one has brought dessert.

Meanwhile, rampant innovation causes supply and demand to misalign until customers catch up to the new products and suppliers get a better handle on what customers like and don't like. The net effect is that supply is plentiful and demand becomes a bottleneck—customer scarcity. While there may, in fact, be a vast number of buyers, that is not the perception of anyone trying to close a sale. This is not necessarily bad news. For those who know how to capitalize on it, the flip side of any problem is an opportunity.

As always, a key to business success is knowing how to exploit scarcity wherever it appears—a concept as useful to modern art dealers, IPO managers, and Ivy League colleges as it was to Scythian goldsmiths three thousand years ago. In the past when raw materials were hard to procure, they were more prized. It was no coincidence that the foremost steel companies owned iron pits and coal mines. If the need for vast manufacturing plants put a premium on capital, the leading companies were those that knew how to accumulate and deploy it. Then the information revolution made talented workers the most vital resource. The ability to attract and retain talent is one reason why businesses like General Electric (number 2 on my current list of new market leaders) and Microsoft (number 3) have maintained their prominence. More than any other factor, it is lack of customers that constrains a company's growth; it is not a scarcity of natural resources, capital, or talent.

In an era when customers are bombarded with choices, the new market leader has figured out why customers favor one choice over another, and more important, uses that insight to improve the odds of becoming their choice—time after time. Today's leader is the company that views customer loyalty as a fragile condition that requires fastidious attention. We are going to explore the realities of competition in markets where customers are, according to my definition, scarce. While *Fortune's* most-admired rankings pay homage to accomplishments from a bygone era, I identify the leaders already shaping the marketplace of the future—the exciting, unorthodox companies that will transform the way we do business in the twenty-first century. (To be fair, *Fortune* now has a separate list of the Internet's top 50 e-businesses.)

It does not matter whether a company's market leadership derives primarily from customer intimacy, operational excellence, or product leadership. (Those are the three disciplines that my coauthor and I identified in our 1995 book, *The Discipline of Market Leaders.* Customer intimacy produced best total solution, operational excellence led to lowest total cost, and product leadership yielded best product.) A market leader must now expect to meet challengers that match or surpass its own expertise.

Intense competition for customers is driving companies to excel at every level. For example, the Home Depot, Inc. (number 6 on my list), is not alone among hardware retailers in its preoccupation with customer intimacy. Wal-Mart Stores, Inc. (number 7), retains its operational excellence but must do battle with a number of other best-cost rivals. And Intel Corporation (number 4) is far from the world's only producer of leading-edge computer chips.

In other words, top performers don't necessarily stay on top. The bar is higher; yesterday's star is today's also-shone. Just as the four-minute mile was converted from an impossible dream to the standard for any world-class distance runner, so a compelling value proposition has become the starting point for today's market leaders.

To dominate their industries, companies must view each and every customer's buying decision—whether it is a repeat purchase or a new order—as a contest to be won against a host of competitive alternatives. To achieve and sustain competitive advantage, the winner must master additional market strategies aimed at coping with the new challenge of customer scarcity. My purpose is to identify those strategies and to show how they apply to all customers, whether businesses or individuals.

The winners of this race—the new market leaders—have discovered how to attract the customers who everyone else seeks.

THE FIRST MEASURE OF A NEW MARKET LEADER

How do you spot today's most influential companies? I evaluated a number of methods with which to answer that question, including the prevailing wisdom that has guided our thinking for decades: Market leaders are the largest companies in any industry. Implicitly, and often without thinking, we have equated leadership with size. But today, size is deceptive. It blinds us to the growing likelihood that giants stumble and that the meteoric rise of up-and-coming businesses will profoundly shake up industries. In the battle between David and Goliath, the giant's size was irrelevant (perhaps even the fatal weakness) when matched against the shepherd boy's agility and technology.

Most important is the fact that size in itself provides no compelling reason for customers to prefer one company over another. Customers gladly patronize smaller businesses if these are more attentive to their needs. This is the reason I decided against ranking companies on the basis of their sales revenues. While that is the method used to rank the Fortune 500 and other venerable lists, it is not designed to detect up-and-coming highfliers. (To illustrate: My top 100 list includes thirty-three companies that were too small to appear on either the domestic or global Fortune 500 radar screen.)

Another method for evaluating companies' influence is surveying people familiar with them, which is how *Fortune* and the *Financial Times* conduct their research on admired and respected organizations. But since that approach is nearly impossible to apply to more than a few hundred companies, all but an established, select group in each industry are excluded.

How about using market share as the guiding yardstick? Again, the drawbacks outweigh the appeal. Beyond the practical difficulty of obtaining this information, there is the problem of defining what constitutes a market. If you define it narrowly, your market share will be higher than if you include all conceivable competitors in the equation. And because market share and sales are so strongly related, we would once again be likely to exclude up-and-coming businesses.

Instead of resorting to these commonly used measures, I look for companies with a proven—by which I mean repeated—ability to win the battle for customers. I want to identify the influential companies whose business strategies make them prosper while others run into difficulty. My ideal company has a special gift for shaping market demand, for changing and raising customer expectations, thereby earning itself the status of standard setter. The single criterion that best exemplifies this is a company's ability to establish and grow customer franchises. Attracting customers is the key to market leadership in this new age, so sales growth is the number to watch. Yet traditional year-end lists of top companies can be too easily swayed by transient results: A new product soars for a year and then fades, for example. So I decided to look at sustained sales growth over the six-year period ending May 31, 2000.

Casting my net as wide as possible, including both domestic and global companies, I gave as much attention to information-based and technology-driven industries as to industrial and service businesses. Both large and small companies were included, and both established and emerging companies were recognized as long as they influenced their markets equally. To reflect today's global business environment, I included companies based outside of the United States whose stocks are traded here or on major international exchanges. However, I excluded privately held companies because they don't provide sufficient information to judge their performances accurately.

Ultimately, the research covered 5,009 companies, about a quarter of which are based outside the United States. Together they account for some 80 percent of the global market value of all stocks.

To level the playing field, I compared each company's growth record with that of a peer group that included twenty other organizations of similar size competing for the same customers. I simply divided each company's sales growth, expressed in dollar terms, by the average sales growth of its peer group and called the resulting number the *sales-growth index*. An index of 1.0 means the company grew as fast as its peers. An index of 2.0 means it grew twice as fast as its peer group average. (Please see the Appendix for more details on the methodology used to compose peer groups and to calculate companies' standings.)

Several factors make the sales-growth index my preferred indicator of a company's competitive prowess. One is that it assumes that customers are the ultimate arbiter of success. The only way to *increase* your sales is to get customers to *change* their buying decisions; merely repeating the same purchases isn't enough. (As I explain in the Appendix, I'm looking at companies' organic sales growth, not growth by acquisition or merger.) Growing faster than your peers requires convincing customers to cast their votes for you instead of others. Another strength of the index is that it compares companies with similar competitors, just as bantamweight boxers square off against other bantamweights, and welterweights against welterweights.

The most surprising statistic I found was that the average sales-growth index of the top 100 new market leaders was 3.1. In other words, their sales grew at an astonishing rate of three times that of their peers. Looking at all of the new market leaders (which I will define shortly) and not just the top 100, we see that their average sales-growth index was 2.0, meaning they grew twice as fast as their peers. Not only has this finding held up over the several years that I have been studying these numbers; the gap between top performers and their peers is, in fact, widening.

Clearly, this is telling us that it isn't enough to perform as well as your peers. The true implication is what I describe as the sales-growth imperative. That is:

Unless you are growing at twice the pace of your peers, you're at risk of falling behind in the race for market leadership.

No doubt this represents a stretch for any company. Yet it is the pace set by new market leaders such as Cisco Systems, Wal-Mart, and Sony, each of which increased its sales in the past six years by more than its four closest competitors *combined*. It's a pace that makes you question whether companies such as the Home Depot, which grew at an annual 28 percent for the past six years, have any room left for expansion. (The answer is that they do.) It's a pace that becomes truly mind-boggling when you consider rapid-growth, Internet-driven markets that are doubling in size each year, making it necessary for leaders such as Ariba, Inc., to grow at more than 200 percent annually just to secure their position.

Yes, growing at twice the pace of your peers is daunting. But that's what defines the winners in the age of customer scarcity, which is the challenge we will focus on.

THE SECOND MEASURE OF A NEW MARKET LEADER

The sales-growth index provides a powerful indicator of a company's ability to win customers. What it does not do is shed light on prospects for continued growth and success. Has growth come at the expense of profitability? Were new customers short-term buyers? Did the company convert its success with customers into solid and sustainable business results? Without answers to these questions, the sales-growth index can be very misleading.

To use an extreme case, consider CHS Electronics, Inc., a computer products distributor that caught my eye a few years ago. Its sales in the previous five years grew at an almost unbelievable eleven times the pace of its peers. Even so, the company ran into serious difficulty, forcing it to file for protection under Chapter 11 of the bankruptcy laws just a year later, despite the facts that the company's sales had grown to $8.5 billion in 1998 and that its high volumes enabled it to negotiate attractive deals with its vendors. Ultimately, the company failed to run a highly efficient operation in an industry known for its wafer-thin profit margins. It didn't help that its overlapping business units often competed against one another for customers. Having a very large customer base was of no import when other performance dimensions suffered.

Clearly, additional measurement tools were needed for determining the value of attracting and keeping customers.

Of course, companies track results in a variety of ways, from operating margins to net profits and from return on equity to earnings growth. Current profitability could have been used as a yardstick. But profits can vary widely from year to year, and moreover, this would have eliminated many successful companies that have temporarily suffered losses—American Home Products, Sprint Corporation, the Seagram Company Ltd., and Toshiba Corporation are examples. Using profit as a yardstick also eliminates many New Economy players, such as Amazon.com and BUY.COM Inc., which influence customers' buying patterns and the evolution of the retail marketplace considerably yet have never shown even a dollar of profit. In any case, these measurements tell only where a company is today.

In time, it became clear that the most useful indicator of a company's future prospects would incorporate the judgment of the millions of people who determine its market valuation every day: stock market investors. That's the logic behind *Business*

Week's Global 1000, *Forbes*'s International 500, and the Financial Times 500 scorecards. But again, looking only at market value would overemphasize size, and most likely not reflect an organization's competitive vigor. Ultimately, I decided to consider a company's market value only in relation to sales; that is, my aim was to figure out what each customer was worth to investors.

This reasoning is not unprecedented. In the spring of 1999, America Online Inc. bought Netscape Communications Corp. for $9 billion, essentially to purchase rapid access to millions of Netscape customers. The industry and the press labeled the practice "capturing eyeballs," and the term was uttered repeatedly in testimony during Microsoft's antitrust hearings. In essence, America Online (and many companies before it) placed a dollar value on each customer, then projected the company's future earnings from that perspective. The phrase "monetizing eyeballs" also entered the vocabulary.

Microsoft followed the same logic in 1997 when it spent close to $400 million to buy Hotmail, Inc., an e-mail services provider. Microsoft was more interested in Hotmail's 10 million subscribers than in its technology or profit stream (which was nonexistent) when it paid almost $40 per customer. Today, three years later, that price seems like a bargain when compared with the value of telecommunications customers. As the *Economist* reported, the German company Mannesmann AG acquired the British telecom company Orange PLC a few years ago for about $9,600 per customer. France Telecom SA paid about 4,200 Euros (or about $4,700) per customer when it bought E-Plus, a German mobile phone firm, while Deutsche Telekom AG acquired a British mobile phone company, One 2 One Personal Communications, Ltd., at a price of about 5,000 Euros ($5,600) per customer.

In a similar vein, I put a price tag on a company's customer franchise by calculating how much a dollar of its sales was worth to its investors. Once again, to maintain a level playing field, I compared each company's numbers with those of a peer group including twenty similarly sized businesses competing for the same customers. Richly valued up-and-comers such as Yahoo! (number 5 on my list) were compared with other richly valued newcomers, which immediately cast their sky-high market values in a different light. Likewise, larger, established businesses were compared with their equivalents. For each company, I divided how much investors were willing to pay for a dollar of sales into the average amount they were willing to pay for a dollar of sales of the company's peer group. For simplicity's sake, I call the resulting number the *market-value index*. As before, an index of 1.0 means you're at par with your peers. (For more details on the methodology, please see the Appendix.)

On the average, the new market leaders in my research had a market-value index of 2.1. That means investors believed each dollar of their sales was worth more than twice that of their peer group—in other words, their customer franchise was judged to be very valuable. It also means that the market leaders had a superior ability to attract investment capital for every dollar of sales, which permits them to fuel their own growth and invest in opportunities unaffordable to others.

A prime example is Cisco Systems. By valuing each dollar of Cisco's sales at 5.5 times that of its not-exactly-undervalued peers, investors boosted Cisco's vast war chest of what analysts called Cisco dollars—that is, highly valued shares of stock. In recent years, Cisco used the equity to acquire sixty-five companies, all to enhance its product and service offerings, and thus to solidify its lead in the marketplace. All in all, the market-value index proved to be an indispensable complement to the sales-growth index for evaluating the 5,009 companies in my database.

MEET THE NEW MARKET LEADERS

To narrow the field to the truly outstanding performers, I focused on companies whose results were better than their peer group average in *both* performance measurements—attracting customers and turning them into a highly valued future customer franchise.

Among the database of 5,009 companies, almost a third, or 1,779, expanded their sales faster than their peers. But of these, 1,139 had a below-average market-value index.

Likewise, a total of 1,642 companies had a market-value index larger than that of their peers, but of those, 1,002 didn't increase their sales as rapidly.

That left 640 companies that outperformed their peers according to both criteria. This is the group I consider new market leaders, which, surprisingly, represents just 13 percent of the investigated companies. In other words, the odds of being above average on the two measures are only one in eight, while seven out of eight analyzed organizations fell short in one area or another.

Of these 640 new market leaders, this book features those that are superior to all others: the top 100 companies. As said, on average they grew three times faster than their peers and earned an annual 48 percent return for their investors. Here they are in order of overall performance:

1. Cisco Systems, Inc.
2. General Electric Company
3. Microsoft Corporation
4. Intel Corporation
5. Yahoo! Inc.
6. The Home Depot, Inc.
7. Wal-Mart Stores, Inc.
8. Oracle Corporation
9. Nokia Corporation
10. AOL Time Warner
11. JDS Uniphase Corporation
12. NTT DoCoMo, Inc.

13. Pfizer, Inc.
14. Dell Computer Corporation
15. EMC Corporation
16. Sprint PCS Group
17. Amazon.com, Inc.
18. Citigroup Inc.
19. QUALCOMM Incorporated
20. Nextel Communications, Inc.
21. Amgen Inc.
22. Enron Corp.
23. Broadcom Corporation
24. American International Group, Inc.
25. Sun Microsystems, Inc.
26. Telefonaktiebolaget LM Ericsson
27. Medtronic, Inc.
28. Network Appliance, Inc.
29. Vodafone Group Plc
30. Sony Corporation
31. Hewlett-Packard Company
32. Softbank Corp.
33. Nortel Networks Corporation
34. Toyota Motor Corporation
35. United Parcel Service, Inc.
36. Palm, Inc.
37. Lucent Technologies Inc.
38. i2 Technologies, Inc.
39. CIENA Corporation
40. The Coca-Cola Company
41. Paychex, Inc.
42. Siebel Systems, Inc.
43. Morgan Stanley Dean Witter & Co.
44. Vivendi SA
45. McDonald's Corporation
46. Medimmune, Inc.

47. L'Oreal SA
48. Berkshire Hathaway Inc.
49. SAP AG
50. The Gap, Inc.
51. Taiwan Semiconductor Manufacturing Company
52. The Charles Schwab Corporation
53. Tyco International, Ltd.
54. Viacom Inc.
55. SK Telecom Co Ltd
56. Wells Fargo & Company
57. Bank of America Corporation
58. Gemstar-TV Guide International, Inc.
59. International Business Machines Corporation
60. Murata Manufacturing Company Ltd.
61. H & M Hennes & Mauritz AB
62. EchoStar Communications Corporation
63. British Sky Broadcasting Plc
64. E. I. du Pont de Nemours and Company
65. PMC-Sierra, Inc.
66. Solectron Corporation
67. Agilent Technologies, Inc.
68. Ariba, Inc.
69. Eli Lilly & Company
70. Schlumberger, Ltd.
71. Infinity Broadcasting Corporation
72. Kohl's Corporation
73. MBNA Corporation
74. Applied Materials, Inc.
75. Genentech, Inc.
76. Comcast Corporation
77. Sage Group Plc
78. Priceline.com, Incorporated
79. Schering-Plough Corporation
80. Fannie Mae

 81. Bombardier Inc.
 82. Royal Dutch/Shell Group
 83. Infosys Technologies Limited
 84. Flextronics International
 85. Allianz AG
 86. Marsh & McLennan Companies, Inc.
 87. The Walt Disney Company
 88. Amdocs, Ltd.
 89. Lloyds TSB Group Plc
 90. Bristol-Myers Squibb Company
 91. Koninklijke Philips Electronics NV
 92. E*Trade Group, Inc.
 93. Cox Communications, Inc.
 94. Forsakrings AB Skandia
 95. Carnival Corporation
 96. Firstar Corporation
 97. Walgreen Co.
 98. At Home Corporation
 99. UnitedHealth Group
100. Omnicom Group, Inc.

The top four—Cisco, General Electric, Microsoft, and Intel—should come as no surprise. They have been touted and well covered in the business press for some time. Others that are high on the list didn't exist six years ago (such as Yahoo!, number 5), or were a fraction of their current size: JDS Uniphase (number 11), a communications technology company, and NTT DoCoMo (number 12), the world's most prominent mobile phone company. Six years ago, AOL was only a tiny, scrambling enterprise. Now the combined AOL Time Warner organization ranks tenth on my list. (This assumes that their merger will be completed. If I were placing AOL alone, I would rank it third. Time Warner alone would rank 55.)

Aside from General Electric, several other very large companies—Home Depot (number 6) and Wal-Mart (number 7)—

grew at an annual 30 to 40 percent rate, a pace normally associated with much smaller firms. Home Depot quadrupled its sales
in six years, while Wal-Mart expanded from $75 billion in 1993
to an astonishing $156 billion at the close of the millennium.

Among the many companies that I will discuss in more detail
later in this book are EMC (number 15), the leader in data storage, and Amgen, ranked 21, which distinguished itself in the
pharmaceuticals field. Moving down the list, Toyota (number 34)
is the only automotive company that made the top 100. UPS, at
number 35, emerged as the leader in its field. Other less known
companies that deserve attention are handheld computer maker
Palm (number 36), Paychex, a provider of payroll services, which
came in at 41, and Solectron (number 66), a contract manufacturer of electronics products.

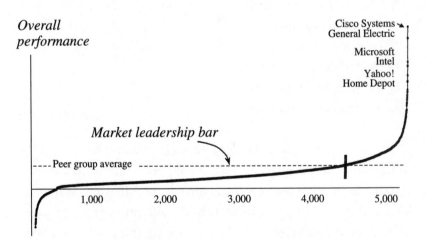

Figure 1. How 5,009 companies fared against one another

To show just how much the new market leaders stand out, I've
lined up all 5,009 companies in my database in order of overall
performance. In the graph (see Figure 1), the market leaders appear at the far right. We can see in one glance that there is a huge
difference in performance between the top-ranked companies and
the rest of the field, and catching up to them will be a tough task

for any challenger. Beyond the top performers, however, the differences become less distinct, with numerous companies within striking distance of the dividing line between leaders and laggards.

In all, the top 100 are a mix of large, small, high-tech, low-tech, service, and manufacturing businesses from all over the world. A quarter of the top 100 companies are based outside the United States, which is consistent with the proportion of non-U.S. companies in the database. While some industries are better represented than others, new market leaders are found in nearly every one.

Covering the top 100 new market leaders, as well as the next one hundred highest-ranking companies, Exhibit 1 (at the end of the book) shows the rankings and other statistics by industry category. Sorting them geographically, Exhibit 2 provides a more detailed look at all of the non-U.S.-based companies that passed the market leadership bar.

In the final tally, some household names did not make the top 100 list. For example, Ford Motor Company, Philip Morris Companies Inc., AT&T Corp., and Eastman Kodak Company are not on the list because their market-value index fell short of their peers. The same is true for BP Amoco Plc, Hitachi, Ltd., and Credit Suisse Group.

Still, let me be clear about the companies omitted from the new market leader list. The exclusion of those just mentioned and others does not imply that they lack either vigor or competitive strength. On the contrary, many of them are fierce competitors with stellar track records. More than a few of their managers could make the case that, judged by other yardsticks, or against a differently composed peer group, their performances were, indeed, above average. Others will argue that investors failed to appreciate their companies' true strengths, hence undervalued their stock. Whether or not we agree, it would be difficult to incorporate such opinions in an objective ranking of this kind.

A natural question to ask at this point is whether the volatility of stock prices undermines the integrity of the ranking approach. The qualified answer is that it does not. After tracking the market-value index for several years, I have found that rankings are not nearly as affected by stock market fluctuations as one might expect, and that market leadership has an enduring quality. In fact, eight out of my top 10 new market leaders also appeared on my top 10 list last year. One reason is that the stock market's effect is muted by the stabilizing influence of the sales-growth index. Another factor is that comparing companies with their peers dampens the market's gyrations. Just as all boats rise and fall with the tide, related stocks tend to move up and down in concert. The strongest companies will rise above the fray whether or not their particular industries happen to be in favor with investors.

The qualifier is that my ranking approach will factor in changes in a company's outlook, as it should. Earnings surprises and other unforeseen corporate developments will inevitably affect share prices and either penalize or bolster the rankings of individual companies. Especially vulnerable are New Economy companies with embryonic business models that are operating in unsettled markets. Examples are Priceline.com and At Home Corporation, ranked 78 and 98, respectively, on my list. In the months following my most recent ranking, Priceline.com's prospects evaporated, while At Home's performance deteriorated seriously.

To illustrate how all of these factors interact, consider the stock market's correction during the early months of 2000, when the Nasdaq combined index dropped 18 percent in value from January 3 to May 31, while the Dow Jones Industrial Average lost almost 7 percent. Among the companies to be hardest hit were Microsoft and the Procter & Gamble Company, both losing more than 40 percent of their market value. Microsoft's peer group as a whole also took a beating, with the exception of Oracle Corporation, whose prospects improved. Microsoft, despite its antitrust difficulties, was able to hold on to its number 3 status, while Oracle moved up to number 8 from its former position of 21. P&G,

on the other hand, tumbled down to 101 from its previous spot at 64, reflecting its weakened outlook relative to rivals.

Clearly, there are no guarantees that the top 100 will continue to command superior valuations in the stock market or that they will be able to sustain their above-average growth. But just as Olympic medalists will be favored in the next race, so are the new market leaders in theirs; current track records and momentum bode well for their future prospects.

Note

When this book went to press in the spring of 2001, the stock market bubble of the late 1990s had burst. Yet, even the fact that many high-flying companies experienced calamitous drops did not affect the essential patterns I described. I ranked my database again in view of these changes and, as Appendix Two reflects, only 15 percent of the top 100 companies lost their leadership position, and did so because of strategic difficulties, not setbacks induced by the drop in stock prices.

CHAPTER 2

Where Do They Lead?

Y ou know the names of the new market leaders. Now let's
look in greater detail at the ways in which the new market
leaders distinguish themselves. In the graph below (Figure 2), the
horizontal axis shows the six-year sales-growth index. Companies located on the right side of the axis grew more rapidly than
their peers; those on the left lagged behind. The vertical axis represents the market-value index, that is, how investors value a
company's sales compared to the value assigned to the sales of
comparable peers. The above-average performers are in the up-
per part of the picture, while laggards ended up in the lower part.
The small dots represent the 5,009 companies in my database. To
illustrate where the market leaders are located relative to others, I
have placed on the graph some of the leaders as well as some laggards. The new market leaders, shown in bold type, excel on
both yardsticks and are located in the top right sector.

The rarefied domain of the new market leaders actually includes 640 companies (13 percent of all companies in the database), but the ones that truly stand out are the top 100 new
market leaders, including Cisco, General Electric, Yahoo!, and

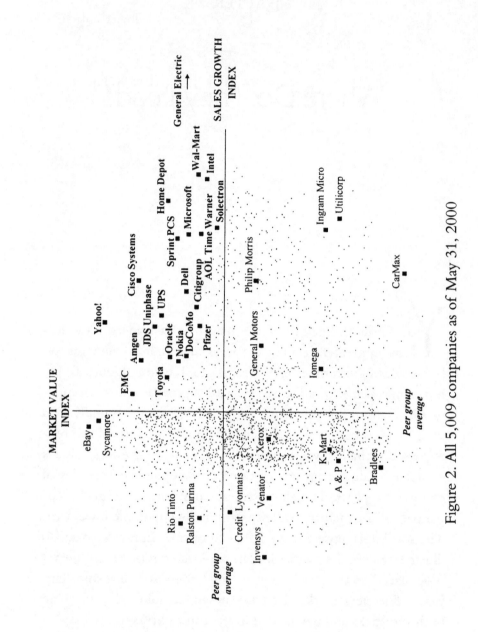

Figure 2. All 5,009 companies as of May 31, 2000

others identified on the graph. It is this extraordinary subset of new market leaders that commands our particular attention.

Another group worthy of note is in the bottom right quadrant of the graph, composing 22 percent of my database. The strong sales growth of these companies testifies to their customer appeal, but their lagging market-value index represents a challenge. On average, their annual return to investors was an unimpressive 13 percent. In a way, investors were saying, "Your sales are growing just fine, but why don't you make more money with that customer franchise?" For example, General Motors' latest 12-month sales of $181 billion were an impressive $43 billion higher than six years earlier, which means that it managed to grow at 2.6 times the pace of its peers. In spite of this accomplishment, its market-value index, at 0.5, trailed its peers. Dollar for dollar, the company's customer franchise was valued at less than either DaimlerChrysler or Ford, even though it surpassed these rivals in sales. General Motors' market value of $44 billion looked paltry compared with Toyota's of $170 billion, the highest-ranking automotive company among the new market leaders.

Given that these companies had about the same net profit margins (3.2 percent of sales), why was Toyota worth more than four times as much as General Motors? Because at the time of the ranking, industry analysts predicted Toyota's earnings would grow at 17 percent per year over the next several years, versus General Motors' at 8 percent. Toyota's valued customers were simply more valued. The implicit message to General Motors is that it must increase its earnings, not just its sales.

That same message applies to others in the lower right quadrant, including Utilicorp and CarMax. The latter had been revolutionizing car retailing, but left investors cold—probably because they couldn't envision how the company would build a profitable business model for the future.

Moving to the top left quadrant of the graph, we find companies that are richly valued by investors even though their sales performance was not up to par. Their investors earned an average annual return of 21 percent. These companies, of which there are two types, made up 20 percent of my 5,009-company database and had sales growth as their primary challenge. First there are entrenched businesses, such as Ralston Purina and Rio Tinto. Rewarded with rich valuations by investors, these companies boasted net margins and profit growth that exceeded those of their rivals. Their challenge was to keep up with their peer group's sales growth. Simply cashing in on a stagnant customer franchise is not a particularly promising strategy for the long run.

The other type of company in the top left quadrant is newer businesses with rich valuations that are based more on high hopes than on proven performance. Good examples are eBay, the online auction company, and Sycamore, a strong newcomer in the communications products area. Their imperative is to expand the footprint in their market and augment revenues aggressively, and in so doing to make it harder for rivals to lay claim to that space. They have the opportunity to convert the riches bestowed on them by investors into sales growth and a solid customer franchise.

Finally, we have the remaining 45 percent of companies, which reside in the lower left quadrant. Neither their sales growth nor their market-value index were up to par. Investors in these laggards had to settle for a paltry 7 percent annual return. For these companies there was not a remedy as clearly mandated as "Boost earnings" or "Grow faster." Prescriptions can conflict with one another, especially when companies are seriously lagging in both performance dimensions. Let's consider the plight of the Venator Group, Inc., a large retailer of athletic shoes, and compare it with that of Bradlees, Inc., a discount store operator. Venator decided to boost its financial performance by closing many of its marginal stores, which improved profit margins but, logically, caused its sales to drop. Bradlees, on the other hand, was able to speed up its sagging sales growth during 1999, but this came at the expense of its financial performance, because promotions and other customer enticements cut into profits.

When companies find themselves in such quandaries, drastic change or a turnaround strategy is often required to prevent getting stuck in a vicious cycle: Weak sales cause weak financials, resulting in little if any revenue left for investments that may boost sales. Breaking out of such a destructive loop was a challenge that almost half of the companies in my database confronted. That pattern stands in marked contrast to the self-perpetuating cycle of reinforcement that market leaders enjoy when their sales growth fuels earnings and market value, which then fuel further sales growth.

Now let's look a bit deeper at a variety of market categories, starting with companies in my database that provide consumer products. In the subsequent graphs, I show all top-100 market leaders that fall into the category discussed, together with a selection from the next one hundred market leaders. As before, these leaders are located in the top right quarter of the graphs, and their names appear in bold type. To keep the graphs uncluttered, I have populated the remaining quadrants with only a sampling of their better known competitors.

CONSUMER PRODUCTS

This group includes 405 companies in two separately ranked categories: nondurables (food products, beverages, health and beauty aids, and apparel) and consumer durables (home electronics, appliances, tools, and recreational products). The companies rated highest are Sony, Coca-Cola, cosmetics maker L'Oreal, and Philips Electronics.

When you examine this graph, you may wonder why some companies (such as motorcycle maker Harley-Davidson or eyeglass maker Luxottica) that clearly stand out in the graph are not included in the top 100. The reason is that my overall rankings

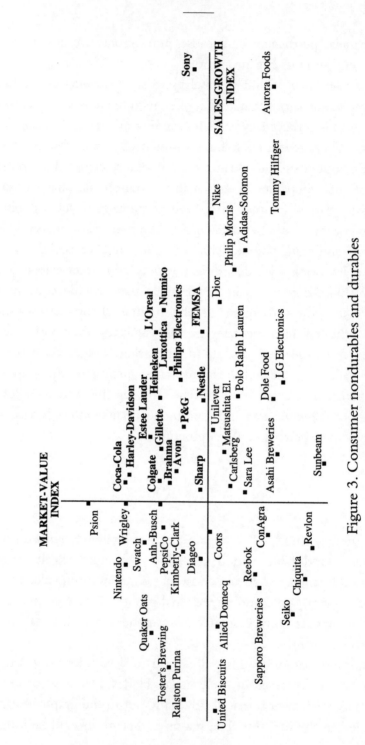

Figure 3. Consumer nondurables and durables

reflect each company's position in the entire universe as well as its standing relative to its peers. Thus, while Coca-Cola and Harley-Davidson were very close in sales-growth and market-value indices, and hence are next to each other in the graph, Coca-Cola's greater prominence among all companies ranked it in 40th place, while Harley-Davidson was rated a respectable 160. (See the Appendix for further explanation.)

As before, relatively few companies fall into this top-grade quadrant; we find the vast bulk in the bottom left. That pattern is not restricted to consumer goods, but is repeated in other market categories, such as retailing, financial services, industrial products, and technology. As a general rule, only one company in eight in any category managed to outperform its peers on both yardsticks. In contrast, the odds of finding companies that lagged in both leadership dimensions were somewhere between 40 and 50 percent. With the odds stacked against success, it is not surprising that market leadership is a sought-after status.

Also relevant across most industries is the fact that market leadership seems to be yoked more with management savvy than with a company's market or even its products. Though competitors may sell nearly identical products, some are far more successful than others in their pursuit of scarce and valued customers. The beer market exemplifies this point.

The best performers are Holland's Heineken breweries, Anheuser-Busch, Mexico's FEMSA (known for its Dos Equis beer), and Brazil's Cervejaria Brahma. While devotees of these beers will be tempted to attribute their superior performance to their superior quality, I believe that it is the companies' marketing and management decisions and strategies that account for their status. It is difficult to explain, otherwise, the fact that Japan's Asahi breweries and Denmark's Carlsberg also attracted droves of customers yet, unlike the market leaders, were unable to exploit that opportunity. This can also explain the lagging performance of the other beers that are shown.

Certainly, customers have many choices of beer, and while other brands are the most immediate and obvious competition, they are not the only rivals. Instead of buying beer, customers may opt for alternative beverages, food, or even other comparably priced nondurables. That's why I considered beer companies in the larger context of nondurables and not just within the limited area of other beer companies.

That rationale is particularly relevant in markets where established companies have been forced to share their market with new rivals that appeal to customers in distinctly different ways. The media and entertainment category is a case in point.

MEDIA AND ENTERTAINMENT

The five new market leaders that ranked the highest in this category are Yahoo!, AOL Time Warner, Viacom, Gemstar, and EchoStar Communications (see Figure 4). These companies compete for customers' time as much as for their money. In a very real way, Yahoo! battles McGraw-Hill; Comcast, a leading cable operator, vies with both; and Infinity Broadcasting, which operates radio stations across the United States, wrangles, too, for customers' attention. From this perspective, in which boundaries between different media have blurred if not disappeared, it is no wonder that America Online and Time Warner decided to join forces, as did Viacom and CBS.

The spate of new offerings of these and other market leaders in the media and entertainment industry has shifted customers' behaviors and priorities, and has placed considerable pressure on other media and entertainment companies, such as Loews Cineplex (which operates movie theaters) and traditional publishers such as Reed International, Reader's Digest, and Scholastic. The last four companies, which we find in the bottom half of the graph, were less prepared to defend themselves against these changes.

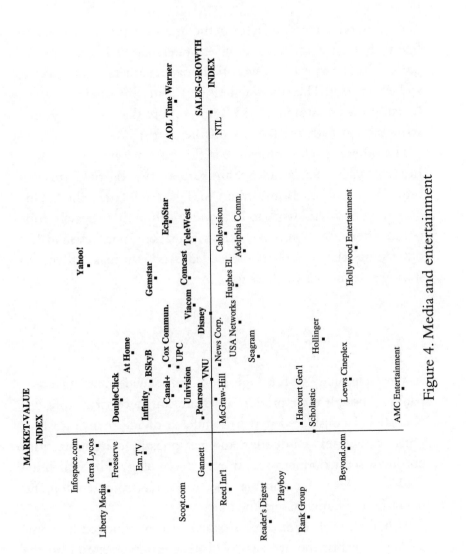

Figure 4. Media and entertainment

HEAVY INDUSTRY

Newcomers are less of a factor in the industrial products arena. In Figure 5 I have included four separately ranked market categories: basic materials, diversified manufacturing, automotive, and energy/oil. The runaway best performer is General Electric, which grew an astounding 13.8 times more than its peer group. (GE's sales growth was literally off the chart.)

The other top–100 companies in this category are Toyota; Tyco International; Du Pont; Schlumberger, the oil-field services provider; Canada's Bombardier; and Royal Dutch/Shell. Undoubtedly, it is hard work to beat your rivals in these heavily contested, often commoditylike industrial markets, but these and 127 other industrial companies succeeded. And that makes them inspiring role models to all of us.

TECHNOLOGY PRODUCTS

In the technology sector, Figure 6 covers a wide range of companies. Though their product lines are not necessarily well demarcated, I considered it worthwhile to divide them into four broad categories: computers and peripherals, communications products, semiconductors, and other technology. The fourth includes a variety of companies that make electronic equipment, scientific instruments, and the like.

As before, each company's performance was judged by comparing it against the averages of a peer group operating in the same category. For instance, Intel was compared against other semiconductor companies.

The top performers here are Cisco Systems, Intel, and Nokia, followed by no fewer than twenty-one other technology prod-

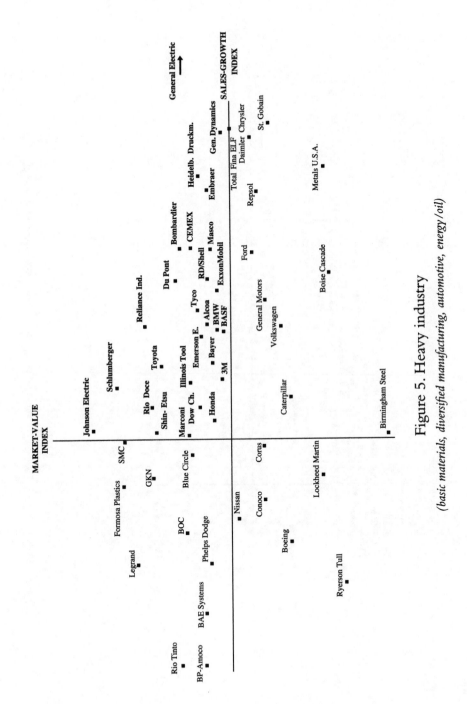

Figure 5. Heavy industry

(basic materials, diversified manufacturing, automotive, energy/oil)

33

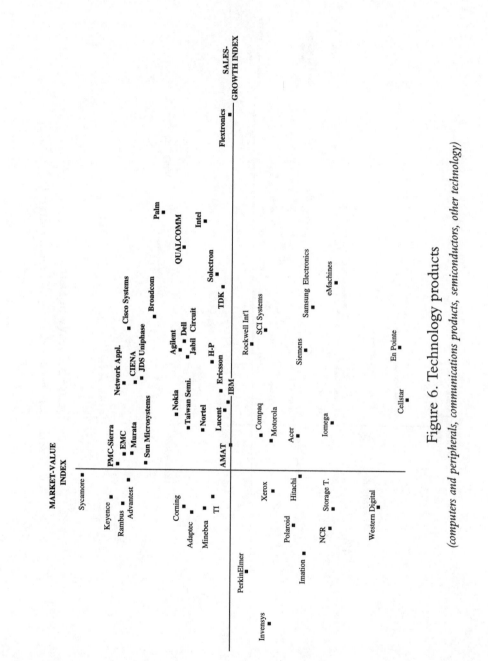

Figure 6. Technology products

(computers and peripherals, communications products, semiconductors, other technology)

ucts companies in my top 100, making technology the most prominent grouping of companies in the research.

Demonstrating that size and revenue cannot alone explain their prominence, five of these highfliers were too small for inclusion on the Fortune 500 list. On the other hand, several large and venerable companies, such as Siemens, Compaq, Samsung Electronics, Texas Instruments, and Xerox, failed to meet the market-leadership criteria set forth in this book.

TECHNOLOGY SERVICES

The second-most-prominent group of companies among the top 100 is computer and communications services (see Figure 7), which counted fifteen new market leaders. This grouping covers two categories: telecom services and software, programming, and IT services.

Microsoft led the technology services grouping, followed by Oracle and NTT DoCoMo, Japan's hot mobile phone company. Once again, the top 100 list included a host of younger and smaller companies whose importance in shaping customer demand outweighed their comparatively modest size. They include e-business solutions providers i2 Technologies and Ariba; Siebel Systems, the star in customer-facing applications; Sage Group, a British developer of accounting software; and Infosys Technologies, a rapidly rising Indian information services provider.

With these and other leading companies setting the market's pace and raising customers' expectations, their well-established but trailing competitors, such as AT&T, Japan's NTT, Computer Sciences Corporation, Novell Inc., Comdisco, Inc., and Bull have their work cut out for them.

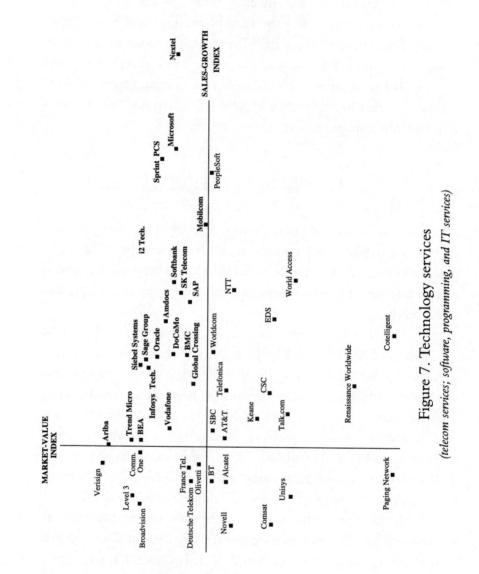

Figure 7. Technology services

(telecom services; software, programming, and IT services)

FINANCIAL SERVICES

Motivated by deregulation and a trend toward globalization, the financial services field continues to consolidate. The distinctions between various kinds of financial services firms are blurring, and from the customers' perspective, much of what their banks are now offering overlaps with what their investment firm or insurance company makes available. That is why I have placed all financial organizations into one category, and compare each company with businesses of similar-size peers that offer any kind of financial service (see Figure 8).

Containing 839 companies (17 percent of my database), this is my largest category. It certainly has its fair share of market leaders, with fifteen financial services organizations making the top 100 list. Three giants occupy the top spots—Citigroup, AIG, and Morgan Stanley Dean Witter.

Mergers of all sizes are rapidly altering the landscape, creating new, larger entities that offer a much broader range of products and services. Yet even a cursory look at the graph shows that size alone does not earn a company a place on the list of top performers. Several of the world's largest and most visible financial institutions performed below their peers on one or both dimensions of market leadership. This includes Japan's Bank Tokyo–Mitsubishi, Switzerland's UBS, France's AXA, Germany's Deutsche Bank, Holland's ING, and Merrill Lynch in the United States. Advantages of scale mean less once so many companies attain them, which is why market leaders have found other ways to distinguish themselves, precisely what the laggards in this industry have been unable to achieve.

It is worth noting that once you move beyond the market leaders, the financial services industry shows less variation in performance than do other market categories. With the exception of a handful represented on the graph, the majority of financial

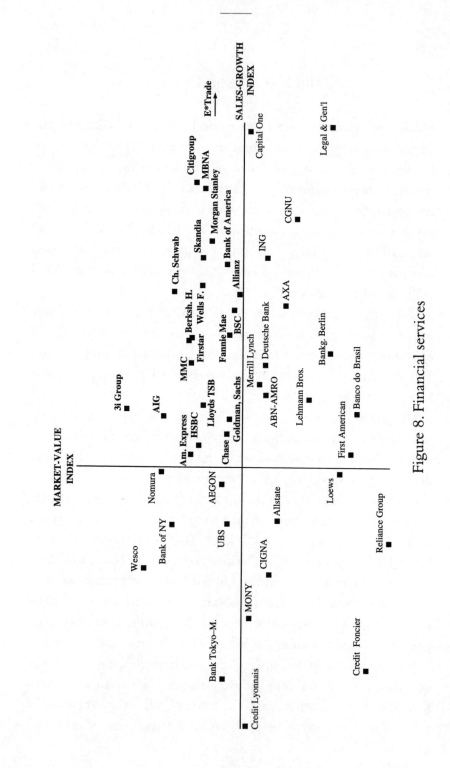

Figure 8. Financial services

services organizations are closely clustered around the averages; that is, they are reluctant or have failed to establish identities that allow customers and investors to separate them from the crowd.

OTHER INDUSTRIES

The final three groupings cover the health care field, consumer services, and all other services. In health care (see Figure 9), Pfizer emerged as the top performer after its merger with Warner-Lambert. The former leader (and current second) was Amgen, whose performance, together with those of Medimmune and Genentech, testify to the rising importance of biotechnology.

In spite of their sky-high market valuations, eminent stalwarts such as Merck, Johnson & Johnson, Novartis, and Roche Holdings just missed qualifying for market-leader status; their peers were valued even more highly.

The consumer services chart (see Figure 10) includes retail and intermediaries, as well as hospitality and food service providers. Home Depot and Wal-Mart were far and away the most stellar performers. Their top status, together with the strong rankings of a host of others in this grouping, suggest that traditional brick-and-mortar retailers are holding their own in the Internet era. More tenuous was the performance of the newer intermediaries and e-tailers, of which only Amazon.com managed to stand out among the top 100.

The last service chart (Figure 11) includes the remaining categories: transportation and logistics, business and management services, and utilities. The companies ranked highest were Enron, UPS, Paychex, and Vivendi. Even a cursory look at the chart will reveal how far these leaders have managed to separate themselves from others in their field, both in customer growth and in market value.

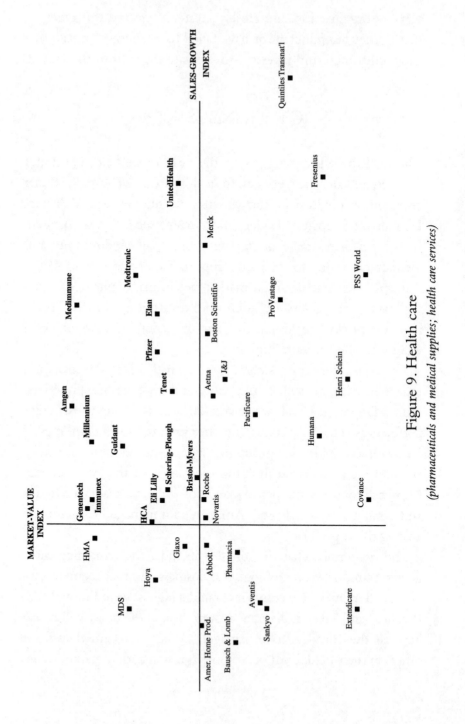

Figure 9. Health care

(pharmaceuticals and medical supplies; health care services)

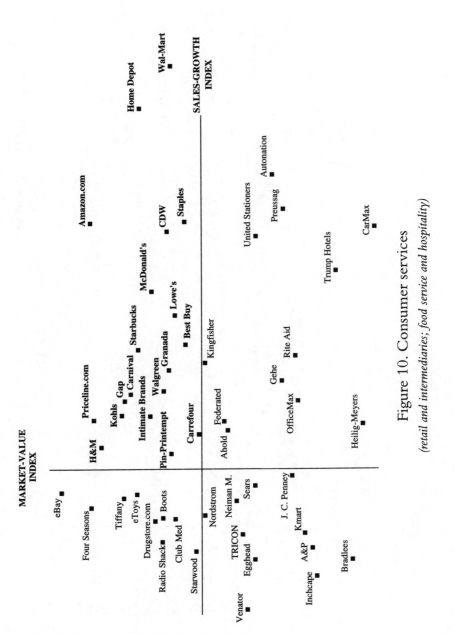

Figure 10. Consumer services

(retail and intermediaries; food service and hospitality)

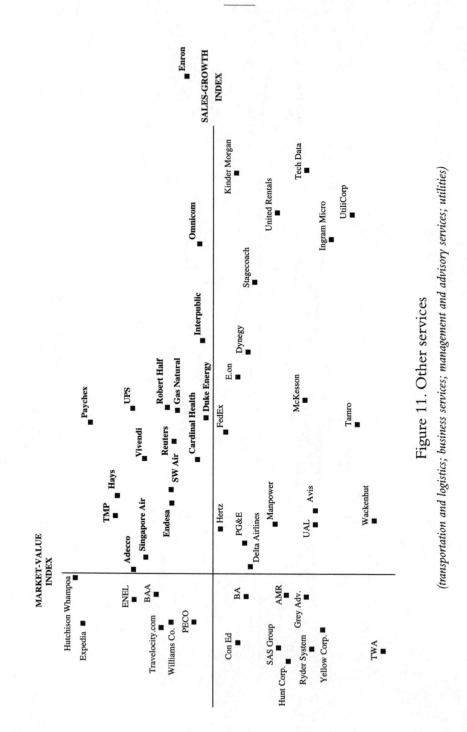

Figure 11. Other services

(transportation and logistics; business services; management and advisory services; utilities)

With this closer look at a cross section of industries, we can see that superior performance is achievable in *any* market category. Market leaders manage to rise above the fray whether their industry is mature or rapidly evolving, commoditylike or innovation driven, product or service oriented.

The charts in this chapter also reinforce the point that size does not equate to leadership. In spite of their prominence, many larger, well-established companies appear to underperform their peers. The same can be said about their highly touted newer competitors. Some of them have managed to join the ranks of market leaders, but plenty of others have yet to show that they can prevail in the battle for customers.

For companies aspiring to leadership, the next steps are clear. First, they need to assess their competitive landscape and determine on what measures they fall short. Second, they need to explore the nature of the new market challenges and adjust their strategies accordingly.

CHAPTER 3

Where Have All
the Customers Gone?

Where have all the customers gone? If the bad news is that your competitors have got them, the good news is that you can win them back or attract new ones.

As we have emphasized, the starkest challenge facing business today is customer scarcity: too many sellers for too few buyers.

In our democratized marketplace, practically anyone can participate in the competitive fray, and to harried managers it sometimes seems that practically everyone has. The result is that despite the fact that customers are more plentiful and richer than ever, each of them is being pursued by more suppliers than ever before. In addition to their traditional rivals, managers face new competitors that have transcended industry boundaries or erupted from the Internet with a new concept that threatens whole lines of existing products. And with the rise in the number and quality of suppliers, it's no longer production that is the bottleneck to growth. It's consumption.

Do you remember when high productivity was the grail we all pursued but never quite grasped? Computers changed all that and transformed business almost overnight. Yet today's huge leaps in productivity have created a classic unintended consequence—a mounting excess of goods and services that clogs warehouses, offends customers, and looks very much like a glut. There is simply too much of everything for customers to absorb—undigested information, miraculous new gadgets, or imitations of existing products.

From a manager's viewpoint, the change has been swift and scary. In just a few years, customers in nearly every field have metamorphosed from dependable, pliant shoppers to elusive, picky know-it-alls who tell you precisely what they want, how and when they want it, and how much they will pay for it. And if for some reason you are unable to gratify them, off they go to find someone who will.

The supply glut and the customer shortage—two sides of the same coin—are a problem that feeds on itself. Striving to attract elusive customers, manufacturers nervously churn out more versions of the same products, as if slicing a salami thinner and thinner. But so many choices can be overwhelming to customers; they create paralysis or resistance, while pouring infinitely more goods into the already flooded market.

Consider:

- The typical telephone customer in the United States gets three monthly bills from three different service providers, while at the same time he or she fends off sales pitches from three or four others. What the telemarketers are trying to sell is the convenience of combining three bills in one. What they ignore is the real nuisance—uninvited interruptions.

- Between 1987 and 1997, the number of U.S. mutual funds mushroomed from two thousand to twelve thousand. As an investor, how can you really tell the difference between one fund and the next? Wouldn't it be much easier to compare several individual stocks instead of trying to make sense of all these funds?

- The 24×7×365 buzz is reaching a fevered pitch. "We need to provide customers access around the clock" is the latest mantra in many service organizations. "That way we won't lose a sale." Never mind that the bulk of our local customers are asleep at 3:00 A.M.

To compound all this mischief, many of our most productive companies are pouring out new products in response to hunches, fads, a competitor's new offering, or merely the fact that technology makes it possible, rather than in response to a genuine sense of what customers want. The end result is a vicious spiral of dwindling profit margins, fragmented markets, and still more competition for ever-scarcer customers.

I often hear managers who are trapped in this cycle fretting about the massive investments they must continually make in technology and new product development, and the impact all this is having on their companies and themselves. "It just feels as if we're all working twice as hard as before just to get the same results," one senior manager told me. "Are we really better off than we were ten years ago?" The answer is yes, but only for those who can turn danger into opportunity and thus win the battle for scarce customers.

Still, a few organizations—such as Carnival Corporation, Cisco Systems, Sony, and Paychex—are inhaling new customers like a great white shark in a feeding frenzy. They are wallowing in customers. What is the winners' secret? In essence, what they share is a thorough understanding of six new realities, which are unusual in that they are causes and effects of customer scarcity. The new realities are:

Competitors proliferate.
All secrets are open secrets.
Innovation is universal.
Information overwhelms and depreciates.

Easy growth makes hard times.
Customers have less time than ever.

Let's examine these new realities in detail.

COMPETITORS PROLIFERATE

Only five years ago, most markets were dominated by a few lead-ing companies, mighty icons with household names that seemed immortal. How quaint all that now seems. Today's competitors are far more numerous, able, and fierce than ever before because they have to be: What used to be outstanding performance is now the norm.

A useful analogy is the sport of speed skating. In the 1980 Win-ter Olympics, American Eric Heiden accomplished an unprece-dented feat—he won five gold medals. Though it was unbeatable in 1980, twenty-five competitors surpassed Heiden's record in Nagano, Japan, eighteen years later in the 5,000-meter race, and did so by at least 12 seconds. The gold medalist, Gianni Romme of the Netherlands, covered the distance in 6 minutes 22 sec-onds, eclipsing Heiden's time by an unbelievable 40 seconds. For that competition, Heiden would not have even qualified.

Of course, the improved scores are at least in part attributable to advances in the state of the art. In skating, the hinged blade of the new clap skate gives skaters a more powerful drive, and aero-dynamic suits also improve performance.

Business practices evolve in similar ways. Products can be man-ufactured faster and cheaper. Just-in-time delivery systems elimi-nate inventories. The Internet, barely a consideration five years ago, is transforming thousands of companies and hundreds of markets. And new software enables customers to bypass interme-diaries and serve themselves on-line, saving time and cash.

But technology and improved methods are only part of the

story. The changing conditions themselves encourage more competition. Like the Klondike gold rush, the Internet is a magnet that lures companies into costly ventures in unknown territory. The high-tech race sets a standard that attracts even also-rans to an expanding field. Those that are unsuccessful don't quit altogether; they just switch to other fields. Lowered barriers to entry and the huge pool of available capital encourage managers to raise their sights and branch into new areas.

Thus, new (and newly) flexible competitors appear not only in cyberspace but out of left field. For example, the Boeing Company is now lending customers money to buy its planes, depriving banks of the loans. Bankers, in turn, are selling stocks and insurance. Stockbrokers have become financial advisers, and insurers enter the medical business in response to their efforts to hold down medical costs.

Entire companies and industries are evolving into others. Publisher Time, Inc., merges with Warner Bros. and becomes an entertainment company, then enters cyberspace to merge with America Online. Two electric utilities, Peco Energy Co. and Utilicorp United Inc. are joining AT&T and ADT Security Services, Inc., the security alarm company, for a combined project that will offer customers natural gas, electricity, phone service, Internet connections, and home security all on a single bill.

For customers, all of this points toward a dazzling new array of choices. For managers, it means learning new tricks to avoid failure.

ALL SECRETS ARE OPEN SECRETS

In an age in which customers are scarce, any company's best practices seldom remain proprietary. Business models are shamelessly imitated with inner corporate workings becoming public knowledge. Best practices travel at Internet speed.

People are becoming masters at imitation. If you don't have a good idea yourself, you can always knock off someone else's product. An imitation is not necessarily an exact copy. You use details to create a difference: the look, the product extension, the packaging—anything that can make the other company's idea look less new. And this is easier than it used to be. If once you could hold on to a secret formula for years or even decades, now it's a matter of months or days before your competitors catch up and replicate it.

One explanation is that the modern need for cooperation between companies forces them to post revealing information on their Web sites, where it is accessible to anyone. But secrets also travel with people. Nowadays there is massive employee mobility from one company to another. Despite noncompete agreements, whatever is learned at, say, Microsoft will inevitably benefit another company that hires a former Microsoft employee.

Consultants carry information and practices from one company to another, too. And software companies survive by encapsulating the leading companies' best practices into a package they can make available to customers. If you don't want to buy or build best practices yourself, you can borrow or lease them, or buy them from an outsourcing provider. Anyone with a great idea that becomes a product or service will see someone else quickly pick it up—and not just replicate it but improve upon it.

Also contributing to the proliferation of best practices is that businesses everywhere are getting much better at organizational change. Any company's first attempt to improve business practices is tough. By now, though, many successful companies have experienced multiple changes and have learned from their battle wounds. Clearly, the company most adept at organizational change has the edge.

One example is Du Pont, which has gone through at least five waves of change over an eight-year period. The first push was to cut costs and raise productivity. In the second, the company integrated its operations to get different parts of the organization to connect and work together. People were just beginning to relax when Du Pont geared up for a third wave, aimed at reengineering its processes to eliminate unnecessary work. Next came a refocusing wave that concentrated on a few high-priority areas; and finally, a wave in which customizing products and services for individual customers was the focus.

The point is that if your company, which has gone through one change, is competing against Du Pont, which has experienced five, which of you is likely to be more skillful at it? Like Du Pont, General Electric is now steeped in change. During the 1980s and 1990s, then CEO Jack Welch led his company through four or five waves of change. That best practices are no longer enough to bring back your lost customers is certain.

INNOVATION IS UNIVERSAL

Innovation has become so commonplace that scarcely any product survives long enough to age. New ideas and items are born obsolete. The cycle never stops. Accordingly, customers and suppliers alike grow dizzy in their futile pursuit of the next best thing.

Last year, consumers in the United States were inundated by roughly twenty-three thousand new packaged goods—about 450 per week. Revlon, Inc., alone introduced four hundred new items. Combine that with the thousands of other new consumer products that appeared, from computer advances to car models, and you get a sense of the plethora of choices, a flood that would have daunted Noah.

If all this makes your head spin, maybe you should consult a consultant. But there is an overload of consultants, too. "The latest estimates suggest that more than 10,000 firms claim to provide some form of Internet consulting or Web design services," reports *The Industry Standard*. If you wait to buy a computer with a hard drive that can hold 10 gigabytes, the 40-gigabyte model will come out six weeks later. In many cases, product proliferation and line extensions begin almost immediately after a basic design is developed. It seems as though some products have come and gone so quickly that their sales brochures were the only thing that ever reached the market.

And this process, too, feeds on itself: The shortened life cycle spurs even faster innovation. If you look more and more like your competitors and your products become less and less distinct, conventional wisdom seeks the answer in new thinking and invention. While all the gurus exhort you to innovate, revolutionize, get out of the box, the quest for something new and different often interferes with more practical measures, such as controlling costs and speeding up deliveries.

We have not overdosed on innovation yet, but perhaps we need to think about what we are doing. In the fantasy of today's high-tech Zeitgeist, every garage tinkerer is tomorrow's Bill Gates. In the business schools, apprentice MBAs express disdain for investment banking or consulting; 30 to 40 percent of them are aiming for their own dot-coms. At the height of the bull market, many venture capitalists threw caution to the wind and snatched at nearly any business plan ending in ".com." If some were badly burned and no longer play the dot-com game, hundreds of other digital dreamers are still hunting the money to fuel talent and launch more innovations. At least some of them will surely find it.

As the new goods and services congest the markets, the pool of potential buyers will not keep pace. In other words, the inflation of innovation causes a deflation of customers.

INFORMATION OVERWHELMS AND DEPRECIATES

Flooded with trillions of trivial pieces of information, millions of human minds are now as saturated as any swamp. Junk mail fills mailboxes; magazines stuffed with ads run as long as five hundred pages and can weigh as much as a newborn baby. Advertisers stamp their logos on every conceivable surface, from cruising blimps and ski-lift towers to e-mail screens and bus roofs. Some television markets offer two hundred cable channels. An Internet surfer discovers a Milky Way of random data, much of it conflicting and some of it stupefying.

According to *The Washington Post,* a study by the Gallup Organization and the Institute for the Future found that the typical office worker sends or receives 190 messages per day. (Yes, per day.) Even if it takes just a minute on average to process a message, the study indicates that dealing with messages consumes three hours a day. How splendid if this means that improved communication is making business smarter and more efficient, but how depressing if it means that three hours are added to the already hectic workday.

The planet-wide Internet now enables virtually anyone to speak his or her mind to most of the human race, start a Web page, barge into chat rooms, and flood the world with e-mail messages. Whether or not the resulting noise makes sense to recipients is another matter. For many, it all seems a bit like being bombarded with popcorn. Much of the Internet's swirling information is ignored and quickly vaporized like a passing rainstorm. If the best of it is a testament to the miracle of worldwide free speech, the worst is malicious gossip, the grammar of paranoia. Not yet equipped with the means of verification, the Internet has more than its share of misinformation dressed in fact's clothing. Sometimes it is hard for anyone standing in the popcorn burst to know which passing kernel to grab, and even the sharpest of us misses key bits.

Information sprawl is also rampant in most corporate settings. As the cost of storing and transmitting data declines, the amount of information collected and circulated becomes a tidal wave. Desks pile high with directives, product data, intelligence on competitors, musings for the coming corporate retreat. When the sales representative takes her notebook home stuffed with product updates to read, how much can she really absorb? The top 2,000 companies in the world are expanding their information storage by 40 to 50 percent per year. That means *doubling* the amount of stored information in two years. Presumably this is valuable information (after all, companies did decide to spend money storing it). But the question remains: How long will it take managers to put it to proper use? Can they truly be expected to keep up with the flow?

The challenge of information processing these days is less about its technicality and more about how to digest it all. And for a customer trying to choose what to buy, too much information is almost worse than too little. The effect is paralysis or denial—and no sale.

EASY GROWTH MAKES HARD TIMES

Because technology raises, if not eliminates, the ceiling on expanding production, managers tend to expand manufacturing capacity without knowing if they have sufficient demand. In their eyes, capacity is a bird in the hand, but demand is guesswork. The frequent result is overproduction and its evil twin, customer scarcity.

For example, the world's automakers can churn out 30 to 40 percent more cars than anyone thinks can be sold. Without building a single new plant, the current overcapacity of 17 million cars is enough to meet projected demand for the next ten years. Nonetheless, carmakers keep building new plants to modernize and handle local needs, so that world capacity will continue to increase but paying customers will not. The industry already produces many more cars in total than customers are ready to buy, which triggers periodic bouts of discounting. Expect shakeouts and consolidations in the auto industry's immediate future.

Airlines have flown into similar turbulence. When deregulation intensified competition, every major line decided it needed to add bigger and newer planes to improve its operating efficiency.

The result was a huge increase in the number of seats. The airlines' solution—to attract more customers by dropping fares and packing more passengers onto each flight—was a good recipe for igniting customer rage.

The telecommunications industry is on the cusp of a similar glut. Internet usage has grown enormously in a few years. But what has grown even faster is the network infrastructure that fiber-optic companies are frantically building in anticipation of even greater demand for bandwidth.

The carrying capacity of long distance networks in the United States is slated for an estimated eightyfold increase over the five years ending in 2001. The result: Bandwidth supply will vastly exceed demand, at least in the immediate future. Moreover, this overcapacity will be exacerbated (and prices slashed) by the advent of far more efficient new technology using packet switching (Cisco's forte, it involves breaking messages into packets that can be sent over many circuits and reassembled on arrival) rather than conventional circuit switching. And that doesn't even take into account the potential growth of wireless communication bandwidth.

It is fair to say that bandwidth supply will outpace demand for some time until customers move toward more data-hungry applications, such as those required to download movies. Meanwhile, fiber-optic companies will battle for a scarcity of customers in ways that resemble how the airlines tried to get rid of excess seats. At some point, the pendulum will swing the other way. Bandwidth demand will pick up, and as it soars, you can be sure that aggressive suppliers will start laying even more fiber-optic cable—thus perpetuating excess capacity.

Similar imbalances afflict semiconductors—an industry in which the requisite state-of-the-art fabs (as they call fabrication plants) can easily cost more than $1 billion apiece to build. To recover that kind of investment, manufacturers understandably run new fabs at full capacity as soon as possible. With many suppliers operating the same way, of course, overcapacity triggers price cutting as well as all the other malign effects of a problematic struggle to win and retain customers.

In pharmaceuticals, the big companies have developed new manufacturing methods that sharply boost their potential output. At the same time, generic drug makers are producing lower-cost versions of the drugs, while contract manufacturers are catering to smaller enterprises that don't want to invest in facilities. Again, the net effect is growing excess capacity.

It is even easier to add capacity in information-based products. There is hardly any physical barrier to reproducing CDs, downloading information from the Internet, or packaging and repackaging data in multiple ways without much cost to the supplier.

In the music business, illegal manufacturing of CDs and cassettes worsens the industry's overcapacity and creates huge piracy losses—well over 20 percent of global sales in 1998. Illegal downloading from the Internet further erodes the customer base, slashing another 15–20 percent from potential sales in 1999.

What brought about this general epidemic? For one thing, replication of practices, processes, and even products becomes quicker and easier once they are debugged and standardized. After you perfect the formula for a new fast food restaurant or retail clothes chain, you can apply it all over the world—as we see with McDonald's, the Gap, and Banana Republic stores.

In a manufacturing era seemingly devoid of constraints, the tools of productivity become the agents of excess. Chief among these are automation and robotics. They flourish as new products escalate and their life cycles shorten (less than six months for cellular phones). They become mandatory as suppliers strive for an edge with customization and just-in-time delivery. All these factors drive a need for highly flexible manufacturing—ideal for robots, which are now used for everything from assembling electronic devices to packaging pharmaceuticals and billing customers.

The ability to make more things faster is both a liberating and an entrapping spiral. Suppose you have learned how to lower your costs by scaling up your operations and running them more efficiently. What's next? You add capacity—doesn't everyone? In business, growth is sacred. But if your competitors all do the same thing, their aggregate overcapacity hurts the entire industry.

When all this imitation and replication multiplies the choices available to customers, overcapacity shrinks the number of customers available to each supplier. It has a relentless logic—fewer sales, lower prices, falling margins.

CUSTOMERS HAVE LESS TIME THAN EVER

When customers lack the time to buy or use things, suppliers lack customers. Of all the new realities, this may be the most important. Time is no longer just money. Time is life itself. In a high-speed era bristling with demands around the clock, the daily puzzle is, how much time can anyone commit to any particular task? Ergo, customer scarcity is often caused by time scarcity.

As managers see it, their challenge isn't creating products, services, information, or innovation. Rather, it is finding ways to get customers to select from, to process, and to digest the abundance of supply. The hardest part may be the first step—to cut through the clutter to get customers' attention and stay on their shortlist.

That, however, is the view from corporate headquarters. Customers couldn't care less. They have problems of their own.

Remember the 1970s, when pundits fretted that people might soon die of boredom during the hours and hours of leisure time that automation would inevitably bring? Fat chance.

Instead, what happened is that most people are working longer and harder, perhaps at two or more jobs. After working, sleeping, eating, and doing chores, what's left of the day? If you're very lucky, maybe three or four hours in which you can read the paper, surf the Internet, play with your kids, converse with your spouse, pay bills, go to church, play golf—or buy things.

We're playing a zero-sum game. As long as the hours of the day are limited, any new claim on your time steals it from something else. If you choose to spend extra hours shopping, you miss the book-club meeting or the big game on television. Quite literally, for the purveyor of goods, the competition is not a rival company; rather, it is the infinite number of other possible ways in which a person may choose to spend his or her time.

This also applies to the business customer. In a buyer's daily welter of meetings, paperwork, protocol, demanding bosses, and office politics, there is no extra time for talking with suppliers who don't immediately have exactly the right answers. As a result, customers of all kinds have very little patience.

The new market leaders are shrewd psychologists and know that people cope with excess by a process of elimination. Customers who are pressed for time and overstimulated by a plethora of choices will simply tune out what doesn't catch their collective eye in the first nanosecond and tune in to what does, just as a car radio scans passing stations.

Market leaders also understand that a company unable to retain customers may be annoying them; perhaps it is burdening people with too much or too little information, or forcing them to squander time on irritations like airline overbooking and automated phone gibberish. The leaders adjust accordingly and make it easy, quick, and as pleasant as possible to do business with them.

Taken one at a time, these new realities of customer scarcity sound familiar to any manager. Together, however, they add up to a formidable challenge. What does a company have to do to adjust to the new conditions? As we will see, all it takes is to divert your customer's attention from the competition; to learn how to operate openly, without secrets; to continuously update your best practices; to innovate constantly without losing focus on the basics; to tighten and focus your flow of information; to resist the temptation to produce to excess; and to help your customer save time. And if all that sounds simple—well, it isn't.

CHAPTER 4

What's New About
the New Market Leaders?

Spotting a new market leader is no more complicated than walking a company's hallways or observing its managers as they work: Do they know who their priority customers are? Are they aware of what this group really wants? Do they stay focused on offering these customers the best value, year after year? And from top to bottom of the company, is the desire and determination to be the company that sets the standards in the marketplace palpable? Ultimately, what proves a market leader is the preoccupation with the fact that the business rests firmly on two pillars—customers and focus. Diminish either and the business flounders.

Of course, customer focus is hardly a novel idea. It lies at the core of such concepts as total quality management and customer satisfaction, as well as their offspring, the seminal Malcolm Baldrige National Quality Award. In fact, all of this could have been said five or more years ago—and was, in *The Discipline of Market Leaders*. That book built on the premise that no company can be all things to all people and exhorted managers to "choose your customers, narrow your focus, dominate your market." What has changed since then is the fervor with which these strategies are being applied. In response to customer scarcity, new market leaders have intensified their attacks on both the customer and the focus sides of the equation.

In the not so distant past when Sam Walton was Wal-Mart's chief executive, it was worthy of mention in the press if a CEO spent substantial amounts of his or her time in direct contact with customers. Now it is news if a chief executive is *not* doing so. These days, too, executives can access a vast trove of knowledge about their customers, much of which transcends market segments and zeroes in on individual customers. Combined with operational and financial data, this permits sophisticated analysis and much more precise interactions with customers. In turn, that sophistication makes it possible to orchestrate the supply chain from the customer to the company's suppliers, and down the chain to their suppliers.

And when managers pay attention to customers and this much information is available, the entire organization is infused with the customers' perspective. Customers are no longer the responsibility only of the people in sales, marketing, and field service. They have become, literally, everyone's business, and staffers from operations to research and development to finance are acutely aware that their company's success depends upon customer satisfaction—and that they, too, will be held accountable for that.

Take a look at Solectron, a contract manufacturer of personal computers and other electronics, based in Milpitas, California. From the chief executive to the warehouse packers, every employee knows precisely what the company's customers want and how their jobs fit into serving those customers.

Each Solectron customer is assigned to a cross-functional customer-focus team, composed not just of salespeople but engineers, program managers, buyers, and quality representatives. Their responsibilities are to ensure that the job flows quickly and smoothly, and toward that end, they actually are in daily contact with each customer regarding scheduling, engineering changes, and any other issue that may arise.

For their part, customers fill out a weekly report card on Solectron's performance, rating it A through D on communication, delivery, quality, service, and overall performance. A grade of B– is enough to prompt a quality-improvement program for the team responsible. A grade of C triggers something like a civilized inquisition: The program manager must respond within twenty-four hours and design a formal plan to resolve the complaint within seventy-two. On average, Solectron reports its grades are A– or better. It is no surprise that this organization won the Baldrige Award, not just once but twice.

Or take a newer market leader, Siebel Systems, a maker of customer relationship management software in San Mateo, California. Here, too, exists a profound concentration on the customer. Thomas M. Siebel, the company's founder, chairman, and chief executive officer, says he spends 60 percent of his time meeting customers. Meaningfully, all of the art decorating the company's halls comes from customers—a poster, a letter of compliment, the cover of an annual report. Every quarter, Siebel's customers are asked to rate the company's service, and its salespeople are compensated on customer satisfaction as well as by the deals they close.

Managers at Ford Motor chose Siebel to provide essential software for a call center that links Ford, its dealers, and its business partners. They report that the reliable Siebel team makes sure that everyone at Ford who needs to understand and feel comfortable with the software does so. The call center's chief says that if he were really unhappy, he could call Tom Siebel anytime, "and he'd take care of it." Other customers are just as happy. Lodging giant Marriott International Inc. has used Siebel software for several elaborate programs and finds that Siebel people are always a step ahead of Marriott's five-year plan. Siebel's mantra, says a Marriott executive, is "How does what we do help your business?"

For new market leaders, such as Solectron and Siebel Systems, it is not sufficient to fill their customers' orders. They are committed to their customers' success, determined that the products or services they sell will bring the results that their customers need. There is an old marketing chestnut worth repeating: Customers don't buy drills, they buy holes. It is results that count. If there is a better way than yours for your customer to get the results she wants, don't wait for her to find it; show her, and find a way to provide it.

The focus side of the customer-focus equation is equally critical. As detailed in *The Discipline of Market Leaders,* focus means selecting your customers carefully and calibrating your operating model to their specific needs. Pursue too many customers or those whose needs don't play to your strengths, and you will strain your operations. Build a general-purpose operating model, and you will be clobbered by more focused competitors who forgo embellishments so they can adhere to precisely what is needed—no more, no less.

Market leaders know that the way to build momentum is to focus ample energy on a well-defined target. Too little energy or too large a target produces a stalemate. Advertisers, politicians, and military strategists have long known that the ability to concentrate resources makes winners, from Alexander the Great to Golda Meir to Norman Schwarzkopf and Colin Powell.

The same logic applies when competition for customers becomes fierce. If two equally matched teams are pitted against each other, the one most focused on the precisely delineated target has the edge: The sharpshooter with a rifle will hit the bull's-eye far more often than those with a shotgun. Similarly, the capacity to focus, to be single-minded, is what gives upstart companies a fighting chance to upset their established rivals, who may be rich in resources but have diffuse goals and less disciplined operations. Clearly, for Solectron and Siebel, nothing has contributed more to their success than their focus and single-mindedness.

Focus means having clarity of intent and direction. Genuine market leaders know and can express without doubt what they are and what they stand for. Managers who waver when articulating their core strengths or defining what distinguishes them from their competitors usually transmit that sense of ambiguity to employees, who find it confusing if not distressing.

You may remember an article in the October 16, 1995, issue of *Fortune,* in which both the outgoing and the incoming chief executive officers of Sears, Roebuck and Co. were interviewed separately on the same day and were asked identical questions about the company's focus and direction. Most striking was that the two men, who had spent several years working side by side to turn around Sears's sagging performance, had views that, in *Fortune's* words, "couldn't be more different." It made me wonder how the people further down in the organization made sense of the conflicting visions. Did they take sides? Did they try to reconcile the differences? Did they pay lip service to the dissonance, or simply ignore it? Whatever their reactions, one suspects the conflict did not advance the aim of revitalizing the business. Don't confuse focus with simplicity. A focused organization such as McDonald's, in Oak Brook, Illinois, may look simple on the surface, yet underneath, it is an intricate and finely tuned operation that for nearly half a century has defeated competitors' efforts to dethrone it. Though rivals copy its store operations and menu, mimic its choices of locations and appeal to kids, they have not found a way to make each of these separate elements come together in the focused manner that lures 27 million customers to McDonald's outlets in the United States every day of the year.

What the new market leaders have accomplished is the elevation of the concept of customer focus. They adhere to four key mind-sets that, together, allow them to break away from the pack, avoid ordinariness, and distinguish themselves in a way that captures customers' attention and loyalty. We will come back to discuss each in much greater detail, but here is the overview.

- First, to make sure they don't get lost in the crowd, *the leaders create a larger-than-life market presence.* That is, they make sure they get recognized. Becoming a well-kept secret just isn't their style.

- Second, *market leaders seek out customers who stretch their capabilities.* To always stay a few steps ahead of rising expectations, they focus not on their average customers but on their most important (and often most demanding) ones. They take all the low-hanging fruit they can reach—but they also make sure to reach for the stars.

- Third, to provide direction and guidance, *the leaders make sure customers realize the full value of their products and innovations.* Less concerned with offering an abundance of new goods and services and more anxious that their customers "get it," new market leaders provide whatever coaching and hand-holding they need to reap the new benefits, even when they might seem obvious.

- And finally, *market leaders act boldly in everything they do.* Obviously, this doesn't mean they are reckless, unprepared, or faddish, and they know the difference. They study their moves, know their markets thoroughly, keep up with the competition, and work out alternative scenarios. Still, faced with a choice between a daring move and a cautious compromise, they invariably choose the more ambitious course. That is their advantage over more timid rivals as they also earn kudos from their customers for their initiative.

Now we'll consider each of the four points individually.

BEING THE BEST—AND SHOWING IT

New market leaders know the importance of building a larger-than-life market presence.

The Discipline of Market Leaders talked about the value proposition—the notion that as long as a company provides the best cost, best product, or best solution, it will catch customers' attention. Though that idea certainly held true when only a handful of market leaders had distinguished themselves, today, offering the best cost, best product, or best solution has become par for the course. Why would customers settle for anything less than the best—whether it is in price, product, or solution—when suppliers are fighting one another to provide all of them? The fact is that unique value propositions such as Wal-Mart's "Always the low price" are simply no longer unique (think of Target Stores, Inc.'s, or Costco Companies, Inc.'s, essentially identical claims). Likewise, McDonald's isn't the only place that offers a dependable hamburger experience, while Nike, Inc., isn't the only athletic shoe positioned as the best product. In the technology field, it is hard to find a vendor today that doesn't claim to be a best-solutions company.

So, while having a powerful value proposition is still the essential first part of building a larger-than-life market presence, it certainly isn't the only part. But because it is indispensable, the value proposition had better be clear, concise, and compelling. There are two acid tests that market leaders apply.

The first I call the *billboard test*. Ask managers to offer ten or fifteen words that they feel capture the essence of why customers choose their product. Think about it as a testimonial that could be put on a billboard.

Simple as this may seem, it is a task that many managers find difficult. But if they can do it, ask them what their current customers would say if they saw that billboard. If they would not say, "Yes, that is precisely why I do business with you," you may not be in synch with their expectations.

Finally, imagine that you replaced your own name on the billboard with your competitor's; would the message suddenly seem strange and jarring to your customers? If so, your value proposition is distinctive. If not—that is, if your rival's name is interchangeable with your own—your message lacks distinction and therefore won't provide a compelling reason for customers to stick with you. It is particularly easy to fail this last part of the test—which is to say that a lot of managers continue to be more confident than correct in their analyses of their product's appeal.

The second test, a variation on the first, applies to industrial products or more complex consumer purchases. I call it the *elevator test*. If you were riding an elevator with a prospective customer who asked you why he or she should do business with you, could you make your case in the sixty-second-or-so ride? If not, your value proposition may not be succinct, or you may not thoroughly understand what is vital to the customer. (Of course, as many a seasoned salesperson will tell you, it may be wiser *not* to attempt an answer even if you have one. Deferring the discussion until after you've learned more about the customer's requirements and priorities would be a more prudent course of action than trying to rush through a hurriedly prepared sales pitch.)

With a solid value proposition in place, the question is, what next sets market leaders apart? The answer: They stand out among all those claiming to be the best because they work hard at being *different* as well as best. Wal-Mart does so by turning its greeters and the folksiness of its staff into a point of distinction. Target runs clever, eye-catching ads that accomplish the same effect. Costco's difference is based on the stores' atmosphere, which resembles an old-fashioned local market where customers can always discover an unexpected bargain or treat. All three retailers know that customers buy the sizzle as much as the steak. They all realize that the right packaging can make otherwise similar goods appear to be anything but. So the second part of building a strong market presence is to enhance a product's or service's core features and give it qualities that make it stand out among its peers.

Importantly, market presence comprises more than advertising. It is equal to the sum total of impressions that shape a customer's perceptions about a product or supplier. As Wal-Mart and Costco know, creating an enticing, out-of-the-ordinary shopping experience is key. In effect, every point of contact with customers or prospects potentially turns into a point of distinction. Consider the subtle differences in the ways companies field customer service calls. Such nuances can account for major differences in customers' satisfaction.

Not all of these formative impressions are under the direct control of the supplier, but that does not make them less powerful. Think about what is said in the press by industry observers or about word of mouth from friends or colleagues and how all of these affect a product's or company's credibility. That is why endorsements and testimonials are such powerful tools and why market leaders frequently showcase their most prominent and prestigious customers.

Glance through the press releases of market leaders and you would find numerous references to other market-leading companies. Siebel Systems counts Schwab and IBM among its customers, and IBM makes it known that it not only is United Parcel Service, Inc.'s, supplier of choice but also is scooping up contracts with several new companies in the e-business field.

For market leaders to construct a larger-than-life market presence, their messages have to resonate with customers. Customers may understand your value proposition, appreciate how you are different, and accept your credibility on the basis of your well-respected customers. But unless they feel that you are committed to their well-being, they may still not pay attention to you.

IBM's managers recognized this sad fact several years ago. Many of the prospects they were wooing didn't fit the profile of their traditional customers—such large, conservative, buttoned-down organizations as Du Pont, General Motors, and Xerox. In the last few years, IBM has aggressively pushed itself into e-business, where, arguably, it is among the most prominent suppliers. Part of IBM's effort required shedding its old uniform of blue suits, white shirts, and military hairstyles. So, in 1996, the company undertook a massive advertising campaign featuring employees who stood in contrast to the stereotype. In these ads, people with long hair and beards wore open shirts and casual attire, chatted around a coffee machine in an office that resembled a downtown loft. That campaign was followed by another in 1998 that emphasized IBM's ambitious efforts to create and shape e-business solutions for customers both small and large. The $75 million campaign implied that IBM is not shaping the future only for global behemoths, but also for organizations of any size that want to benefit from emerging e-business opportunities. It featured close-up profiles of a diverse group of employees at IBM Global Services—using real names and real job descriptions. The intended underlying message: We are approachable; we are with you; we understand you; we resonate with you.

Also positioning itself as a company of the future, seven-year-old Siebel Systems used the opposite method to connect with its customers. Most of them are large, well-established, traditional companies, and many have higher-than-average risk aversion, especially when buying systems or software for a mission of critical importance. Accordingly, Siebel shied away from casual dress in its California headquarters and stayed away from New Age antics in its ads and annual report. The Siebel image reflects professionalism, even traditionalism. The antithesis of flaky and certainly not laid-back, Siebel Systems is all business.

However, every piece can be in place and a company can still fail to create a powerful market presence simply because it remains unknown. It is no good having the best steaks and the most wonderful ambiance in town if diners don't know about your restaurant or can't find it easily.

Thus, the last step in building market presence is to make sure that your message gets noticed. As any advertiser knows, it takes an awful lot of momentum to launch a campaign, and it is far easier to err by doing too little than too much. If you want to be heard above the din, turn up the volume. If you want to get through, you had better keep repeating your message. It is an old advertising rule: Unless your audience hears or sees your message at least three times in a four-week period, you might as well keep your money in your wallet.

That truth didn't escape IBM when it ran its 1996 and 1998 campaigns with such weight and frequency that it was hard not to notice it or take in its message. America Online launched a similar campaign when, in its early days, it handed out millions of free software diskettes and CDs, hoping that recipients would sign up for on-line service. AOL didn't send just one diskette to a customer, either. It sent several. Total overkill? Not necessarily. By traditional standards it was certainly excessive. But what seemed like overkill was, in fact, a calculated and well-executed move to accelerate the company's rise to prominence. The risk was that it would spend a lot of money with little payoff, but the potential was enormous. The company quickly became the largest on-line service provider in the world, with more than 21 million subscribers—about four times as many as its closest competitor.

AOL's bet looks modest in comparison to the make-or-break wagers that many new companies are placing today to build their market presence. Some spend the bulk of their investment capital on advertising and promotion rather than on infrastructure or other operations. Maybe it is AOL's good fortune that inspires them, or maybe they feel it is their only chance at gaining visibility in the supercrowding of cyberspace. Regardless of the rationale, these companies' chances for success are diminished unless they have well-crafted value propositions, are recognizably different from their competitors, and can find ways to resonate with their intended audiences. Without those, one questions the wisdom of nearly a dozen dot-com unknowns that staked an average of $2.2 million on a thirty-second advertising spot during the Super Bowl of 2000.

In short, if you want to really be noticed in the crowd, you had better make sure you are on the customer's wavelength, have a clear, concise, focused, and compelling message, and broadcast it loud enough for people to hear.

THE CUSTOMERS WHO
CAN MAKE OR BREAK YOU

Market leaders choose their customers very carefully because they know that they will be judged by them: Nothing says more about a business than its customers. Unfortunately, conventional wisdom can't help in this task. The first rule in sales is, go after the low-hanging fruit—that is, the easy-sell customers—rather than clamber for what is hard to reach. But this is good advice only if there is a plethora of fruit on the low branches, and in the era of customer scarcity, the pickings are getting slimmer. The real plums are in the high branches.

Market leaders deliberately pursue some of the most difficult and demanding clients they can find because they know that satisfying these customers will stretch their abilities and help them become better at what they do. I call these *stretch customers.*

But not all tough customers are desirable matches. Some of them are simply the wrong ones to have because their demands don't play to a company's strengths. That doesn't necessarily mean they are undesirable for other suppliers. Picky, critical eaters who want personal service could be ideal stretch customers for a swanky full-service restaurant but a very bad match for McDonald's.

Who are the desirable stretch customers? As it turns out, for companies that sell to other companies, many of them are other market-leading companies. It is easy to see why. By definition, market leaders are the pacesetters in their fields, and they didn't get there by moving slowly. Their success depends, at least in part, on their ability to motivate their suppliers to perform consistently at elevated levels. It is also important to have them as customers because they are growing faster than their peers, as we saw in Chapter 1.

Consider the makers of consumer packaged goods, whose immediate customers are retailers that sell the products. Procter & Gamble and Gillette discovered long ago that they had to do whatever it took to get their diapers and razors onto the shelves of the notoriously demanding Wal-Mart Stores. They could not ignore the enormous buying power of this giant, which grew in the six years through May 2000 from $76 billion in sales to $167 billion. That $91 billion increase represented the single largest growth opportunity for both P&G and Gillette.

Since its inception in 1993, Siebel Systems, too, has made a point of pursuing stretch customers, such as IBM, Microsoft, Yahoo!, and Schwab, enterprises on the forefront of their industries. Catering to them has propelled Siebel into the lead and insures that it won't design solutions for yesterday's problems.

Not only do stretch customers help you grow; they keep you on your toes and tone up your muscles. Toyota, for example, heaps enormously tough demands on its suppliers, who often have to struggle to keep up, to improve quality, costs, delivery time, and efficiencies. Yet after they successfully meet such high standards, they find themselves in far better shape to deal with their other customers.

While there is nothing intrinsically wrong with low-hanging fruit—without such attractive, easy customers, even market leaders would have trouble making money—companies that settle for them alone inadvertently risk defining themselves as reactive followers, unwilling or unable to tackle challenges posed by more demanding customers. On the other hand, catering to companies like GE conveys a different story. Being a key GE supplier means working harder, and that effort speaks volumes about a company's determination to keep up with the market leaders.

The implicit message in all of these examples is this: If you want to be a market leader, do business with others who already are. If you want to grow, go after customers who are growing. And this advice isn't limited to companies that sell to other businesses. It is equally relevant for about half of the 5,009 companies in my database that sell directly to consumers.

McDonald's, for example, is constantly investigating new ways to appeal to the roughly 20 percent of fast food patrons who eat at this kind of restaurant four or five times a week. These superfrequent customers account for 80 percent of all fast food revenues. Clearly, they are not complaining. Equally clearly, it behooves McDonald's to cater to their needs and work to understand how they are changing over time.

Tests of new product lines, such as Mexican dishes or pizza, found little enthusiasm among the superfrequent crowd. But McDonald's recent adoption of a speedy custom cooking technology has been a hit. Not only does the technology improve the burger's taste; it speeds preparation time while cutting down on wasted food. McDonald's knows that what its superfrequent customers value most is the "fast" in fast food.

Does all this mean that the new market leaders go after only those customers who will stretch them? Not at all. A useful way of thinking about this is to imagine the customer base as divided into three separate groups. In the first are stretch customers, who spur a company to improve its business practices. Managed properly, they are a vital source of progress. They may not be the most profitable customers. Wal-Mart, for example, is known to drive a very tough bargain, and Toyota is certainly not every supplier's idea of a lucrative account. Having too many stretch customers can therefore put excessive pressure on the bottom line and overextend the organization. As a rule of thumb, stretch customers typically don't make up more than 10 percent of the market leader's customers. (Often the percentage of sales is far higher: Wal-Mart, for example, accounted for some 18 percent of P&G's diaper sales a few years ago.)

The second group in the customer base is made up of demanding customers who do not meet the criteria of the stretch category. These customers should not make up more than 10 percent of the customer base either, but for different reasons: They are the wrong match.

Customers may be wrong for a variety of reasons. They may be altogether too demanding, or they may ask things from an operational standpoint that don't mesh with what a company is trying to do. Or they may turn off—and turn away—other, better customers.

One way to deal with them is to try to change their demands and turn them into more desirable patrons. Whether or not that works, there is a real risk in overservicing them, which ultimately hurts other, more valuable customers. That is why it is good to know who these customers are and to hold the line on the amount of energy and resources that is spent on them. Saying no to undesirable customers is a practice that many market leaders have become very good at. (Of course, it would have been better to have screened them out altogether before they became customers. In practice, however, that isn't easy. Even managers who use sophisticated approaches to assess their prospects will be unable to avoid a few that simply don't belong. Ask any banker whose carefully selected customers default on a loan.)

That leaves the 80 percent who are the bread-and-butter customers in most thriving businesses. This core group typically is the most profitable and thus is worth holding on to. Even though this group may not be as vocal or demanding as the others, market leaders know how important it is to give its bread-and-butter customers the benefit of the progress generated by stretch customers. Thus, they achieve a proper balance between stretch customers and this core group.

MAKING SURE CUSTOMERS "GET IT"

Especially for companies on the cutting edge, the greatest challenge of the New Economy isn't coming up with a new product but making sure that their customers understand what it can do and how to use it. The new market leaders have mastered this problem with powerful tools of persuasion and assistance. Not only do they focus on their customers; they also work hard to make sure their customers accept the new ideas, fully understand them, and benefit from any available improvements and innovations. This is no easy task.

Human willingness to change behavior is clearly limited. One example that comes to mind is the Massachusetts Turnpike. Some time ago, the Mass Pike introduced new electronic tollbooths for its *fast lane*. After arranging to prepay the toll fees or have them automatically deducted monthly from a bank account, drivers could zip through the toll gates while a windshield-mounted gadget recorded their passage.

I signed up for the timesaving innovation before it was even operational. But to my surprise, few other travelers did the same. Even today, with the fast-lane technology in place for almost two years, I see only a fraction of drivers taking advantage of it. Of course, I am not complaining about zooming past lines of waiting cars, but I am baffled. Even allowing for infrequent users and out-of-state drivers, I am astonished that so many people continue to inch forward at a snail's pace when, simply by signing up, they could enjoy life in the fast lane.

The point is that despite an innovation's merits, people do not relinquish their habits easily, a fact that the new market leaders are exquisitely sensitive to. But as we will see in later chapters, customers adopt innovations at different speeds and with different levels of enthusiasm. Figuring out how they might be tempted into changing their buying and consumption habits, even when the advantages of doing so are apparent, requires more than a casual approach.

Here again, focus is crucial. The new leaders know that the problems of dissemination are now even more important than creating additional goods and services. As Siebel Systems did with

Ford Motor, leaders make sure that customers "get it" by providing training, hand-holding, and whatever else it takes.

Think of Dell Computer. Its ostensible claim to fame is its direct sales model, which allows customers to buy Dell products extremely efficiently at good prices. But this accounts for only part of the company's success. What sets it apart, particularly for repeat customers, is its superior customer support, which ranges from user-friendly Internet assistance to around-the-clock telephone access to technicians ready to resolve the inevitable hiccups that personal computers seem prone to. And when neither self-help nor technical support can resolve a problem, same-day or next-day on-site support from a qualified service provider is available.

The same kind of attention to customer needs helps explain the extraordinary success of IBM's global service operations, the most profitable and rapidly growing branch of IBM by far. Siebel Systems, SAP, and Oracle Corporation are among other technology companies whose successes are strongly coupled to their ability to get customers up and running.

For years, SAP has relied on an army of strategic partners to implement its software applications. It has also developed its own methodology—aptly named ASAP—to help customers install and configure its applications. What SAP and other technology companies have recognized is that if their growth has a bottleneck, it is where customers get stuck and need help to understand, accept, and use the goods and services already available.

That customers want and expect more advice from their suppliers is apparent, and in response, market leaders are experimenting with new kinds of relationship with their customers. These new relationships help the market leaders gain market share and, at the same time, translate into profits. First, the extra services themselves are sources of revenue; second and more important, once customers are comfortable with innovation, they are ready to buy more of it.

OUTSIZED AMBITION

In the age of customer scarcity and the Internet, the boldness and ambition of the new market leaders are unprecedented. Like their market presence, their aspirations are larger than life. They stretch their resources to the maximum and set unprecedented goals for businesses still in their infancy. They are determined to rule their markets and have no qualms about making the serious and risky commitments necessary to do so. Such spirit stands in marked contrast to the traditional manager's tendency to spread risk and exposure, to take small, well-tested steps forward, and to avoid putting all the eggs in one basket.

Not long ago I spoke to the leaders of a company in the cut-throat communications field that, in terms of its competencies and operating model, looked very promising. But one vital element was missing: The leaders' aspirations were woefully inadequate for the battles that lay ahead.

Instead of making the courageous decisions required to become the undisputed market leader in a chosen segment, they were spreading their resources over a host of different technologies, markets, and customers—trying to avoid becoming overly reliant on any one. In spite of its talent and reputation, this company set itself up to flounder for at least the next few years, becoming easy prey for rivals with fewer resources but more focus and gumption.

You don't have to look far for leaders and companies that exemplify boldness. One is Qwest Communications International Inc., a telecom company with sales of barely $70 million just six years ago. After hiring former AT&T Corp. executive Joseph Nacchio in 1997, the company embarked upon a huge acquisition spree, initially gobbling up LCI and then agreeing to a merger with US West. The 1999 sales of this combination exceeded $17 billion. Just imagine this jump: from $70 million to $17 billion in six years. If Nacchio was a flea setting out to attack an elephant, he wasn't fazed. Rather, he figured out how it could be done—and did it.

Qwest's founder, Denver oil baron Philip Anschutz, gambled against conventional wisdom by laying nearly nine hundred thousand miles of fiber-optic cable, building bandwidth at a time when experts said it would not be needed. Now, with data traffic quintupling every year and the competition scrambling to catch up, Qwest has a clear lead.

With the capacity to transmit 31 million phone calls simultaneously, Qwest needed customers, and Nacchio set out to find them. Initially at least, he bought them in a spectacular series of acquisitions, primarily using other people's money and his own soaring stock price to swallow up much bigger companies.

In 1993, Amazon.com didn't exist. Less than seven years later, it ranked 17 on my list of the one hundred new market leaders. Its aspirations are enormous. As CEO Jeff Bezos told *Business Week* magazine, "We want to build a place where people can find and discover anything they might want to buy online." Books and music were only the beginning. In short order, the Internet retailer has expanded into clothing, collectibles, electronics, photography, and a myriad of other product categories. On-line auctions and referrals to other merchants are among the latest initiatives. Amazon.com is in a super hurry to cultivate customers and put together an efficiently scaled infrastructure. With expenditures amounting to $1.50 for every dollar of sales it brings in, its efforts certainly amount to an audacious bet on the future.

At number 2, General Electric was the highest-ranking of the old blue-chip companies, in large part because it is as bold, if not bolder, than any newcomer. Just listen to the language that Jack Welch used in a recent speech: "Reality in the Internet world means moving at a fanatical, maniacal pace everywhere in GE!" As anyone who is familiar with the company can tell you, these aren't empty words: GE is surging ahead at Internet speed.

Again, the market leaders' boldness should not be confused with recklessness. Yet their willingness to place much larger bets in order to pursue outsized opportunities represents a fundamentally different approach to life. They have much more than grandiose fantasies; the new market leaders have the capacity to make their visions come true even if others think them ludicrous.

A decade ago, Qwest's meteoric rise would have been considered impossible. Five years ago, anyone who predicted that Amazon.com's market capitalization would surpass that of Caterpillar, Volkswagen AG, or Campbell Soup Company would have been told, "You're out of your mind."

Today, business works on a totally different scale with different standards and different expectations of performance. The horizons are boundless, the pace is quicker, the growth is bigger—and its essence is boldness.

CHAPTER 5

Discover the New Customers

Imagine a modern Rip Van Winkle waking up from a twenty-year sleep. He would surely be amazed at how the world has changed: He would be bewildered by new technology, bowled over at the speed and clutter of life in 2001, dazzled by the sheer abundance being thrust at him. The torrent of new products, goods, services, ideas, and innovations vying for his attention would be shocking.

How would he react? I suspect, like people through the ages in suddenly changed circumstances, Rip would reset his bearings from his old perspective before cautiously testing the new water. Like a child who clings to a teddy bear well into adolescence, or a lottery winner who repaints the old house, he would cling to the familiar and be slow to embrace what is new.

As customers of the New Economy, we all share that shock to one degree or another. Unlike Rip or a lottery winner, we didn't suddenly face a totally new landscape. Our horizons have expanded more gradually. And as I will explain in this chapter, Rip's reaction is only one of four distinct behavior patterns we display when confronted with major changes in our environment. But for us, too, the proliferation of choices and new riches create anxiety and discomfort, as well as opportunity.

Of course, this isn't the aspect of the New Economy that the media celebrate. Journalists searching for a fresh story focus on the opportunities, not the hesitations. Yet even the most enterprising and open-minded customers in today's cornucopia can find themselves in a quandary. No one is inclined to throw out his or her comfortable old shoes or reliable two-year-old computer simply because a new style or an improved model has appeared. They may not be sure they need a new one; they don't necessarily want to spend the money; and they surely don't have the time to choose between all the different-sounding yet similar-appearing alternatives.

Unfortunately, buying something doesn't usually resolve your problems. The purchase is just the first step; then you must use and extract value from it. Will it be compatible with what you already have? If not, how hard will it be to learn how to use it? Are you buying more than you can consume? Will your new book from the on-line retailer lie unread in the pile on your bedside table? Will you feel guilt for spending money, regretful for not having enough time, or anxious about keeping up with what seems important?

These are real feelings that nearly all customers share, at least to some extent, so managers who fail to understand them or don't take advantage of the various ways customers adjust to the new conditions will never be among the new market leaders. But this misreading of the market is pervasive. Business publications are rife with references to "fickle," "disloyal," and "whimsical" customers—as if it were the customers' fault that companies can't sell them goods and services. In reality, the flighty customer is a self-serving rationalization for failing managers who can view the world only from their own perspective, not the client's. Certainly, today's customers are intolerant of shortcomings. That they have many alternatives from which to choose only makes them more demanding than ever. But to call them disloyal or fickle is merely to duck the hard work of understanding what drives them and avoids your need to adjust your operations accordingly.

The new market leaders have done just that. And they have found and attracted customers who are ahead of their competitors in resolving their quandaries. The message these customers are sending to suppliers is clear: Don't just tout your product. Help us make the right choice, then teach us how to use it.

When uncertain, customers gravitate toward sellers who inspire trust and are committed to delivering results, not just products. These suppliers have value propositions that leave no doubt as to the benefits of their products or services, and their offerings are clearly distinguishable from their competitors'—as the examples in the previous chapter reflected.

These complex relationships between buyers and sellers aren't limited to consumer markets. Business customers feel the same ambivalence. They, too, flounder to keep up with their evolving world. Witness the revolving fashions in management concepts: from yesterday's TQM, mission statements, service guarantees, and business reengineering to today's customer relationship management, electronic marketplaces, virtual organizations, e-learning, and e-engineering.

Surveys indicate that the success rate of management initiatives is far from perfect: Less than half of the companies that have adopted them report feeling "extremely satisfied." And no matter what survey I look at, the life span of new initiatives, already less than three years, is getting shorter. In other words, the majority of new concepts that companies put in place don't last beyond three years or end up disappointing their sponsors. All of this proves, if proof were needed, that corporate customers are having as much trouble as the rest of us in absorbing change.

Customers differ in their problems. What's daunting for some is the sheer variety of choices; for others, it is the concern that they won't extract enough value from their purchases. So it's important for managers to understand the varying ways their customers behave in the new marketplace. After all, there is money to be made from shoppers of all types. Insights into their motivations and shifting priorities give companies the inside track on the concerns, preferences, and comforting factors that count the most in their buying decisions.

The new market leaders know that the greatest constraint on today's customers is time—more critical even than money. The broader choices, the constant stream of innovations, and the pace of contemporary life conspire to crowd people's schedules. Whether you're in the market for a CD player for home or a new supplier of components for your company, you don't have time to evaluate every option, consider every shred of information, and explore every contingency—even though it would probably be useful to do so.

Time is a flexible commodity: We willingly spend more of it on some activities than on others. A busy manager for whom every minute counts will happily spend hours on the golf course, but an easygoing person with time to chat will hang up angrily on a telemarketer who calls at dinnertime.

Yet time is also rigid: There are only twenty-four hours in a day, and allocating them is a zero-sum decision. Time spent on any activity takes away from time available for any other. The time you spend deciding what to buy and actually buying it could also be spent on a host of things: mowing the lawn, surfing the Internet, watching television, attending your child's soccer game, reading a novel—name your favorite activity.

In general, the less time and effort it takes to get what we want routinely, the more time we have for complex situations that require choices. Thus, zipping through the no-brainer chore of buying pencils and stamps is prerequisite to, say, a romantic dinner at a great restaurant, since it buys time for checking out the restaurant critic's review, choosing the right wine, and lingering over dessert. So what's at work here is the customer's personal priorities about using time.

Different people make different compromises. Even identical twins will not spend time in exactly the same manner. Moreover, any given person will allocate time differently from one situation to the next. Nearly everyone takes longer to consider a dinner menu than to pick up coffee and a muffin on the way to work. Even so, some will ponder the dinner menu longer than others, considering more possibilities, perhaps even trying something new—and that type of person, in the morning, may pause long enough to switch occasionally from a muffin to a cinnamon roll.

Customers making purchasing decisions are solving problems. Some are enjoyable (making vacation plans, looking for new golf clubs); some are not (having a tooth pulled); most fall somewhere in between. In general, the amount of time a person spends shopping for and buying a particular item is directly proportional to how weighty he or she considers that particular problem. What else has to be accomplished with the time is also a factor. For people with an active curiosity, hours of Web surfing may be well spent and pass quickly. For others, with more pressing problems, five minutes adrift in a gigantic Wal-Mart store may be monumentally irritating. Most people facing a major purchase problem—anything from buying a wedding dress to approving a new fighter plane—consider it eminently worthwhile to let it consume a significant block of time. Yet even in this position, some buyers prefer to solve the problem by getting advice and help from others rather than making the decision alone.

In the end, the intersection of abundant choices and limited time evokes two issues for customers—and two key insights for managers into their buying decisions. The first is how open to change the customers are: Are they willing to free up time to explore multiple alternatives, or will they try to limit their time and effort, and thus their choices? The second issue is how ready they are to leverage their time by relying on others: Do they prefer to be self-reliant, or will they call for advice and assistance?

From this view, all customers range along two variable lines—their willingness to change and their willingness to leverage others for help and advice. Each variable is an axis of a matrix that divides the customer universe into four quadrants (see Figure 12).

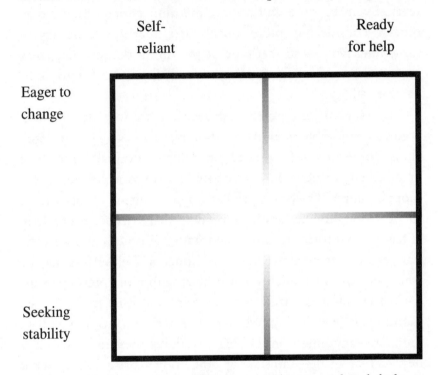

Self-
reliant

Ready
for help

Eager to
change

Seeking
stability

Figure 12. Customers' willingness to change and seek help

We'll come back to this graphic view in more detail later in the chapter. For now, note that the quadrants don't mark abrupt divisions: Each axis of the matrix is a continuum, so that eagerness to change shades gradually into unvarying routine, and self-reliance yields by degrees to acceptance of help and advice.

No individual consumer behaves consistently in all of his or her purchases; for instance, we might want automatic reliability in our newspaper delivery service but spend weeks deliberating which of two paintings to buy. Similarly, the customer who feels confident and secure in choosing her own automobile may want help and advice in buying stocks and bonds.

From a seller's viewpoint, however, these individual inconsistencies hardly matter. Some businesses (newspaper delivery, for one) attract customers who, at least in that context, fit the bottom half of the matrix, and some (cutting-edge computer lessons, for instance) are for people in their change-ripe mode. Some products and services appeal to do-it-yourselfers (for example, gourmet cookbooks) and some to consumers who like to be pampered (luxury tours).

What every manager needs to know is what kind of customers she is serving, and thus how to meet those customers' needs and keep them coming back. There's money to be made in every quadrant of the matrix—but only by those companies that thoroughly understand the vagaries of their markets.

Now let's look in more detail at the vertical axis—openness to change.

FROM STATUS QUO TO WHOLESALE CHANGE

With all the demands on our time, it's not surprising that for the most part, most of us value our routines and aren't about to embrace every conceivable new possibility that comes our way.

We're willing to examine options when we're excited about a new product or service, or frustrated by what we have. But if we're enjoying our current condition (or disliking alternatives), we will be in no mood to change, much less spend any time listening to a sales pitch. "Give us more of the same, and don't bother us with the newfangled stuff," we say. Like the worker who prefers his familiar job to the uncertainties of promotion, we resist any unfamiliarity. We would rather spend our time preserving and building on what we have than exploring what we could be doing instead.

When buyers aren't ready to change, they see the abundance of choices in today's markets as a potential disruption of their status quo. New suppliers aren't going to get their attention unless they recognize and find ways to deal with that problem.

One alternative, of course, is simply to give the customers more of what they have been getting. But even in businesses firmly rooted in the bottom half of the matrix—commuter railroads, for instance, or heating oil suppliers—there are, in fact, two ways to persuade customers to accept change.

The first method is to ease into it: Don't put pressure on the customers' time, make no sudden moves, disrupt them as little as possible, and gradually nudge them to the realization that yes, there is merit in making a move. Automatic payment by bank transfer, for instance, would make commuting or feeding the furnace even more hassle-free, and change-averse consumers can be persuaded to try it.

These customers respond better to gentle and gradual changes than they do to drastic ones. A lot of the prevailing wisdom about customer service and nurturing repeat buying patterns is based on this concept: the mantra "Make it easy for the customers to do business with you, empathize with and delight them, and above all, don't rock the boat."

This is the logic underlying the no-haggle approach to selling cars that has gained popularity in the past decade. The idea was to appeal to people who disliked the usual experience at a car dealer's showroom so much that they would drive their old car for a few more years rather than undergo it. To win these customers, companies such as Saturn and dealers such as CarMax and AutoNation offered fixed prices, so that customers wouldn't have to spend time, effort, and psychic capital to negotiate a deal. This method also minimized disruptions and intrusions on the showroom floor, again helping to soothe customers' nerves.

Many clients welcomed this civilized approach and rewarded these companies with their business. But it was not an unqualified success. When the new dealers' sales numbers were compared with those of the more assertive old-style showrooms, the latter typically did better, primarily because, though the customers in the low-pressured settings enjoyed the experience, they took longer to decide. The conventional dealers knew how to exert pressure to get wavering clients to make up their minds.

The second way to persuade reluctant customers to accept change is to blast them through it: Make it imperative for them to act, then guide them through the process with as much speed as possible. "Just get it over and done with" is their watchword. A dentist's patient, for instance, knows that having a tooth pulled will hurt only briefly and will soon be forgotten. Customers tend to approach buying a new computer system in the same fatalistic spirit.

Even the most change-averse customers will endure intrusions if they are perceived as inevitable, sporadic, and brief. Still, a be-grudging assent to a onetime big change doesn't mean that a steady stream of disruptions will be tolerated.

Again, for these customers the amount of time demanded is crucial. They prefer to get the house remodeled all at once, rather than spread the project over several years. Once they take the leap into a new computer system or an e-mail provider, they don't want to think about upkeep or other hassles. In fact, the less they have to think about their system for any reason, the more content they will be. Constant reminders and offers of new bells and whistles will be resented unless they require little, if any, time and effort, like AOL's automatic upgrades that simply take over the customer's PC and feed themselves into the system. Of course, not everyone is averse to change. For example, the customers represented in the top of our change axis are ripe for it. Far from savoring stability, they are motivated by the promise of new possibilities. Their problem is the opposite of preserving the present; they are figuring out ways to tap the future. They want as many options as possible and are more than willing to spend time making them. Not that it takes them very long to decide; on the contrary, their needs are so pressing that it is hard to describe them as patient folk.

They want action and don't want to be slowed down by suppliers. They want to be showered with information, offered free product demonstrations, and provided with unexpected technical support. They would rather deal with a new product's inevitable glitches and shortcomings than wait out a delay in its introduction. Though they will complain—loudly—when anything goes wrong, they won't drop you as a supplier as long as you keep them involved. They want to be listened to and want suppliers to solicit their input, particularly if that fuels further innovation and improvements.

That is the whole idea of what seems, at first glance, to be a high-risk gamble in the software industry: Companies launch new products by giving free copies to thousands of hackers and other venturesome users. In practice, the giveaway pays dividends. The early users form, in effect, worldwide communities of test-drivers who reward the companies by suggesting new twists and refinements and by getting rid of their products' bugs and errors. The companies have identified and capitalized on one of the most change-avid audiences on earth.

With change-ripe customers, the supplier's challenge is not to get their attention but to retain it. Their attention span is a practiced flicker; they're eager to check you out, but you won't merit a second look unless they considered the first one worthwhile.

What they value are activities and products that make them feel special, in control, or ahead of the pack. This may include keeping up with the latest fashion, having the newest technology, going on the most exotic adventure vacation, or even driving the hardest bargain for a car (these people actually enjoy haggling or anything else that gives them a sense of accomplishment and a feeling of control). These customers have a permanent appetite for the latest and greatest, the better alternative, and the most unexpected deal. "If you surprise us and give us more," they tell their suppliers, "we'll make time for you." Likewise, as business customers, the change-ripe are hungry for what is new and different. They are always on the prowl for better ways to run their operations and exploit the riches of the new marketplace. Their use of time is linked to their business priorities. Some spend it hunting for alternative sources of supply or for better prices. Others will use time to update business practices and make their offerings stand out. As a supplier, you earn their time by understanding what they want and helping them achieve it. But if you don't keep up with them, don't be surprised if they find other sources of supply.

Again, no consumer behaves the same all the time. We tend either to welcome change or to seek the comfort of stability, but for some purchases our attitude will alter. Still, the message is clear: To appeal effectively to different kinds of customers, suppliers need to know how open each customer is to changing and exploring alternatives. What appeals to one kind of customer can be a turnoff for others. If you are too gentle or too staid or don't offer enough choice, the fast changer's attention will be lost. Meanwhile, stability seekers won't give you their time if you move at Internet speed or overwhelm them with alternatives.

FROM SELF-RELIANCE
TO THE CATERED LIFE

The horizontal axis of our matrix represents the degree to which customers are willing to seek advice or help.

The self-reliant people, in the left quadrants, like to mow their own grass, but those on the right prefer to hire a maintenance service and free up their time for other tasks. In a restaurant, some prefer to help themselves at the buffet or use the take-out service, while others don't mind waiting to be served at the table.

There's more at work here than time pressure alone: Customers clearly occupy a range of attitudes, from do-it-myself independence to a heavy reliance on others. A supplier who confuses one type ("I'm just browsing; I'll call you when I need help") with the other ("Could you show me what's available and help me make up my mind?") does so at her peril.

In the process of purchasing, a customer's decision to rely solely on himself or to leverage others depends mainly on how complex he perceives the decision will be.

When the task at hand is simple, self-reliance may be the answer. But in other cases, we have no choice but to call on others. As technology keeps adding layers of complexity to life, it often seems that the more intelligence is embedded in our products, the more human intelligence it takes to acquire, use, and repair them. Fewer and fewer people can fix their own cars or upgrade the hard drives in their computers.

Even if consumers are not entirely prepared to perform a specific task, they may treasure their independence or just not feel like bringing a supplier up to speed on a complex problem. Suppose you have just completed your tax returns but would like a CPA to check your work. Your accountant, however, requests all sorts of documentation to feed his computer programs and generate his version of your returns. He also expects the same fee he would charge had he done the returns from scratch. "Too much trouble," you decide; "I'll take my chances alone." In other words, customers are likely to balk when the cost or effort of switching from self-reliance to leveraging others is greater than they are willing to expend.

In a heavy surf, even a good swimmer may need help. Customers are no different. If your septic system needs replacement, if you need surgery, or if you want to sell your company, it is time to relinquish your self-reliance and hire the best help you can afford. But the greater the scope of the buying decision, the higher the stake, so it is crucial that you scrutinize your prospective suppliers. It is logical that the quality and quantity of your help increases as the problem becomes bigger and more complex. You need a supplier who you trust, who genuinely understands your aim, and with whom you can share your sense of apprehension. This is especially important if your bias is to be self-reliant and you are only reluctantly asking for help.

To this point, we have considered the willingness to change and readiness to accept help as separate ways to sort out customers. But it is where the two axes intersect to form the quadrants as we have defined them that gives managers their most useful view of the changing priorities of the customer universe. The customer who combines self-reliance with a fondness for routine behaves quite differently from the consumer who is just as change-averse but wants help and advice. While variations along each axis create an almost infinite number of customer types, the four main classifications are essential to managers trying to understand their markets.

Here is the previous matrix, with additional labels in each of the four quadrants—searchers, streamliners, delegators, and collaborators (see Figure 13). As the arrows suggest, the more the market is fluctuating (which means heightened change pressures and complexities), the more we will see customers' priorities shifting away from the center toward one of the four distinctive behavioral patterns.

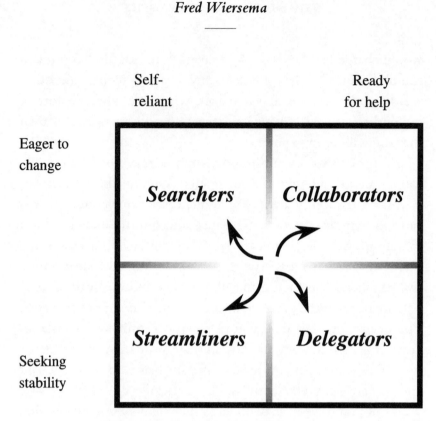

Figure 13. Customers' buying patterns

Let's apply the matrix to a single set of decisions and examine how various shopping types might buy their dinner. The top left quadrant, which holds the searchers, as I refer to them (self-reliant and open to change), would be represented by a gourmet who plans a menu, shops carefully at a different store for each ingredient, cooks for hours, and relishes each bite. At the bottom left is the streamliner (self-reliant, but at the same time relishing routine)— in this case, a stereotypical bachelor who buys a case of baked beans once a month and eats a can for dinner every evening. Moving to the top right (collaborators), the gourmet who is willing to accept help with new experiences could go to a restaurant and spend half an hour reading the menu. (A representative of the group at the extreme top right, in full collaboration mode, could call in advance to discuss the day's special possibilities with the chef, planning the meal with his suggestions and advice.) Moving to the right in the bottom tier (delegators), the change-averse bachelor who is more willing to accept help could order a ready-cooked dinner for delivery—possibly the same dinner every night. Someone meeting the criteria for the extreme lower right would, in full delegation mode, let the take-out cook who knows his preferences plan variations on the meal for him.

In the following pages, we will examine each of the four customer buying patterns. Later in the book, separate chapters are devoted to the care and feeding of customers displaying these patterns, analyzing not only how the new market leaders have learned to capture them but how they perpetuate their leadership.

SEARCHERS

Consumers in this category—self-reliant, open to new experiences, and ready to spend a lot of time at the task—are consummate shoppers. They read *Consumer Reports,* examine stores and Internet sites, and constantly pursue sales, bargains, and innovative products. Some virtually live to buy; all regard shopping as time well spent.

Searchers relish the feeling that they are in charge of their lives and like to participate directly in whatever is the task at hand. Driven by curiosity, a sense of anticipation, and an itch to be in the forefront, they like to be first on their block to own a new product. They boast of getting the best deal and return home from an exhausting shopping trip with a real sense of victory: They have made their own decisions, and they were the right ones.

This person is open to new things, including your arrival in the market, provided that you introduce yourself in a simpatico way and maintain a larger-than-life market presence. Making a big splash will attract the attention of the search-and-browsers, and with them, free publicity is more effective than costly advertising.

Richard Branson, adventure-loving founder of the offbeat Virgin Atlantic airline and its many spin-offs, has a penchant for publicity stunts. In 1994, for example, he filmed an episode of television's bikini-bopping *Baywatch* while riding water skis pulled by Virgin Atlantic's company blimp. He lasted 1.5 miles. Not only did this get enormous media coverage, but Branson became one of only four blimp-powered water-skiers on earth.

Four years later, Branson issued a challenge to Jeffrey Taylor, chief executive officer of Monster.com, the world's biggest on-line site for job seekers. Besides acquiring 12 million accounts and 7 million résumés, Taylor's company owns a 165-foot blimp named *Trump.*

Early in 2000, Taylor blimp-water-skied behind *Trump* for 3.3 miles, erasing Branson's record. Naturally, Branson promptly challenged Taylor to compete in a blimp-to-blimp water-skiing race in Las Vegas. By no coincidence, Branson planned to be there, launching Virgin Atlantic's new service between Las Vegas and London.

If we take it on faith, for now at least, that Branson and Taylor know what they are doing, then clearly their efforts are aimed at searchers—the novelty lovers most likely to see merit in any company that makes a joyful noise. Having done just that, Virgin Atlantic and Monster.com boosted their name recognition all over the world. To search-mode customers, at least, these two companies will always be first in their fields.

STREAMLINERS

Self-reliant and change-averse, these customers shop for themselves but streamline the process by eliminating variety. They spend as little time and effort as possible. Rolling their carts through a supermarket once a week, they spend most of their lunch hours at the same fast food restaurant and promptly renew their magazine subscriptions. They want their choices narrowed;

they form buying habits easily and will endure a lot of aggravation before looking for a new supplier.

We are all streamliners in some facets of our lives—the heating-oil contract, newspaper delivery service, and so forth. Some customers want similar hassle-free interactions with as many suppliers as possible. This may reflect a simple yearning for comfort and peace of mind, or a sense of priorities: The less time a painter spends worrying about her supplies, the more she can ponder her creative problems. She pays top dollar for trouble-free, high-quality brushes and paint from a dealer she trusts—and keeps going back for more.

DELEGATORS

On the bottom right of the matrix are the change-averse, help-seeking shoppers who delegate as much of their buying as they can to suppliers or intermediaries. They prefer not to spend time at the chore and don't want to get personally involved if they don't have to.

Delegators will sign up for a cruise to avoid planning their own travel itinerary. In buying computers, they hire experts to take care of everything, from purchase to installation to remaining on call in case of glitches. Delegators are the perfect turnkey customers. Convert any of their needs or problems into a comprehensive package and they will be drawn to it.

Like streamliners, delegators are trying to off-load the pressures and complexities of buying decisions by making them as automatic as possible. But they go a step further in looking for suppliers who are market leaders and can do the job better than the delegators themselves could. They count on a creative approach that will solve problems for them without involving their own time and thought.

The legendary newspaper correspondent Richard Harding

Davis was delegating when he hired a London messenger boy in 1915 to deliver invitations to a party. He was delegating when he gave the boy a letter proposing marriage to his sweetheart in Chicago, and left it to him to figure out how to get there. (The messenger took the *Lusitania* and came back eighteen days later with the reply. She said yes.)

A corporate example of a delegator is DaimlerChrysler. This automaker has transcended rivals General Motors and Ford in outsourcing such major components of its cars as exhaust systems and entire power trains, preserving for itself only those systems and activities it does best.

COLLABORATORS

The fourth quadrant comprises change-ripe customers, who, like the delegators, hire expertise they themselves lack but, unlike the delegators, insist on staying personally involved in the job. In remodeling a house, for example, a collaborator would not only team up with a designer; he or she would work side by side with the expert to create the best-suited outcome.

Collaborators are not to be confused with kibitzers, meddlers, or control freaks. An authentic collaborator genuinely appreciates the depth of knowledge and practical skills of well-chosen experts. Such collaborators respond well to suppliers—such as a truly devoted banker—who offer themselves as coaches, mentors, or partners in launching a customer's new business venture.

Some collaborators go a step further: They hire professional expertise and guidance to attain better results than they could achieve on their own, but they are convinced that their own insights and knowledge of their field will be critical aspects of the eventual solution. However talented the collaborator's architect is, this client needs to tell him or her that the manufacturing area of the new plant will almost surely shrink in five years as outsourcing progresses. Then the client and architect will work together to plan what will expand into that space and how it can be designed for both uses.

The Internet has vaulted collaboration into one of the world's growth industries. By 2003, some analysts predict, 62 percent of all industrial spending on e-business will go to support the implementation and maintenance of new technology. Only 29 percent of the spending will pay for hardware, and a mere 9 percent for software. As in the emergence of railroads, the digital evolution has progressed from creating technology to applying it—in a word, to services. The winners are service providers so reliable that their customers increasingly make them partners.

When market leaders understand the shifting attitudes and priorities of new customers, they find it much easier to evaluate the buying decisions of those customers. One reason that the laggards can't catch up to the leaders is that the less vigorous companies fail to recognize customers' distinctive purchasing patterns; hence, they treat buyers as a generic group.

I am not the first to note that New Economy companies, in particular, are sending mixed messages to the marketplace by appealing to customers in contradictory ways. If one day they speak to search-and-browsers, the next day it is toward streamliners or delegators that their efforts seem aimed. As a result, customers are confused, which inevitably translates into sales lost to rivals that position themselves consistently. This is a self-inflicted wound at the moment when clarity is the most direct and best route to a customer's heart.

CHAPTER 6

Entice the Searchers

J ust three thousand souls gathered in an insufferably hot tent when the Computer Dealer Expo, the annual Las Vegas computer show better known as COMDEX, opened for the first time, in 1979. Twenty years later, two hundred thousand visitors and twenty-one hundred businesses jammed into a million square feet of blissfully air-conditioned convention space—making COMDEX the world's largest technology convention, and possibly the most important.

Steven Jobs introduced Apple's revolutionary Lisa computer at COMDEX in 1983; Microsoft introduced Windows there in 1985; the term "hacker" was coined at COMDEX in 1988; and it was there, in 1992, that IBM unveiled its ThinkPad laptop computer.

COMDEX is a search-and-browse customer's paradise, a place where change-avid customers who enjoy conducting their own research on a given purchase can indulge their desires to their hearts' content. The convention works as a kind of laboratory for attracting and keeping searchers—a model that market leaders are quietly adapting to lure customers to their own businesses.

Searchers, as you remember, are independent, skeptical, and like to keep everything in their own hands, where they can control them. They want to be first, will struggle against constraint, and they seek empowerment. COMDEX empowers them. In fact, since searchers desire a world full of possibilities, COMDEX is their Valhalla. There they can play with and compare new products at their leisure. They can talk to the technicians who designed them, the product managers who know them inside and out, and they can discuss them endlessly with their fellow searchers.

The customers at COMDEX, of course, are mainly computer aficionados who love technological novelty above all else; they are not the typical search-and-browsers we all want to have as customers. To reach this larger, general population, we have to modify the model, softening the edges while holding on to its core.

One market leader, Cisco Systems, has done just that. As the provider of most of the infrastructure for the Internet, Cisco shot to stardom on Wall Street in the mid-nineties. In May 2000, it enjoyed a 75 percent share of the market for routers (the devices that guide the traffic flow of information on the Internet) and was a premier provider of a host of other communications products and network management services.

In 1998, in response to increased competition from start-ups as well as from established companies including IBM, Cisco began in all seriousness to buy up smaller companies as a way of expanding its product lines and enhancing its market presence. By 1998, under president and chief executive officer John Chambers, Cisco's market capitalization exceeded $100 billion. It was the youngest company ever to reach that milestone.

Cisco is a product-leadership company: It generates an endless flow of innovations, each of which seems to spawn its own product smorgasbord. But as its managers realized early on, being a product leader is not enough to qualify as a market leader in the New Economy. To attain that level of success, a company must give its customers the tools that allow them to conclude that its products are superior. The company has to provide a participatory experience.

Corporate attitudes toward customers are making a 180-degree rotation, from excluding to including them. Today's smart manager doesn't tout a product; rather, he or she gives savvy consumers the information they need to form their own judgments. Smart companies are committed to helping their customers arrive at a sophisticated understanding of products and innovations—and here, the COMDEX convention does provide a model.

For many years, Cisco aimed its sales efforts at network administrators. In general, this group resembles the technology-oriented people who attend shows like COMDEX. A few years ago, Cisco managers decided to sell directly to the end user, the person who applies the product to perform a business function. That meant reorienting its sales efforts to target line managers and business managers. At the same time, Cisco realized that the managers have an abundance of similar products or systems from which to choose.

Cisco jettisoned its customary selling practices and began teaching potential buyers how to make informed choices. With all of its wares on the table, including non-Cisco products, the company held candid discussions of the pros and cons of each and let customers make up their own minds.

Today that idea has grown exponentially. At its two executive briefing centers in San Jose, California, Cisco's educational facilities cater to approximately thirty-five different customer groups every day, with anywhere from six to sixty people in each group. Typical sessions, which last from four to six hours, deal with business and technology issues and trends, or whatever a customer chooses to bring up. The response has been overwhelmingly positive. General Electric alone has sent no fewer than fifty teams of managers to San Jose during the past year. Cisco CEO John Chambers considers the program so vital that he personally attends nearly 150 sessions a year, which translates into about 20 percent of his working days. The education effort ranks equally high in the priorities of his senior staff.

Donning masks of neutrality, Cisco people share their insights with an audience that is eager to learn about the business potential and technology challenges of cutting-edge applications in general, not just Cisco's products. It is an invigorating and empowering experience, and one that reinforces Cisco's market leadership. Surely, it brings in sales, but the benefits reach deeper: The company learns much about its customers, including their needs, frustrations, and biases—knowledge that contributes to keeping Cisco ahead of the curve.

Yet, beneficial as the sought-after executive briefings are, they extend Cisco's reach to hundreds of thousands, not millions of potential customers. That means the next challenge is scalability, to use a much-uttered Silicon Valley term that refers to the ease with which some approach can be put to much-expanded use. Awkward as the word is, it somehow is a good fit for the bold aspirations that drive the market leaders as well as the vast and yet to be explored potential of the Internet.

Cisco's latest initiative to scale up its influence in the marketplace is both imaginative and self-evident. Launched in July of 2000, it is called e-learning. Its purpose is to leverage the Internet to help companies and individuals deliver and absorb knowledge and expertise better, faster, and more flexibly, thus helping them become more agile and stay abreast of rapid change. As Gary Daichendt, executive vice president of worldwide operations, puts it, "E-learning is the initiative that we have in place that makes most efficient use of [our people's] time and their resources, [and] allows them not to have to travel. And in this technology business, where it's so important to keep updated on the latest information, on the newest products that are coming out in industry trends, we have the capability to do that."

Cisco uses its own experience with e-learning to set a compelling example for other companies. What better way to develop and test a new approach than to apply it to one of the toughest customers around, in this case your own company? In a multi-hour briefing on the Web, Cisco team members explain how they are rolling out their e-learning initiative internally, and with a partner and reseller base consisting of about thirty thousand entities in 137 different countries. In one case study, in the sales-and-service organization, Diane Bower, senior manager of e-learning solutions marketing, explains how twelve curriculum tracks were developed within eight months, giving Cisco's field sales engineering organization access to up-to-date information and fully customizable training modules anywhere in the world. The contrasts with traditional education and training methods are stark. Says Bower, "You'll have moved from running an internal training program to managing an internal dot-com." Aside from its much broader reach and its inherent efficiency, e-learning can be self-paced and suited to individual needs; real-time virtual classes let students connect into a live session to collaborate with other learners and interact with the instructor on-line; and robust tracking capabilities provide instant feedback to learners and their mentors.

In the words of John Chambers, e-learning "represents the biggest payoff opportunity of the Internet economy." That is not a surprising statement coming from someone who fervently believes that, going forward, the two pivotal forces in life are the Internet and education, and whose company would be the first one to benefit from searchers' quest for empowerment in a networked world.

WINNING MARKET STRATEGIES

Cisco's success embodies a variety of success strategies used by market leaders to appeal to search-and-browse customers. It provides an abundance of product or service choices; it offers access to a lot of information to educate and empower the customer; it consistently pioneers new products and services; and it enriches and expedites customers' buying experience. Whether applied in combination or on their own, each of these strategies capitalizes on the shifting priorities of this demanding group of customers. Let's take a closer look at how some other companies apply each of these strategies.

Offer Choices—the More the Merrier

The abundance and sumptuousness of its food characterizes the Club Med vacation. Breakfast, for example, is a smorgasbord of fruit, all styles of eggs, pancakes, French toast, hot and cold cereals, and even steak and fish dishes. When vacationers first encounter this display, most sample as much of everything as they can. After a few days, however, most settle on a few favorites, blithely ignoring the rest. But don't make the mistake of limiting their menu. What seduces the searchers is the liberating effect of choice. Actually availing themselves of the cornucopia comes second.

That reaction is typical of today's searchers in any market. They want to consider the widest possible range of products, options, configurations, features, and alternatives, which is why astute market leaders offer them their competitors' products in addition to their own. And even if you are the smallest company in the field, searchers expect you to provide the most extensive access to alternative sources of supply.

Searchers can actually help you do that. Cisco Systems, as we learned, consults with its search-and-browse customers, who are always scouting new ventures. Let's suppose that a Cisco customer needs a certain piece of Internet hardware that is made by only three companies in the world: a three-man shop in Taiwan, a fifty-person factory in Silicon Valley, and a small team in Michigan. Not convinced that any of the three venues is appropriate, the customer talks to his or her Cisco sales representative. The representative asks for a week to work on the situation. The next day Cisco puts up $1 billion to buy the Silicon Valley company. By the end of the allotted week, Cisco, which has by now acquired the company, can assure its customer that everything produced by the Silicon Valley company will work flawlessly. The customer's problem is solved—and Cisco has one more line of business.

The automobile industry has also gotten the message. Buying a car today is not the experience it used to be. If you bought a car ten years ago, you probably initiated the process with a look at some reviews or a visit to a dealership. Today, your first stop is more likely to be a Web site devoted to cars, especially if you're in search mode. Automakers such as Toyota and BMW thoroughly understand this. Toyota's Web site invites side-by-side comparisons of its own models with competing ones from Ford, Nissan, Mitsubishi, or any other brand you may be considering. BMW's site allows you to "build your own car" in any of a wide range of colors and configurations. It covers about any option you might want to explore, short of taking a virtual test drive. Even that possibility will be a reality in the not too distant future.

Saturate Customers with Information

Home Depot's vast assortment of building supplies shows that it, too, knows that customers savor choice. But an even more important reason for its lasting success is that it knows how to capitalize on a customer's wish to perform a task him- or herself. Home Depot employs our second strategy to attract the searchers, showering them with advice and insight.

This paradise for those who subscribe to do-it-yourself turns modestly competent amateurs into confident renovators and barely competent fumblers into people capable of remodeling their kitchens. Home Depot's employees don't do the job for you. Instead, they make accessible the information, products, and people you need to complete it for yourself. You feel capable of improving your own skills, which is exactly the feeling that searchers are seeking.

In the same way Cisco complements its in-person customer briefings with electronically delivered education, Home Depot uses the Internet to broaden its reach. Its Web site resembles the self-help section of a bookstore or library, offering a wide array of instant advice and step-by-step guidelines for beginners and more advanced customers. Fix it, build it, grow it, decorate it, or install it—whatever the project, Home Depot clearly wants to become the searcher's preferred source of empowerment. On-line training seminars should be the next logical step.

The smart company pursuing searchers knows the value of keeping them informed and educating them about their products. Sony, for example, devises more technological gadgets than the average consumer can even imagine. Though its strategy used to be to flood the market with a wide assortment of products and then focus on those that created their own demand, lately Sony has been making sure that its customers explore all of the benefits of its products.

For example, in its brochures and on its user-friendly Web site, Sony teaches people how to use PlayStation, its new video game system. It figures that a customer who has been educated by Sony is less likely to defect to Philips, Sanyo, Sharp, or any other brand.

Searchers soak up information like a sponge. For them, knowledge and content is king, and that's why deluging them with meaningful information is a winning strategy. When they surf the Web, they nourish their appetite by clicking on every promising link to related Web sites. They also enjoy exchanging thoughts with like-minded folks, either in person or in chat rooms on the Internet. Among their favorite suppliers are new media companies such as Yahoo! (which is the topic of our next chapter) and Internet retailers like Amazon.com.

To appreciate Amazon.com's appeal to searchers, ignore for a moment its wide assortment and the convenience it offers of being able to order from your home. Instead, imagine what it would be like if Amazon.com were a bricks-and-mortar retailer. Stripped of its Internet roots, Amazon would still cut a strong profile in the marketplace, as long as it continued to seduce the customer with knowledge. For searchers—a large proportion of its customer franchise—Amazon's true value lies in the treasure trove of information it makes available on the merchandise it sells—whether it is books, CDs, vitamins, or toys suited for twelve-to-fourteen-year-olds. Amazon is popularizing an alternative way of doing what smart retailers have always done: showering interested customers with information, advice, and recommendations. What's different is the scope, nature, and timeliness of what they provide. In a matter of minutes, customers can find the most comprehensive list of books on even the most esoteric topic, or check what other people in their company or community are buying. Within hours of the launch of the latest and anxiously awaited Harry Potter blockbuster, customers can peruse reviews and share their joy with others.

Searchers clearly value information at the time of purchase. But that's not the only time when information matters. It can be equally useful in making customers more proficient after the sale—when they're using or fixing the product. Examples of companies catering to searchers' desire to be self-reliant and fix their own problems aren't hard to find. Just take a closer look at Hewlett-Packard's or Microsoft's Web sites, and you'll find a host of diagnostic tools, knowledge bases, and other sorts of information that help customers troubleshoot their printer or word processing software on their own. Another look at these sites also shows that they are geared toward a higher level of sophistication than what would be suited for the average customer. And that's exactly what makes them a searcher's dream.

Stay Ahead of the Curve

Companies that have attained the status of market leaders are not content to rest on their laurels or on their existing products, nor should they be. They accept the unending responsibility of exploring uncharted terrain to imagine and design new products with original features and unique benefits. Market leaders are always thinking about the future, working to anticipate not-yet-recognized needs.

They also know that customers—especially searchers—are not necessarily looking for what they are selling. Often people want something that doesn't yet exist, or they have a problem to which there is not yet a solution. Historically, market leaders made sure that their pipelines were filled with a steady stream of new technology, distinctive designs, and original gadgets. Today, a full pipeline is not enough. To satisfy searchers, market leaders must try to answer questions that have not yet been asked.

Searchers may not know exactly what they want next, but they're more than open to new products and services. "Surprise us" is their mantra, which distinguishes them from streamliners, for whom surprises are generally unwelcome.

Searchers are particularly fond of companies that are constantly innovating and introducing new, better, and different items with which to woo them. This customer group is first to seek out the latest offering, whether it's Disney's stream of new movies, Sony's perpetually full pipeline of new electronic toys, or Nokia's conveyor belt of sleek and colorful new cell phones.

In *The Discipline of Market Leaders,* my coauthor and I made the observation that product leaders tend to be companies that lead by staying ahead of the curve. Staying ahead isn't something a company does once—it is an organization's sustained state of existence; once inside this perspective, you and everyone in the company are vigilant about the fact that breakthrough innovations are copied or imitated faster than ever before. Converting this frame of mind into a durable strategy requires the new leaders to hone their skills in detecting customers' needs, to expedite product development and output, in general, and to distinguish themselves from the plethora of less-than-original thinkers, that is, the imitators swarming the marketplace.

Nokia is a company that understands the importance of this. Founded in 1865 as a pulp and paper mill on the banks of the Finnish river with the same name, Nokia abandoned its roots and, in the 1990s, completed a radical transformation, becoming a powerhouse in cellular telephony with a strong market presence in 140 countries around the globe. By the year 2005, Nokia expects to have no fewer than 1 billion global subscribers. In each country where it operates, Nokia customizes its products in accordance with whatever characteristics are unique or particular to that country. It has always promoted a global perspective, evidenced by its choice of English for the company's official language and by the fact that it encourages all of its managers to accept assignments abroad.

In addition, from its earliest days Nokia has emphasized research and development, and today, approximately thirteen thousand people work in research and development—key to the company's success. No sooner has one product been released than the next, slightly more sophisticated, is readied for launch. "You always need to have a tease," Olli-Pekka Lintula, a director of product marketing, told *The Economist*. "You always need to move the customer up the value chain."

Current works in progress include Nokia "hot spots," which are set up in hotels and airports to allow travelers to make wireless connections to the Internet and video telephones. The company emphasizes the product's color and design and plans to introduce new models every year, employing the same strategy car manufacturers do with new styles each year. All of these approaches target searchers.

Looking forward, Nokia is betting that their search customers (or trendsetters, as this company calls them) will focus on the handset's visuals as they tap into the device's data capabilities that will link them to the Internet, word processing programs, a network diary, information services, e-commerce activities, and even allow them to view moving images. In the not too distant future, the handsets will enable traveling Nokia users to get news and information from home by downloading, say, a local newscast to the nearest television set.

Five years ago, Nokia shared cellular phone dominance with Motorola, Ericsson, QUALCOMM, and Sony. As these companies evolved, Nokia and Sony concentrated on producing flashy products; QUALCOMM concentrated on research and development; and Ericsson, on infrastructure. Each manufacturer attempted to stay ahead of the curve with distinct strategies, with Nokia and Ericsson representing contrasting poles.

By emphasizing sleek contemporary design and offering phones in a rainbow of colors, Nokia pursued searchers by making the company synonymous with hip, stylish phones for savvy consumers. Ericsson, which came of age as a supplier of telecommunications equipment to the Swedish government, stuck to utilitarian designs in basic black and concentrated on infrastructure.

In February 2000, Nokia reported a 92 percent year-over-year increase in handset sales for a total of 78.5 million units sold in 1999. Profits for the fourth quarter of 1999 were up 52 percent over the same quarter for the previous year. Today, Nokia accounts for nearly 27 percent of the market worldwide and predicts net sales growth of between 30 percent and 40 percent in 2000.

In Europe and the United States, Nokia is well poised to continue its dominance of a market that is expected to double over the next two years. But in Japan, it's a different story, which brings us to NTT DoCoMo, the company that is undoubtedly, by anyone's standards, ahead of the curve. It is an offspring of Nippon Telegraph & Telephone Corp. (NTT), Japan's equivalent of AT&T.

When NTT took DoCoMo public in the fall of 1998, the offering was 2.5 times oversubscribed and raised a record-setting $18.3 billion. DoCoMo instantly became the third-most-valuable company on the Nikkei index after Toyota and NTT. By mid-2000, it had become the largest market-cap company in Japan and continued to dominate the mobile phone market with a market share of 70 percent.

Its most recent innovation, a breakthrough called i-mode, allows customers to access the Internet via their cell phones, turning the wireless Internet into a reality. Japanese teenagers wear little i-mode handsets in "honey platinum" and "time gold" around their necks like pieces of jewelry. These are the devices that will provide high-quality streamed video and audio in the not too distant future. I-mode has turned mobile Internet access into Japan's latest craze, and since DoCoMo dominates that market by an immense amount, it is currently Asia's biggest success story. Because of DoCoMo, nearly everyone in Japan is surfing the net, gossiping, swapping e-mails, listening to music, making stock trades, getting the news, and playing games on their palm-sized DoCoMo phones. According to *Fortune* magazine, sales are running at fifty thousand *per day*. Users pay less than $3 a month, in addition to charges based on the amount of data they send or receive. (To give you a general idea, it costs about twenty cents to download a weather report.)

"Cell phones here [in Japan] are fashion accessories and toys above all," says Tim Clark, president of Internet consultants TKAI. Some DoCoMo handsets come in clamshell designs that open to reveal a screen up to three times larger than Nokia's. Some have full-color displays and plug-in keyboards, while still others recognize spoken commands.

I-mode is most popular among users aged twenty-four to thirty-five, roughly the same constituency that dominates traditional on-line usage. The heaviest i-mode users are women in their late twenties. Japanese magazine stands are packed with publications comparable to *TV Guide* that are chock full of i-mode offerings. The current projections estimate that 63 percent of Japan's population will be using mobile phones by next year.

DoCoMo sets a shining example for other market leaders intent on staying ahead of search-and-browse customers with a penchant for innovation.

Enrich Their Buying Experience

For years, E*Trade was content with the small piece of the stock brokerage business it had carved out by being the lowest-cost trader on Wall Street, an achievement made possible by automation and the no-frills service it offered. For the most part, its sixty-five thousand customers were independent, cost-conscious people who were comfortable making their own investment decisions and pleased to be paying about $15 to $20 per trade, compared to the $65 or so charged by most brokerage houses.

But E*Trade's complacency was shaken in the mid-nineties, when Charles Schwab launched a new division that offered trades at $29.95, encroaching dangerously on E*Trade's bargain-basement strategy. The company responded by hiring a young, ambitious chief executive officer, Christos Cotsakos, who quickly took the company public and released a flood of advertisements designed to raise its profile. At the same time, E*Trade focused on making its Web site easy to access and, even more important, fun to navigate.

Riding a bull stock market and the expansion of cable television networks devoted solely to investors—CNBC and CNNfn, in particular—E*Trade saw its accounts soar to nearly 2.5 million by May 2000. At the same time, a flood of imitators, some offering even lower costs to trade, entered the fray.

E*Trade credits its success to its focus on what it calls self-directed investors—search-and-browsers. These are the engaged clients, as Pam Kramer, E*Trade's chief content development officer, puts it, "who feel confident and want to make their own financial decisions." Kramer notes that E*Trade, like most market leaders, places enormous emphasis on its market presence, which is particularly relevant to searchers, who tend to have fleeting attention spans.

Perhaps the most important change in E*Trade's way of doing business is related to the company's vision of itself as, in Kramer's words, "not just an on-line investing company, [but] an all-electronic financial services company." Innovating new services is one of the highest priorities, if not the highest. "Most other on-line trading companies," Kramer continues, "are waiting to see what everybody else is doing, and behave accordingly. We continue to . . . [kind of] push ahead even in the face of other people . . . [on occasion] saying, 'Gee, I don't know if that makes sense.'" In January of 2000, for example, E*Trade bought Telebanc, the parent of an Internet-based savings bank. "We pushed ahead because we knew that's what we had to do to transform into a broader financial service company."

At the same time, raising customer expectations puts pressure on the entire company, as E*Trade learned the hard way when system blackouts incensed customers and triggered a rash of critical news stories. Kramer acknowledges that "the stakes are higher now. We've got more customers. . . . [We've got] more people running the company, certainly higher visibility. The pitfalls are, we have to continue to deliver on the brand."

Kramer credits chief executive Cotsakos with putting Internet trading in the public eye and with attracting Wall Street's attention through a very clever advertising campaign. The son of a Greek short-order cook from Paterson, New Jersey, Cotsakos, a decorated Vietnam War veteran, worked his way up the ladder at Federal Express before joining the research firm A. C. Nielsen, where he eventually became president and co-CEO.

Like most CEOs of market-leading companies, Cotsakos looks at his task with a fresh perspective. "I never viewed [E*Trade] as a brokerage company," he said. "I've always viewed this as a technology company that leverages information through an all-electronic business model." On top of that basic model, he explained, "you could add banking, brokerage, stocks, bonds, investment banking, insurance, and you could also build out a mall, if you will, a mini shopping mall."

Cotsakos personifies another market-leader characteristic: a belief in his organization's ability to influence other, much larger competitors. He believes that even if his company does not "unseat the Merrill Lynches and the PaineWebbers of the world, . . . we are going to force them to fundamentally change the economics of their business model."

———

Whether Cotsakos and other market leaders succeed in changing their industries depends on more than their collective ability to attract and retain searchers, despite their well-conceived strategies, including an enriched shopping experience. After all, genuine and dedicated search-and-browsers are a restless, critical minority, while most other customers are searchers just for a short phase before they settle into what are for them more comfortable routines.

The real challenge is whether there is a way to turn the searchers' break from the mundane into a mainstream trend that creates and sustains demand. They are trailblazers with the potential to generate such a shift. Scouting out new terrain, searchers will find the areas that streamline customers and delegators may eventually move into. Closely monitoring the searchers—and the market leaders catering to them—is crucial to any organization's success.

Undoubtedly, remaining attentive to customers in search mode is a more tumultuous process than tending to customers with any of the other three buying patterns. Pursuing searchers is not for the fainthearted, but you ignore them at your peril.

CHAPTER 7

Case in Point—Yahoo!

W e actually make the assumption that our users are smart, and don't need to be hand-led to things. So we just want to make sure they know that we have everything they need. We need to make it easy for them once they choose to try something, but we don't want to force the decision on them."

That's Karen Edwards talking. She is caretaker of the Yahoo! brand, and she has just spelled out the nutshell version of the gospel on catering to search-and-browse customers. And she should know: With searchers as its key clients, Yahoo! has zoomed, in an astonishingly brief five years, from a nerdy Web guide to one of the top five sites on the Internet—and a new market leader.

Yahoo! Inc. has evolved from a simple search engine to a full-fledged Web portal, and increasingly to an e-commerce mall and a broadband entertainment site. As of June 2000, its 156 million users (who make up 63 percent of the entire Web population) were hitting Yahoo! for an awesome 680 million page views every day, and 3,675 advertisers were sending the users paid messages. Yahoo! had alliances with twenty-three companies in eleven countries, giving it the strongest international presence of any

Internet portal. Its revenues in 2000 were expected to reach $1 billion. And by some accounts, it is already the most powerful name on the Web. Interbrand, an international consulting firm, calculates that Yahoo!'s brand value rose 258 percent from 1998 to 1999, to $6.3 billion. Such Internet powerhouses as AOL and Amazon.com were valued at $4.5 billion each.

By the time you read this, however, those numbers will be thoroughly obsolete. Yahoo!'s growth is as amazing as its statistics. The e-mail traffic on Yahoo! Mail and Yahoo! Messenger, for instance, jumped from 3.6 billion messages in March 2000 to 4.4 billion just three months later—an annual growth rate of 88 percent.

The rise of Yahoo! defies a good deal of conventional wisdom. Consider these paradoxes:

- Everyone knows that to be successful in fiercely competitive markets, you can't be all things to all people. Yet Yahoo!'s goal is precisely that. It aims to be "the only place anyone ever has to go to find information, to get connected with anyone, or to buy anything."

- Everyone in the cyberworld knows that losing money is a badge of honor. Yet Yahoo! has been earning healthy profits since its third year of existence, racking up operating earnings that were expected to total $284 million in 2000.

- Everyone knows that to build a strong market presence fast, Internet companies pour buckets of money into promotion, marketing, and advertising. Yet Yahoo! is stingy; instead of big, splashy campaigns, it relies on creativity and ingenuity.

- Everyone knows you should put your money where your mouth is. Yet here is a company trying to sell marketers on the Internet as an advertising medium but spending most of its own ad dollars on the traditional media it is trying to supplant.

In fact, all these apparent inconsistencies are well-thought-out strategies aimed at snaring search-and-browse customers—those independent, do-it-myself, dying-to-be-first consumers forever looking for the next big thing. Yahoo!'s success can be traced to three successful efforts: the cultivating of that target audience, the shaping of its own hugely successful brand personality, and the creative, imaginative use of media channels and services to reach its customers. Let's take the three in turn.

CULTIVATING THE SEARCHERS

From the day in 1994 when Stanford graduate students Jerry Yang and David Filo first compiled a list of their favorite Web sites to share with their friends, they were aiming to make the Internet user friendly for nontechies. In fact, Yahoo! has never seen itself as a technology company—and that is what gave it the potential to be a media business in the mass market.

Every time the company has come to a crossroads, that key decision has been reaffirmed: Rather than limit its appeal to the high-tech population already using the Web, Yahoo! would reach out to the newbies as well and make it easy for them to join. Yang has said that he is technically oriented enough to have been tempted to move Yahoo! higher on the scale of difficulty, but Filo always resisted. "He was insistent on the human touch," says Yang. Filo also warned that if Yahoo! were to abandon the newbies, it would never be able to change its mind and get them back.

And almost by definition, that decision meant that Yahoo! was targeting searchers as its key customers. The newbies were adventurous enough to be looking for a new experience on the cutting edge, and they weren't about to let anyone tell them all about the new Web world and where to go in it. They would explore and find things out for themselves—and then triumphantly e-mail all their friends whenever they were first to find something new and interesting. What they wanted was someone to flood them with information and choices, and then get out of the way.

In another key decision, Filo and Yang realized early that they had no experience and needed help in running a business. So they brought in experienced people—notably including Tim Koogle, an eight-year veteran of Motorola, to become chief executive officer; Jeff Mallett, a former Novell executive, as president; and Twentieth Century Fox marketer Karen Edwards, whose title is vice president of brand management.

The first rule of catering to searchers is, *give them lots of information.* Which is, of course, where Yahoo! began, with directories that would tell surfers how to find things on the World Wide Web. The key difference between Yahoo! and the competition, however, is that Filo and Yang began with their own favorite sites and arranged them like branching trees, with a logical progression from a subject through its associated topics. Great Britain, for instance, would have categories including history, economy, travel, sports, and the like, each of them with subcategories. Most other search engines start with a word or phrase (Prince Charles, the Millennium Dome, Hadrian's Wall) and list every Web site that mentions them—which is the main reason surfers run into so many numbing announcements of 38,542 possible answers. Put another way, Yahoo! resembles a book's table of contents, presenting information in an orderly, logical way. Most rivals are more like an index, giving locations where random topics are discussed or names are mentioned.

Yahoo! also retains the human touch that Filo prized so highly: Its directories are maintained by people, who find new sites or explore and classify sites reported by clients. Other search engines use sophisticated software to prowl the Internet, find sites, and glean hints of what's there. (For people who insist on high technology, Yahoo!, too, does automated searches. But its directories remain the heart of the matter.)

The second essential for dealing with searchers is, *offer them lots of choices.* Yahoo! floods the zone. Unlike America Online, for instance, which screens and preselects sites for clients who tend to be streamliners and delegators, Yahoo! wants its customers to have virtually unlimited choices.

The services it offers are mind-boggling. You can go to Yahoo! for message boards, chat rooms, and in-depth discussions. You can find wireless services, instant messaging, driving directions, and telephone numbers. You can stream or download music and television. You can shop with any of 11,300 merchants. If you manage a business, you can have a customized information portal to talk with your partners, suppliers, and customers. If you buy at auctions, you can sign up for shipping and escrow payment service. The list is virtually endless.

At the same time, as Edwards noted, Yahoo! is careful to avoid forcing you to choose—or even jogging your elbow as to what you might prefer. It shuns exclusive arrangements with merchants or data sources, in order to maintain full availability of everything. And its directory listings impose only the lightest of value judgments to indicate which sites Yahoo! finds interesting. In the directory branches, the site listings are always comprehensive and alphabetical. Just a tiny symbol—a pair of sunglasses, saying "cool"—sets off the preferred sites.

Unlike most portals, Yahoo! doesn't even try to get you to stay on its pages. Its main commitment to users, says CEO Koogle, is to make it easy to find and get connected to content, no matter where or whose it is. So, "We don't try to figure out ways of tricking people to stay on Yahoo! But as we extend our value to users, we find that they come back and stay longer. It's a subtle difference, but it's profound."

It's also effective. With or without tricks, Yahoo! is truly addictive. According to Nielsen NetRatings, it is the number-one site in time spent on-line by users: an average ninety-five minutes on Yahoo! in June 2000.

Yahoo! is also tireless in applying the third formula for snaring searchers: *Constantly pioneer new products and services.* In the second quarter of 2000 alone, according to its earnings report, the company offered eleven wholly new products and services, ranging from a printing center for small businesses to an on-line employment site in Australia. In the same three months, Yahoo! launched its twenty-third overseas company, formed three new foreign alliances, and expanded countless existing products and services into new territories.

Yahoo! has moved aggressively to fatten its e-commerce presence. While it has collected thousands of on-line retailers who pay the portal a fee for bringing surfers to their sites, people don't yet automatically associate Yahoo! with online shopping. So, in late 1999, the company added a prominent shopping icon to its home page and began an advertising campaign (the clever Eskimo spot, with an Inuit family finding on-line relief from its wintry habitat and fishy diet, was especially memorable).

And Yahoo! is preparing for the coming world of broadband, in which most Internet users will arrive on high-speed connections and expect a full range of instant downloading, multiterabyte data banks, and streaming video. Koogle plans to "serve them with things that we think are going to be compelling, which is seamless integration of text, fixed graphics, and moving stuff—video and audio—all in one place."

The final lure for searchers is, *enrich the buying experience with added value.* From the beginning, the Yahoo! strategy has been to provide as much as possible to broaden its users' horizons. While it refuses to add content that would compete with the sites it catalogs, it does offer functions and facilities that compete, including calendars, chat rooms, games, instant messaging, and auctions. And true to the ethos of the Web, wealth is to be shared. Yahoo!'s services—even e-mail—have always come free, which keeps customers coming back to be exposed to the ads that provide the bulk of Yahoo!'s revenues. "Our core conviction," says Koogle, "is that if we take care of people, they'll keep coming back. They'll trust us."

THE WEB'S LIVELIEST BRAND

In the beginning, Filo and Yang called their directory Jerry's Guide to the World Wide Web. But the name began to grate on them as hopelessly nerdy, the antithesis of cool, and one night they set out to improve on it. They wanted a twist on an acronym then fashionable in Internet circles: YACC, standing for "yet another compiler compiler." In the often-told story, they surfed their on-line dictionary until they arrived at "yet another hierarchical officious oracle," giving them the acronym "YAHOO," which they liked for its mischievous flavor and the dictionary meaning, "rude and uncouth." "It fit us," said Filo. "We were well-regarded yahoos."

In everyone's hindsight, the name was a stroke of genius. It was nonintimidating, friendly, and plebeian; after the addition of an exclamation point, it was also exuberant and playful. Karen Edwards says it establishes Yahoo!'s personality as genuine, authentic, human, and endearing, with a sense of humor and self-deprecating modesty. I can't imagine a name better calculated to appeal to searchers. Yahoo! is the brand, Edwards says, that people "want to see win," and it is so strong that she modestly says that her job is a snap. Ninety percent of Yahoo!'s success comes from the name alone, and "maybe ten percent is not screwing it up. The reason I deserve a raise is that I didn't screw up the brand this year."

But there are subtleties involved in avoiding mistakes. For one thing, says Edwards, there are different ways to establish a global brand. Some brands, like Coca-Cola, "actually mean different things in different markets. Disney, on the other hand, really does mean the same thing in almost every culture and every market. We're aiming to be more like that." Not, she hastens to add, that there's anything wrong with Coke, but Yahoo! needs to be understood in the same terms by people (read: searchers) all over the world.

Next, she says, the company has to deliver what its brand personality promises. (Searchers are a skeptical lot, constantly testing.) "If your brand is about being honest and fun but your culture is not that way, you're in big trouble," she says. "We've benefited from positive media exposure primarily because we're honest and straightforward."

Yahoo!'s image has also changed subtly over the years. Early on, the Niehaus Ryan Group public relations agency pushed the story of the two young entrepreneurs and their chaotic shop, full of barefoot programmers and surfers working impossible hours with irrepressible zest. (Searchers always like underdogs and questioners of authority.) But as the public offering approached, the story changed. "Yahoo! had to present itself as a grown-up, serious company," says Edwards. The Jerry-and-Dave show gave way to articles in the business press quoting CEO Koogle and president Mallett. *Fortune* found Yahoo!'s offices in Santa Clara "whisper quiet . . . no parrots, no sleep tents—not even a sock puppet. The most exciting thing at Yahoo! is the exclamation point that officially goes at the end of its name." The magazine quoted Mallett: "Inside, we're wickedly boring and have been from Day One." He pictured himself poring three times a day through the four terabytes of statistics on Yahoo!'s users that the company compiles every week.

At bottom, however, the story remains the same: Yahoo! is a media company and always has been, and its name is perhaps its strongest asset—$6.3 billion strong, if you credit that Interbrand study.

CREATIVE MARKETING 101

However serendipitous the Yahoo! name may have been, getting the market to notice the brand was serious work—and here Yahoo! and Edwards get high marks for creativity and ingenuity in their use of media channels and services calculated to appeal to the search-and-browse customer.

When Edwards joined Yahoo! early in 1996, most Internet companies were advertising on-line or buying space in magazines aimed at people who were already surfing the Web. Since Yahoo! aimed to become a mass-market brand and to be perceived as pop culture rather than high-tech, she figured she had to reach the nonusers. And that triggered the revolutionary decision to advertise on television. Perhaps inevitably, that brought charges of hypocrisy: Why was she using old media to persuade people to advertise on-line? Her answer: Seventy-two percent of the people using the Internet were already Yahoo! visitors. The newbie customers she wanted had to be found elsewhere.

Edwards also signed on a second PR agency, the Wasserman Group, a Los Angeles shop that had handled publicity for such world-famous entertainers as the Beatles and the Rolling Stones, to help with the quest for young, entertainment-oriented customers.

But what message was Yahoo! trying to send? It would have been logical to differentiate the brand from the rival search engines by highlighting the human-touch directory approach, the number of Web sites being offered, and the speed of loading pages. But Edwards was after bigger game—the searchers, looking for experiences they hadn't tried. "We just tried to show people the benefits of the Web," she says. "Our strategy was to grow the category, not differentiate the brand based on comparative benefits. That was a risky decision." But it also set the tone of the basic message, with key words such as "friendly," "reliable," and "nonintimidating."

Edwards brought in Black Rocket, a hot San Francisco boutique ad agency (one of its founders sparked the "Got Milk?" campaign). The result, only four months after her arrival at Yahoo!, was the brilliant national-television fisherman spot, in which a forlorn angler found bait and fishing tips on-line and used them to land a monstrous fish. It was Black Rocket, too, that came up with the Eskimo spot—and with the slogan "Do you Yahoo!?" which converted the brand into a somehow understandable verb.

But the fisherman ad could run for only two weeks before Yahoo!'s meager advertising budget was spent. Edwards took the public relations approach, getting news coverage of the ad (and the attention of searchers) in such prestigious publications as *Time* and *The New York Times*. "Then we did a lot of barter and guerrilla marketing at street fairs and community outreach," she says. "It's amazing how creative you can be when you have no money."

Amazing indeed. Her guerrilla marketing became a legend in the business; Yahoo! posters and logos turned up on construction sites, at concerts and sports events, and on NASCAR race cars. Gleeful searchers could spot the logo on golf balls, Visa cards, shirts, beach balls, Ben & Jerry's ice cream lids, even on the Zamboni ice grooming machine of the San Jose Sharks. Five Yahoo! employees got the company to shrink-wrap their cars with the yellow-and-purple corporate colors and drove around as mobile Yahoo! logos.

To this day, while upstart rivals are spending their IPO capital on advertising campaigns to become known, Yahoo! continues to be frugal in its marketing. In 1999, for instance, at a point when its major competitors were advertising at an annual clip of $400 million, Yahoo! was spending at only a $258 million pace. "Marketing is a very low percentage of our revenues," says Edwards. "That's a cultural thing here. We're really cheap. We still have to be creative, out of necessity."

But that creativity ensures that Yahoo! gets far more bang for its buck than its rivals enjoy. And the truth is that such "cheapness" and ingenuity appeal far more to the search-and-browse set than do money-splurging, attention-wrenching campaigns that saturate markets with heavy-handed slogans. Searchers prefer a twist of wry: Do you Yahoo!?

———

A few months ago, stock analysts and pundits were wondering gravely whether Yahoo! could make the transition from an Internet portal to the full-fledged age of e-commerce. The problem, said *Adweek*, is that Yahoo! customers are used to getting everything free, while people arrive at Amazon.com with their wallets open as buyers, not browsers. Was Yahoo! really trying hard enough? Patiently, Mallett explained that Yahoo! is in the media, communications, and commerce business; that it doesn't sell things but enables its customers to buy and its merchants to sell. The stock took a hit, but profits kept rising.

More recently, the conventional wise men were even graver in asking whether Yahoo! could make the leap from its undoubted success in narrowband information to the world of broadband entertainment. "The skills of the portals need to change," *Fortune* quoted a Wall Street analyst who follows Internet stocks. Patiently again, Koogle explained that Yahoo! had indeed noticed the trend, and that in fact it was ahead of the crowd: It was getting a lot of traffic that originated from workplaces, which are already fitted out with "fat pipes"—the high-capacity connections that can transmit broadband signals. Yahoo! decided that this was a ready-made test market and has begun serving it with *Finance-Vision*, a live business-news television show being streamed over the Web to Yahoo!'s customers.

At bottom, however, Yahoo!'s managers know that neither e-commerce nor broadband will be the be-all and end-all of their business. Both are important, and both are being addressed. But the business remains where it began, centered on information. "Navigating the Web will never go away," says Tim Koogle. "If you do that well, it gives you a platform on which to grow." Or as Karen Edwards puts it, "People will always need information, and you never really know what type of information you will need."

Whatever it turns out to be, Yahoo! intends to supply it. "You never turn your back on the open ocean," says Jeff Mallett. "As we grow, there's more people standing on the shore with us, looking out at the ocean. You see Michael Eisner there, Jack Welch, and Bill Gates. The winners are going to be the ones evolving the business to keep up with the customers."

For Yahoo!, the key customers are still the searchers, and the permanent challenge is to keep them coming back. The last word goes to Jerry Yang, whose directory it was in the first place: "If the user experience is something they must or want to come back to, it doesn't matter how much other stuff you talk about."

Yahoo!

CHAPTER 8

Reassure the Streamliners

I magine that you are an Internet e-tailer and your business is utterly dependent upon the uninterrupted flow of data from your computer system. Although everything appears to be running smoothly, you get a call from EMC Corporation, the company whose data storage devices you're using. (It's also a business you'll hear more about in the next chapter.) An EMC service person informs you that something is about to break down and asks if he can send someone to look at it. Somewhat shaken, you say sure; she arrives the next day, replaces a couple of logic boards, gives the unit a pat, and leaves. Disaster has been averted. And you never receive a bill for the call—it's on the house.

How did the EMC service person know that your system was about to go on the blink? Each of EMC's roughly forty-five thousand data storage systems in operation worldwide is connected to one of three Call Home centers, located in Hopkinton, Massachusetts; Cork, Ireland; and Tokyo, Japan. Whenever an EMC unit anywhere in the world senses something wrong or on the verge of becoming wrong, it automatically reports the problem to the nearest center. Service to prevent, not repair, is indeed service par excellence.

The success of this sort of preventative maintenance makes it likely that car manufacturers will soon build the same kind of diagnostic capabilities into cars. Whenever they sense a mechanical problem, their onboard computers will beep to a global satellite. Monitors will alert drivers of the problem, or perhaps even solve it by remote control. The customer may not even know that anything has happened to his or her car until the bill arrives for services rendered. (Giving service away isn't quite in vogue in the car industry.)

Even today, reliable service is vital to every customer. Still, for streamliners, those independent consumers who want to handle their own chores, but with the smallest possible allocation of time, service arrangements are particularly significant. All consumers streamline when it comes to routine purchases—for example, we want our heating oil tanks filled when they get low and we expect to be billed monthly without having to prompt the company. Business customers, too, try to streamline purchases of raw materials, office supplies, cleaning services, and the like. But some customers aim to streamline as many facets of their lives as possible; these people set up automatic payments on their credit cards; they establish routines for buying clothes, going to restaurants, even taking vacations. Market leaders in the age of consumer scarcity know that catering to their needs can be profitable, indeed, but learning how to do so requires a thorough understanding of the streamliner mentality.

If streamliners do not feel completely secure in their business relationships, they have no peace of mind. Because they strive to minimize risk, they are comforted by the knowledge that their suppliers are the leading companies in their fields. They are reassured, too, by any measures their suppliers take to provide even more automatic, dependable service; streamliners are looking for solutions that can be incorporated into their lives with as little effort on their part as possible.

As recently as a decade ago, EMC sensed an opportunity in the fact that computer data storage systems experienced frequent breakdowns. In those days, computer-reliant companies guarded against failure by maintaining decentralized systems, making backup tapes at frequent intervals, which they stored in distant warehouses in case of fire or flood. When something did go wrong, they resorted to what was facetiously known as CTAM— the Chevy truck access method. Workers at a warehouse stacked tapes on a truck, drove to the site of the problem, and made copies. It took at least two days.

EMC has replaced CTAM with a backup system that clones and files data as it goes along, so everything is automatically backed up and stored. If you were to buy one of EMC's storage boxes at a cost of $1.5 to $2 million (the top-of-the-line model), you would get something radically different from what was available to you ten years ago. Today's largest EMC box is about the size of a large desk, but it holds 19 terabytes of data—19 trillion bytes—enough to contain every word in every book in the entire Library of Congress, or more than twice the number of words ever published in *The New York Times, The Wall Street Journal,* and two or three other newspapers combined.

When you buy a storage box from EMC, in addition to massive capacity you get years of free service and the assurance that the equipment will work summer or winter, rain or shine. Of course, the boxes themselves are well designed and built, and each one is torture-tested in extreme temperatures for more than twenty days.

Whenever a computer calls home, the call pops up on a computer screen. Within three minutes an engineer in, say, the Hopkinton emergency center (resembling, incidentally, Hollywood's idea of a war room, replete with lighted maps and dramatically blinking monitors) is dealing with it. If nobody has picked up the call after three minutes, it is automatically forwarded to war rooms in Cork and Tokyo. Within fifteen minutes, it has to be answered. The system works so well that EMC's error rate is close to negligible.

Because EMC's software engineers are involved in these real-life problems, they develop a feeling for the nuances of what does or does not go wrong, and what may need improvement. As a result they have a truly close connection to the user.

Surely there are cheaper solutions to the problem of data failure, but none inspires the peace of mind that EMC offers. As a result, two-thirds of the world's critical data is now stored on EMC products, and virtually every major business with a stake in data storage signs on with that one organization.

EMC's forte is to make sure streamline-minded customers feel totally secure. The strategy is similar to Intel's marketing of the phrase "Intel Inside," which was intended to reassure consumers that their computers are reliable. The message from both EMC and Intel is: You may not know how your system works, but we do and we'll make sure everything is fine and dandy.

In this chapter we examine three market strategies that new market leaders use to capture and retain streamliners. Each of them builds on the recognition that in a world in flux, people derive comfort and reassurance from tried-and-trusted routines.

DELIVER DEPENDABILITY

Nothing is more important to streamliners than being able to depend on their business relationships. Far from lazy, this group just doesn't want to spend time rethinking its decisions. They want to know exactly what they will be getting, time after time. Beware the company that strays from the predictable, as Coca-Cola found out when it introduced New Coke some years ago, unleashing uncounted protests from customers who liked Coke just the way it was. Coca-Cola hastily, and with some embarrassment, reintroduced its old Coke, renaming it Classic Coke.

Streamliners don't like surprises, and particularly not the disruptive kind. They value market leaders they can rely on, who, when needed, will guide them through changes with a steady hand.

Charles Schwab, the financial services firm, clearly understands this. Throughout its more than twenty-five-year history, the company built its business on the assumption that culture and people are its greatest asset. Reassuring customers is its mission, or as co-CEO David Pottruck is fond of saying, at Schwab "we want to be the custodian of our customers' financial dreams." Linnet Deily, vice chairman, echoes Pottruck's sentiments: "This is a very customer-driven organization from top to bottom [and] I've sat in many meetings here where the question is, over and over again, 'What's the right thing for the customer?'"

With the Internet rapidly transforming the investment management field, Charles Schwab's challenge was to steer its streamline-minded customers through some pretty dramatic changes. Starting in 1993, it introduced them to on-line trading, over time lowering customers' average cost per trade some fivefold, to $29.95, and putting $250 million of annual net profits at risk. "Fortunately," says Pottruck, "the gamble paid off—we strengthened our existing customer relations and gained a large number of new customers."

Of course, when a company is dealing primarily with streamliners, change must be introduced with care and subtlety. Deily recalls a presentation to a group of investor customers in which she used a chart that described fifteen current Schwab programs. Only when the chart was projected on a screen did Deily realize that "we were only doing one of them two years earlier. But the changes had built over the last couple of years, bits and pieces every month, until suddenly, when I looked back over a two-year time frame, we had changed things fairly dramatically. But it never felt like a dramatic change."

For market leaders appealing to streamliners, brand building is another priority. "We have put a lot of advertising weight behind [our] brand and we would say that has helped us differentiate ourselves from a lot of the competition," says Deily. As is to be expected, the company's ads stress peace of mind and empathy with the customer. After all, that's what is important to its customers.

Another industry where dependability counts is fast food, or as it is more formally known, the QSR (quick-service restaurant) business. To hold on to streamline-minded customers, some of the better known fast food brands invested billions of dollars in a market that even ten years ago was already deemed mature.

The conventional wisdom that was frequently reported in the press was that there was a massive fast food oversupply, and analysts predicted the industry was headed for trouble.

If you were competing in the QSR marketplace, your initial step in confronting the problem would likely have been to analyze customers' needs. First, who uses these restaurants and what do they want? As it turns out, the majority are streamliners. As far back as 1959, Fred Turner, one of McDonald's founding fathers, recognized the company's appeal to streamliners, though he didn't use the term, when he challenged the fledgling company and its franchisees to "achieve standardization without regimentation." As Claire Babrowski, executive vice president, worldwide restaurant systems, puts it, "He was looking for some level of standardization and consistency in what the customer got so that we could have a clearly identified brand that people could recognize and be comfortable with."

In time, as we know, people became very comfortable, indeed, with McDonald's golden arches and its various imitators. In fact, roughly 35 percent of the U.S. population visits a quick-service restaurant on an average of ten times a month, and some people—the frequent users—eat in them five or six times a week. In all, the 35 percent of the population that seems devoted to fast food restaurants accounts for 80 percent of all visits to QSR facilities.

Competition is fierce. In any given year in the United States, about ten thousand new QSR restaurants will open. "The barriers to entry for the restaurant business are pretty low," Babrowski points out. "Anybody with enough money to line up rental space and get a little bit of equipment in it, and knows how to cook, can at least attempt to start in the restaurant business." This means, she adds, that "there is almost a limitless stream of competitors," though it is the "branded, organized competitors," as she calls them, that McDonald's concerns itself with most: Burger King, Wendy's, Hardee's, Taco Bell, and Roy Rogers.

Streamliners look to these branded restaurants for speed, low cost, and dependability (consistency). Of these, speed is the most important. Fast food customers may not have finely honed taste buds, but they do have well-oiled body clocks. Time is their priority. Since all fast food restaurants are competing for the same customer base and the number of restaurants exceeds the need, the challenge lies in providing even faster, more dependable service without diluting the customer base.

Within the fast food business, each chain seeks a feature to set it apart from the others: Some strive to be the cheapest, others the fastest, still others the tastiest. Wendy's has the most variety in its menu choices; Taco Bell is the cheapest; and McDonald's is generally regarded as the fastest and most consistent, which is precisely how it wants to be regarded, since speed and dependability are what the fast food business is all about.

Taco Bell's response to its industry's glut was to cut costs and lower prices. McDonald's, too, expended a huge effort to decrease its costs. But its analysis of the market went considerably deeper and led to a bold and surprising course of action.

McDonald's realized that among frequent users, about a third were so devoted to them that they would patronize another chain only when the McDonald's nearest to them was too crowded. Another third of the frequent users preferred other brands; McDonald's picked up only occasional business from this cohort.

And the final third didn't care for McDonald's at all, and wouldn't go there under any circumstances.

McDonald's managers tried to figure out how to attract the one-third who preferred the competition. They decided that since speed was the crux of the matter, it made sense to make the service faster. And they concluded that the speed equation had to include the time it takes a customer to get from his or her home or office to the nearest McDonald's restaurant, as well as how long it takes to be served. The only way to shorten the arrival time, they finally realized, was to build more restaurants.

The logic was as powerful as it was counterintuitive: The more outlets there were, the closer one would be to a higher percentage of customers. That the industry appeared overbuilt did not stop McDonald's from embarking on a massive construction spree. In ten years, McDonald's grew from approximately 8,300 restaurants in the United States (3.4 outlets for every 100,000 people) to 12,600 (4.7 for every 100,000 people). The gambit worked, bringing in more customers, most of them streamliners, for whom the restaurants were now closer and therefore more convenient.

McDonald's next appeal to streamliners took the form of a new speeded-up cooking process called Made For You, which was more than a decade in development. As early as the mid-1980s, McDonald's was working on equipment that would allow outlets to cook to order without making customers wait. But it took until 1997 for the company, working in partnership with its equipment suppliers, to finally perfect a critical component called the universal holding cabinet, a piece of equipment that allows McDonald's restaurants to preprepare hamburgers and chicken in such a way that they don't dry out or get cold. In addition, says Babrowski, "a modification to our cash register system allows us to read in the kitchen what is being sold at the moment of sale." The customer gets a fresher burger made to order; McDonald's gets less waste, which translates into more profit.

Toward that same end, McDonald's came up with proprietary software that monitors sales in sixty-second increments, so that if there's a sudden run on cheeseburgers, says Babrowski, "we have the opportunity to get just a bit ahead of it." Babrowski says she was in one busy outlet recently, and even after a very busy lunch rush, "there was one quarter-pounder with cheese sitting there to be thrown away." "Waste not, want not," times thousands.

With innovations like these and the patience to stick with them over a multiyear development period, McDonald's clearly makes for a determined competitor. Not only did Made For You take more than a decade to conceive and implement, but the company also persisted for nine years to turn breakfast into a profitable business. Today, breakfast accounts for almost 25 percent of McDonald's business, which, remarkably, represents nearly 75 percent of the total number of breakfasts that are eaten in restaurants each morning. "People finally agreed that McDonald's could be good at eggs," says Babrowski with considerable understatement.

MAKE ROUTINES ROUTINE

If the first strategy with streamliners is making sure your operations run dependably and consistently, the second is getting your customers to behave consistently and predictably as well. This strategy taps into streamliners' craving for routine by creating and reinforcing their habitual, or "sticky," behavior—in other words, making routines routine.

In a recent speech, Bill George, chief executive officer of Medtronic, Inc., the world's leading medical technology company, advanced the thesis that as a maker of pacemakers and other electronically based products for people with chronic diseases, Medtronic should be a part of a patient's life for a quarter of a century or more. Now, there's a vision of stickiness.

On a more modest scale, ExxonMobil encourages sticky behavior by allowing its gas station customers to merely wave their Mobil SpeedPasses, which some keep on a fob on their key chains, in the direction of the pump in order to fill their cars' tanks with gasoline. The SpeedPass automatically identifies them, releases the pump, and bills their account. The process may be just slightly easier than inserting a credit card into a slot in the pump, but streamliners appreciate even modest savings in time and energy. Furthermore, the very act of waving the SpeedPass makes streamliners feel as though they're somehow insiders; many take pleasure in the fact that "their" company, ExxonMobil, is demonstrating its position on the cutting edge.

In response to increased competition, the drug industry has also had to focus its efforts on stickiness. Historically, a single successful drug could earn its discoverer huge profits for a very extended time. But there are so many new drugs on the market today, as well as new and different approaches to managing various diseases, that pharmaceutical makers have had to work harder than ever just to keep revenues constant.

Based in Thousand Oaks, California, Amgen is the biggest biotech company in the world. And the giant pharmaceutical company's drugs Neupogen (which treats the side effects of chemotherapy) and Epogen (which is used to treat anemia in patients undergoing kidney dialysis treatments) are among the best-selling prescription drugs of all time. Even though the drugs proved their efficacy long ago, Amgen must wage a never-ending battle to persuade its customers (patients as well as health care professionals) not only to use them but to use them appropriately, which is not as easy as it may sound. Although it is clear that proper dosage and timing vastly improve the drugs' benefits, Amgen learned long ago that moving through the doctor–patient pipeline takes a lot of sweat and tears.

"It's not enough that the drugs are great products," says Kevin Sharer, Amgen's president and CEO. "We have had to continually support them by working very, very closely with at least four separate customer groups to make sure that patients are able to receive the drugs and prefer ours over alternatives." In other words, making routines routine isn't an issue that involves only the patient—everyone in the drug chain needs to cooperate as well.

The first group Amgen tries to educate is professional medical caregivers, physicians and nurses, people not inclined to take direction from anyone who lacks professional credentials and a deep knowledge of medicine. This is why, says Sharer, "we go to extensive efforts to be seen by physicians as a science-based company." Amgen sales reps must have the appropriate knowledge of science down cold and must be able, says Sharer, "to talk with physicians in great depth about the latest studies, the latest advances in the areas of medicine that the physician is interested in. In the case of Epogen, those physicians are kidney specialists, so our sales representatives are very, very knowledgeable about treating anemia in patients who have failed kidneys and are on dialysis. It's a highly skilled and focused sales force." It is also an extremely loyal one. While the national average turnover rate is 17 to 18 percent, Amgen's is a mere 5.5 to 6 percent.

Bill Ashton, vice president of corporate accounts, explains how educating doctors and nurses works: "We have what we call an Anemia Management Institute, where we train nurses and health care providers to be better at everything associated with managing anemia of a dialysis patient," he says. "For example, when you go into a dialysis center, and the patient's hematocrit [the ratio between red blood cells and white blood cells] is not going up as it should be, and you are increasing the dose, what's the cause of that? Well, it may be they have an infection. It may be that they've got hemorrhoids and they've got bleeding. They may just be nonresponders, and they have low iron levels—we've done a lot of research around that particular area. In fact, we have almost written the book on quality guidelines about how to treat anemia, basically through our own research and our own databases. So we're actually training nurses—we put them through a two-day training program that teaches them how to treat the anemia better."

The second group Amgen targets for education is made up of people who own and operate health care facilities—hospitals, clinics, and the like. Toward this aim, Amgen invites health providers to submit their patients' hematocrit levels to them for evaluation. "We make sure that their patients are within what's been clinically judged to be the right range," says Sharer. "To do that, they must use our product. So it economically makes sense for us, but more importantly, it makes sense for the patient."

Again in Ashton's words: "It's our job to try to help customers solve their economic problems, so we're really trying to teach our people to be much more business-driven and less sales-driven. In dialysis, six customers represent nearly sixty percent of our business. We have one customer that does almost $500 million with us. That customer is as big as a lot of pharmaceutical companies, so the management of that account is very critical to us.

"For example, we negotiate a contract every year with them and a lot of the contracts that we've negotiated are based on two things. A quality measure that simply says the number of patients that are being treated are being appropriately treated. That's A. Second thing is that a lot of these are volume performance incentives. It's like okay, this year, you grew at fifteen percent, next year, to get the top-tier discount, you've got to grow another fifteen percent, and they will say, 'If that's fair because I grew fifteen percent last year, can I grow fifteen percent on a much larger base?' So it's that kind of discussion that goes on with these guys."

The third group that Amgen feels must be educated is the actual payers—Medicare, Medicaid, and insurance companies. "We try very hard to make sure that physicians and patients can get reimbursement," Sharer explains. "It's not always easy. We have people who are focused on the insurance companies to make sure they are educated about the benefits of our drugs, and that's a lot of time and effort." In fact, this requires an Amgen unit dedicated to no other function. "So if somebody says, 'Gee, Aetna isn't paying for your drug, and that's why I'm not using it,' we have a team that can be mobilized to find out why. Sometimes it's just a simple coding error; sometimes it's the educational training of the medical director; sometimes you'll find that the people deny-ing the claim are just high school graduates who are expected to process some seventy-two claims a minute. They see one and they think an eight is a five, and they put it aside and that delays payment. So we have a team that works actively with that. That's another service we provide our customers."

Wholesalers—the people who actually distribute the com-pany's products to hospitals and doctors' offices—comprise Am-gen's fourth target group, and the fifth and final group is what Sharer refers to as patient-related organizations and individuals.

"Communication with the patients is more and more impor-tant," according to Sharer. "Patients are participating in their own care much more than they ever have been and I think we're very effective there." He also takes note of the many patient advocacy groups that lobby for legislation, usually devoted to specific dis-eases. And he communicates with large national organizations, such as the American Cancer Society and the National Kidney Foundation. These, he says, "can really be helpful as a focal point to bring together the interests of physicians, patients, and providers and be able to work out industry standards that are helpful and try to bring the best thinking to bear."

Sharer attributes Neupogen's and Epogen's dominant market share as much to these educational programs as he does to the fact that the drugs themselves are extremely effective. "That combi-nation is powerful," he says, "and I believe it is the explanation of our success."

LEAD THE WAY

Another means of attracting streamliners is by asserting leadership. As a group, they require reassurance, and as stated earlier, they are comforted by the fact that their suppliers are market leaders. Streamliners tend to be other-directed, to use Harvard sociologist David Riesman's well-known term, which refers to people who take their cues from watching others and make decisions based on what their neighbors and friends do. They are risk-averse, so one way to diminish their anxiety is to team up with companies that are synonymous with reliability and service and will be in business tomorrow and the day after.

Thus, it is important for companies to be seen as market leaders. If you are Nike, you must expend enormous effort to ensure that your running shoes are perceived as the leading brand and, therefore, the only ones to buy. No wonder market leaders spend millions of dollars to "prove" that they are, in fact, number one.

In the business-to-business arena, the same dynamics operate: People want to be linked with the leaders in their field, which, on the Internet, are EMC, Cisco, Sun Microsystems, and Oracle. In e-business software, the leader is Siebel Systems. "We have Citicorp as a customer and Charles Schwab as a customer," Siebel says in its promotional materials. "If you are a financial services firm, you cannot afford not to be part of this team."

In fact, no company has pursued the leadership strategy more aggressively than Siebel, founded a decade ago by ex–Oracle supersalesman Tom Siebel, now forty-eight. The company, which makes software that lets far-flung corporate marketers or salespeople tap into vast pools of data, has been described by the *San Francisco Examiner* as "the nation's fastest-growing tech firm." Siebel himself carries the notion even further. "We started this business in 1993," he often tells prospective clients. "We have sixty-eight percent market share. We are one of the fastest-growing companies in the world."

He may be right. In February 2000, Siebel, which had seen its stock skyrocket twelvefold since its 1996 IPO, signed a global deal with IBM providing its software to Big Blue's more than fifty-five thousand employees, thirty thousand business partners, and millions of customers via the Web. "IBM," Tom Siebel said at the time, "represents both our most strategic partner and our largest customer."

The IBM alliance also reinforces Siebel's very deliberate strategy to identify and partner with industry leaders, from Microsoft, with whom Siebel worked closely in its early days, to financial firms like Charles Schwab, to consulting companies, such as Accenture, formerly known as Andersen Consulting.

"Everything we do," says Siebel's cofounder Pat House, aims "to send the message that we're a global leader. We hope that all roads lead back to Siebel." Many roads do. The company has successfully wooed international clients, including Siemens Business Services, GE Capital, Ford, Bank of America, and Hoechst Marion Roussel. "We used to tell the customer how to do business with us," Siebel told journalist Michael J. Ybarra, listing the well-known names of banks, insurance companies, and automakers that he counts as clients. "I'm the world's largest provider of software to every one of these businesses." According to Ybarra, Siebel then put his hand over his heart. "The customer," he said, "is the only reason we're in business. We don't want to be as good as IBM. We want to be the best. We will do whatever it takes."

One thing it takes is a strong presence at industry shows such as COMDEX—annual events that display the wares, show off innovations, and provide opportunities for networking and job hunting. In most industries, only a few of these shows can garner a huge turnout, while the rest attract a fraction of the potential audience. The leaders, of course, are the companies that sponsor the successful show.

For years SAP AG, the big software company, has been organizing enormous events—Sapphire Conferences—all over the world, from the United States to Japan and Australia. Attracting nearly everyone seriously looking at systems and software solutions, the conferences bring in outside speakers and display new technologies. But the events' implicit message is that SAP is the leader, and customers don't forget it.

Many companies try to hold on to lifetime customers—people who will do business with them as long as they live. Yet remarkably few succeed in this. How many companies have you had a relationship with for fifteen or twenty years? If you're like me, probably not too many. I have been going to McDonald's for thirty-five or forty years, and I've had my American Express card for twenty-six. (I know because my card reminds me: "Member since 1974.") Other than those two, I can't think of any companies with which I've done business for decades.

McDonald's and American Express keep my business because they have allowed me to streamline my life and, at each stage of it, incorporate them into my behavior patterns. When I change my habits over time, they have accommodated and kept up with me, if not even moved a step or two ahead.

If I ask that same longevity question in the business-to-business field, it's telling how often the answer includes IBM. It is an organization that companies have conducted business with for thirty or forty years, in the same way that sports fans root for the same teams for decades—win or lose. Even in the depths of IBM's dark days in the late eighties and early nineties, many customers—streamliners, in particular—quietly rooted for Big Blue to get back in the game. Such customer loyalty over a prolonged difficult period helped Lou Gerstner, the American Express superstar who took IBM's helm in 1993, get the company moving again.

Surely, there are other companies that have held on to customers for life. Sears comes to mind; the Big Three U.S. automakers may still own some of that loyalty. And there are companies like AT&T, producers of raw materials, railroads, and utilities, that have lifetime customers. But they are exceptions; most companies don't achieve it.

Streamliners want to be sure of their supplier's leadership. Unless a supplier continuously conveys its superior effectiveness through advertising, and with new products and services, its customers will eventually choose to root for a different team.

If your customers don't root for you, you're in trouble. (Conversely, as the IBM example shows, loyal fans can play an important role in getting a team winning again.) But if your customers are on your side and believe that you are a leader, they will forgive errors here and there, as long as you actively address the problems and continue to assert your leadership.

That it behooves managers in every kind of company to think hard about streamliners is an understatement. At first glance, they may appear less critical than the fast-moving, creative, search-and-browse customers. But just as we are all streamliners in some phases of our consumer lives, every market has a streamliner segment.

In the end, market leaders never forget that no matter how customers change, predictability is a core component of everyone's life, and one well worth catering to.

CHAPTER 9

Case in Point—EMC

A few years back, *Wired* magazine called it "the most important company you've never heard of," and that was dead accurate. These days, EMC Corporation is a bit more familiar—when your stock rises by 80,575 percent in a decade, people tend to sit up and take notice. But most people would find it hard to say exactly what EMC does, except that it's vaguely high-tech.

EMC has a lock on a business that, until recently, no one else much cared about: electronic memory, or data storage. Since the early days of computers, the details of where and how all those billions of 1's and 0's were stored and retrieved has been the boring side of the business. The glamorous (and profitable) side was the computers themselves—mainframes, PCs, laptops, and then network servers—and the software that kept them running. But times have changed. Demand for memory storage is exploding at a rate of 86 percent a year, and if EMC is right, the market for storage will leap to $100 billion over the next five years, twice the size of the traffic in servers themselves. And though such formidable rivals as IBM, Hewlett-Packard, and Sun are now taking a lively interest in storage, EMC still has a lock on the business. Its success is a case history in how to cater to buyers in streamline mode—and in the attention to detail, customer care, leadership, and marathon persistence that market requires.

When it comes to storage systems, nearly all customers are streamliners. They don't really want storage units; they want what the machines can do for them, and they want it with as little hassle as possible. Streamline customers need reliability and responsive service, and they want their suppliers to be around five to ten years from now. They are settlers, not nomads, so they want suppliers who can settle in with them. They don't really trust overnight success stories; what they want is a market leader with the solid discipline to stay on top for a generation or more.

"Choosing information infrastructure used to be called a bet-your-career decision. Now, it's a bet-your-company decision," says Mike Ruffolo, EMC's executive vice president for global sales, services and marketing.

"Before I joined EMC, I saw the company from the perspective of a marketing partner, customer, supplier, and even competitor," says Ruffolo, who previously headed the document solutions group at Xerox after serving as CIO at NCR.

"I was always impressed by three things about EMC," he says. "The high quality of their products and service, their hard-charging culture and their talented team of professionals. Now, from the inside, I can drive these considerable assets to even greater success in the marketplace."

EMC has proved itself a caring supplier and a master at keeping up with a market that changes at breakneck speed. The company has gone through five major business reinventions and five product generations in just ten years, and is in the process of accelerating its evolution to what its managers call TNT: the next thing. These people are nothing less than serial disrupters of their own business model and technology—yet somehow they manage to do this so seamlessly that their streamliner customers barely notice it.

In 2000, EMC was on course to chalk up $8.5 billion in sales.

By the end of 2001, it plans to be a $12 billion company, with its customer base growing at 50 percent a year. In its managers' view, EMC is losing market share if it grows at anything less than 35 percent a year.

In the previous chapter, we got just a glimpse of EMC's spectacular Call Home system: Its storage boxes call their maker and alert EMC technicians when something is about to go wrong with them. This service is only part of the care and feeding that EMC gives its customers, but it underscores and illustrates the company's basic strategy for dealing with streamliners.

"Only ten percent of our job is fixing problems," Joe Walton, EMC's senior vice president in charge of global customer service, puts it. "The other ninety percent is predicting, preempting, preventing problems so that customers can get on with their business." Even better for the customers, EMC's customer engineers follow a "guilty until proven innocent" policy in dealing with problems. Whether the glitch originated in an EMC product or another part of the customer's system, EMC will keep on trying to fix it until it's clear somebody else was to blame. That approach surely plays to the streamliner's urge to make a purchase and have no hassle about it, but it also helps EMC design better boxes. And that saves a lot of money. As CEO Mike Ruettgers told me, "We believe the old adage that if you fix a problem in design, it takes one unit of effort. If you fix it in manufacturing, it takes ten units. If you have to fix it in the field, it's a hundred units."

The value of the Call Home support centers isn't merely that they provide customers with peace of mind today. In the long run, they are also incubators of innovation at EMC. The company's mission is to make its storage solutions better and better to keep the industry leadership that its streamliner customers crave, and the support centers are closely linked to the engineering and R&D operations. Thus they provide EMC engineers with an intimate connection to their customers and the customers' experience with EMC's products. "We can read our customers' minds," says Walton. That interaction becomes a key factor in EMC's innovation process—and in its moving on to TNT.

EMC pays a hefty price for this relationship: Unlike most others in the information technology industry, EMC manages customer service as an investment center, not as a profit center. For the first two years after a customer buys a storage box, service is free. By contrast, IBM's global services are its most profitable line of business. But sacrificing this flowing profit stream is only tactical. EMC's obsession with performance and reliability makes its streamliner customers willing to pay considerably more than rock-bottom prices. The service philosophy has paid off in loyalty, too: 80 percent of sales are to current customers, and EMC's customer retention rate is 99 percent. The idea of "customers for life" is a lot more than an empty slogan at EMC.

All this is a far cry—and a painful journey—from the day in 1988 when a blunt new executive vice president arrived at EMC, handed out airsickness bags to his senior managers, and announced: "The quality of our products makes me want to puke." Mike Ruettgers went on to spearhead the revolution of the company—and in the next decade, as president and then CEO, to transform it four more times to stay ahead of the pack.

The first revolution came in 1989 when EMC, to the derision of industry observers, took on giant IBM to go after the mainframe storage market. EMC had been founded in 1979 as a maker of add-on memory boards; after ten years it was still an upstart on Boston's Route 128, with some bright ideas but a quality image that Ruettgers rightly called awful.

But Ruettgers knew that IBM was vulnerable because of its growing arrogance: Big Blue was terrible at listening to its customers. It didn't help that IBM and its major competitors were focused on their expensive mainframes, disdaining storage as a tedious necessity. EMC was already reforming its culture to center on customers, and one of its bright ideas was a revolutionary approach to storage. Instead of trying to compete in the ever-growing complexity of memory, EMC's engineers assembled a lot of small, low-priced disks and linked them into what was called a redundant array of inexpensive disks (RAID).

This approach, while as reliable as existing devices, offered a big advantage in speed and a small footprint. EMC overcame initial skepticism by offering the devices on a trial basis—and lo and behold, many trials turned into purchases. In 1990, EMC made its storage systems independently intelligent. Within three years, it had become the market-share leader in mainframe storage.

By that time, however, customers were shifting away from mainframes to decentralized computer networks, with servers linking dozens of outposts. But the server makers, like the mainframe producers before them, left an opening for EMC by treating storage as an afterthought.

EMC caught that wave of change by transitioning to so-called open systems in 1995, creating one box to handle all the storage needs of a company's mainframe as well as all the additional computing platforms found in many organizations. In essence, this was one giant hard disk with a lot of computers hooked on to it, permitting better management of data. Another advantage was that companies could upgrade or replace their computer systems without having to reinstall all the data in the memory. And because the storage devices were compatible with a wide variety of computing platforms, versatility improved and data could be exchanged between networks.

Also in 1995, EMC went through yet another significant transformation by getting seriously into software and services to make their boxes more independent and able to deal with still more varied platforms. With the new software, customers can actually set up duplicate storage systems, recording everything simultaneously in two locations to ensure that the system will never be down for more than a second or two. Some Wall Street houses now flip back and forth between the duplicate locations every day, using each in turn as the primary system and thus making sure both stay fully up to speed. What better assurance could a streamliner ask?

A few years later, EMC moved rapidly into the emerging market for storage networks, in which a large number of servers are connected to a large number of storage units. The latest reinvention is still happening: the move from enterprise storage networks to a whole new infostructure to deal with what EMC calls the "Content Big Bang"—an Internet-based information explosion over the next five years that will dwarf all previous market forecasts for information storage. We'll come back to that.

Each of EMC's serial disruptions required foresight and the commitment to enormous investments in R&D ($5 billion over the past ten years, and another $2.5 billion planned for the next two). But what stands out most is that all these innovations and changes were somehow implemented without major interruptions for the customer.

In fact, says Frank Hauck, executive vice president for products and offerings, seamless product transitions are an EMC core competence. And while that sounds glib, it includes an intermeshed set of tasks that would challenge any organization. To achieve seamlessness, EMC must develop several technologies concurrently; start working on the next breakthrough before the current one has even reached general availability; make its own products obsolete in their prime; and preserve its customers' investment by offering software that works across generations.

All this would seem incredible if the incredible had not become commonplace. To give the storage explosion some perspective, Mike Ruettgers points out that forty years ago, a terabyte of data would have required a storage facility the size of Argentina. Now EMC stores 19 terabytes in a box the size of a desk, and a single company, British Telecom, has a storage capacity of 85 terabytes—more than all the information contained in all nine thousand mainframe computers used by all the companies in the world just ten years ago.

In part, the explosion has happened simply because it was possible: As the cost of storage has been driven down, it becomes easy and affordable to keep nearly everything anyone might want. Since it's never clear which bit of information might come in handy, nobody works very hard at managing data and weeding out chaff, and the boxes keep filling up. For every price drop of 1 percent, EMC says, demand for storage rises by 4 percent.

What's more, globalization and the Internet have combined to require mission-critical computing: Nearly all the systems must work twenty-four hours a day, seven days a week, 365 days a year. Just five years ago, Ruettgers says, a company could assemble the components of a system, make it work, and handle any glitches with its own IT staff. If the system crashed, the IT staffers would be heroes for working until 5 A.M. to get it back up. With mission-critical systems, however, any crash is intolerable. That means that systems have to be designed and tested as a whole, made as foolproof as possible, and then duplicated to provide an emergency backup.

But there are major differences between EMC's two main kinds of customers: the dot-com Internet companies and the global 2,000, the two thousand biggest companies in the world. In some ways, the most demanding of the two are the dot-coms—Internet companies that were built around their computers, whose need for storage doubles on average every ninety days. They must also be ready to scale up operations almost instantly to meet rising demand. One mobile phone company, Ruettgers tells me, planned for sixty thousand customers in its first six weeks. In twelve weeks, it had six hundred thousand customers and had to pull out all stops to provide them service.

Dot-coms typically want change faster than EMC can provide it. In May of 2000, Amazon.com alone had roughly 35 terabytes—35 trillion bytes—of storage (most of it from EMC). Amazon.com's storage requirements were growing at a pace of about one terabyte per week, which meant that by the end of

2000, it would need storage for roughly 60 terabytes, which would contain three times the entire Library of Congress.

NTT DoCoMo's hot new i-mode, which enables mobile phone users to access the Internet, has an even greater appetite for storage. Within eighteen months, the count of i-mode subscribers soared to 9 million, placing enormous strains on DoCoMo's systems. In a brief twelve months, DoCoMo purchased 265 terabytes of storage from EMC—thirteen Libraries of Congress.

By contrast, the average company in the global 2,000 thinks EMC is changing too fast. A global 2,000 company doubles its information needs every year—fast, but only a quarter the rate of dot-coms. But because these companies are larger organizations than dot-coms and have much more existing infrastructure, they find it far harder and more complex to make changes.

For the dot-coms, says Ruettgers, changing is like digging the tunnel under the English Channel: hard and expensive, but relatively straightforward. Change for the global 2,000 is more like Boston's Big Dig, the project to modernize the much shorter tunnel to Logan Airport. The channel tunnel cost $6 billion over six years, while the Big Dig has been going on for fifteen years and is now estimated at $18 to $20 billion, at least eight times the original estimate. The difference is mainly that the Big Dig must replace the old tunnel, disrupting thousands of existing infrastructure connections, and traffic must keep flowing around the work all the time.

Given that complexity, Ruettgers says, the global 2,000 must put even more effort into change than the dot-coms, and what they need is whole new systems that will work flawlessly with their existing organizations. So EMC collaborates with the major hardware and software companies to build and install complete infrastructures, delivering the highest possible reliability and providing service that anticipates problems and solves them before they happen. When a customer has to change its system, EMC engineers will preview the change and test any questionable features in the EMC laboratories, using equipment that matches the customer's system. If anything goes wrong after that, EMC will fix it at no charge. For streamline customers, it's the ultimate reassurance.

"Quality isn't really optional today," Ruettgers says. "It's like poker. If you have to have jacks or better to open, that's what you need to play the game." EMC's customer satisfaction rate of 99.4 percent is by far the highest in the industry, he says, reflecting its continuing investment in quality, its engineers' close involvement with the customers, the reliability of its products, and the company's expertise in product research and development.

Most electronic products go through lengthy tests in a customer's shop before they are installed, but Ruettgers says customers tell him that EMC's boxes "are the only products they will literally take from the shipping dock and put into production." Still, given the number of chances for things to go wrong, "it's amazing, frankly, that there aren't more disruptions."

To maintain close relations with its streamliner clients, EMC has set up customer councils. Customers' engineers and designers meet with their EMC counterparts in separate technology councils. And every day, an average of twenty-five client companies send groups of two to forty people for customized briefings on industry trends and possible solutions to their problems at special briefing centers at EMC's three regional headquarters, in Massachusetts, Ireland, and Japan.

EMC also tailors its sales and support staff to its customers, with one style for the relatively buttoned-up global 2,000 customers and a younger, hipper approach to the dot-coms. EMC staffers on the global 2,000 beat tend to work from 9 A.M. to 7 P.M., and may even wear suits. Those working with dot-coms dress and talk accordingly, and work from 10 A.M. to 10 P.M. When Ruettgers goes visiting dot-com customers, he says, "I notice that the sales guys that go with me have a slightly different scent—the scent of moth balls. They've been bringing their suits out because I'm in town."

And always, EMC staffers pay heed to their commonsense mantra: Listen to the customers, discuss their problems, hold their hands, and help them find solutions, big or small. Not long ago, Ruettgers himself met with executives from Disney who needed help in reorganizing the computer system in their resort hotels. "They told me it takes too long to check in because the people on the front desk actually have to toggle through three different systems in order to register somebody," he says. "And they don't even know whether you've been there before. Now, a hotel that knows that you've been there before makes you feel good. 'Nice to have you back again . . .' Well, we're going to help pull it together so that they only have to deal with one system, and they know what the customer is doing—where you've been, what you buy, all the rest."

EMC is well along in preparing for TNT—this time the Content Big Bang, which Ruettgers says will make today's speeded-up world look positively primitive. With annual storage costs down to a penny per megabyte, world demand for storage will rocket to 10,000 petabytes—10 million trillion bytes, fully fifty times today's total capacity. The fiber-optic infrastructure will have grown a thousandfold, to 20 billion miles, and data compression technology will multiply transmission and storage capacity another thousandfold.

The possibilities are staggering, for better or worse. Jim Rothnie, EMC's senior vice president and chief technology officer, talks of "the coming of the personal terabyte"—when any person might generate a trillion bytes of stored information, ranging from medical records, school data, and personal history to photos, videos, shopping, and credit card records, and every e-mail she ever sent or received. All of this could be organized and indexed for rapid, meaningful retrieval.

A hospital emergency room could find out everything the doctor needs to know about the victim of a traffic accident in time to save his life. Or as Ruettgers visualizes the brave new world, an individual driver on Interstate 80 could be advised by her cell phone that if she wants a new high-definition VCR to replace the one she bought five years ago, there's a sale going on at a store just off the next exit.

This big bang of nearly infinite, virtually free bandwidth and storage will be far more powerful than any previous stage of the information revolution, in EMC's considered view, and the company is ready for the challenge. "EMC has never been better positioned to capitalize on the tremendous opportunities ahead of us," says Ruettgers. "For the past decade, we have seen the next wave in storage before our competitors, and we have executed at least two years before any of them to achieve the technology and market leadership we now hold."

Ruettgers takes nothing for granted. He knows, he says, that there's no guarantee of continued success, and he promises "continuous reinvention and investment, seamless product transitions, and superior execution on a global scale." In the old days, he recalls, EMC could afford to make only one bet at a time, but now it's putting up $2.5 billion over two years for the simultaneous tracking of "two or three" promising new technologies that could revolutionize the storage world again. So his customers can rest assured: Whatever happens, EMC will be expertly leading the charge. It will be there for them, discussing their problems, holding their hands, and helping to find solutions. And as long as there are streamliners, that will be the formula for finding and keeping them.

CHAPTER 10

Free Up the Delegators

I f your company developed a new operating system and software platform that became the world's de facto standard in the
field, gaining you a market share three times larger than that of
your nearest rival, you would probably be pleased. If your new
product earned cult status, won award after award, sold 7 million
units in the four years following its release, causing industry analysts to predict a 40 percent earning growth rate for the next several years, you would probably be elated. That is, unless you're
Palm, Inc., the world's leading provider of personal handheld
computing devices (also referred to as personal digital assistants,
or PDAs).

Palm's sleek electronic organizers took off faster than color
TVs, cell phones, and CD players, and now account for approximately 70 percent of the worldwide market, but nipping at the
company's heels is its key rival, Microsoft, whose PocketPC operating system (a modified version of Windows CE) was chosen
by Hewlett-Packard to drive its Jornado, by Compaq for its
iPAQ, and by Casio and Siemens for devices that will compete
with Palm's.

To add to your headaches, there's a new company called Handspring, run by two of Palm's well-respected cofounders, which came up with an eye-catching new product they claim is even better than yours. Furthermore, the powerhouses that license your operating system—Sony, Nokia, and QUALCOMM—are speedily designing new products based on your technology that could render your version obsolete.

It's not surprising that Palm, which ranked 36 on my list of the top 100 market leaders, feels under tremendous pressure. In this brutally competitive and time-starved world, no one can do everything alone. More people and organizations are asking: What can I off-load onto someone else? Put another way, the question is, what can I delegate? You want someone to assume the elaborate, difficult, tedious, or resource-consuming jobs—those you would prefer not to think about and can trust others to perform, so you can pursue more pressing matters.

For Palm, which designed its breakthrough product, the Palm Pilot, around the idea that simplicity is a virtue, the answer has been to delegate everything except the business's core functions. In June of 2000, Palm employed just 951 people, who, among them, produced $1.06 billion in revenues. That's more than $1.1 million generated per employee. To put this number in perspective, compare it with Microsoft's $730,000, GE's $345,000, and Sony's $317,000 of sales per employee.

Palm's vital functions are product design and engineering, which employs 364 people, or 38 percent of the company, and marketing and sales, with 342 employees, or 36 percent of the total. Among the remaining employees, 154 are in general and administrative jobs, and 91 take care of supply, service, and support activities. The majority of the latter activities are delegated, thus keeping Palm's operations highly focused.

Palm does not have an operations center where all of its PDAs are made and serviced. Instead, Flextronics International and Manufacturers Services, Ltd., take care of prototyping, manufacturing, procuring, testing, and handling the logistics for its product. Regionally based third parties look after Palm's customer service, tech support, and product repair, while its network operations are outsourced to Houston-based Network Inc. And to top it off, Palm encourages some seventy-seven thousand third-party volunteers to enhance the functioning of its products by developing new and improved software and applications.

Of course, not all customers, corporate or consumer, delegate their tasks to the same degree that Palm does. There are aspects to our lives as customers that we enjoy taking care of ourselves, whether as lone search-and-browsers or in collaboration with others, and we streamline some of our buying to make it as automatic as possible. Yet for most of us, delegating whole jobs to trusted surrogates is increasing. As consumers, we are trying to free up time and make our lives more convenient, in addition to shedding those tasks that we aren't comfortable handling ourselves. We want to reduce our risk, worry, and anxiety. When we hire delegators, we are buying relief.

Companies that cater to delegators understand that frame of mind. They circumvent the scarcity of customers, and make themselves indispensable by creating new demands for their services, and they do so for both consumer and business customers. Managers know that delegators crave solutions like one-stop shopping because these customers want to devote as little thought as possible to the job they are off-loading; they actually welcome having narrow choices. Once the clients trust the quality and reliability of the service they buy, they will return repeatedly to that supplier, rather than switch to a new one. Above all else, delegators want peace of mind, and will prefer "reliable" to "exciting" any day. Their mantra might be "Just don't make me have to think about it." Or as they say at Palm, simplicity is a virtue.

Now let's examine four market strategies aimed at winning delegators.

CHOOSE FOR THE CUSTOMER

Most consumers in delegation mode are following the first of the four basic strategies: Let someone else shop for, select, and buy a particular product or service. The responsibilities of a delegated personal shopper include, but go beyond, selecting and buying. The supplier becomes involved in various activities on behalf of its customer, and has to be skilled at *one,* sourcing, that is, locating suitable offerings; *two,* negotiating, particularly on price; *three,* bundling and prepackaging solutions, meaning putting together the pieces of the desirable package; and *four,* seamlessly managing the delivery of the goods to the customer.

A prime example of the first strategy is the intent of the cruise vacation—a delegator's dream of one-stop shopping, requiring just one decision and one payment. Once the reservation is made and paid for, everything is taken care of: voyage, cabin, meals, entertainment, and activities for kids. The vacationer's only added expense is souvenirs and cocktails; her biggest decision is whether to work out in the ship's gym or visit the casino.

The industry's growth is testimony to the rise of delegation. In 1980, an estimated 450,000 people bought cruise vacations in the United States. Ten years later, that number had grown to 3 million annually. In 2000, 6.5 million passengers are expected to spend about $7 billion cruising. And the industry leader, with two million passengers spending $3.5 billion in 1999, is Carnival Cruise Lines.

The market has grown so rapidly mainly because cruise companies have managed to make these vacations affordable. Twenty years ago, people who took cruises were regarded as an elite group. In 2000, Carnival Cruise Lines offered a one-week cruise to the Caribbean for $549. With the industry's capacity now growing faster than the market, Carnival's seven-day trips have been discounted as low as $389. Carnival, which enjoys a 30 percent share of the cruise market, has been growing through acquisitions. More important, its expansion comes from new and repeating customers. Bob Dickinson, president and chief operating officer at Carnival Cruise Lines, reports half of its clients are first-time cruisers, while 80 percent of the other half have previously cruised with Carnival.

The line's Fun Ships offer swimming, movies, casinos, disco, shopping, food, and more food, with excursions and shopping at ports of call. You can eat around the clock in the pizzeria, then work off the pounds on the treadmill or climbing machine. It's prepackaged fun for everyone. Carnival works tirelessly to deliver the fun it promises; it trains crews to interact with passengers at every opportunity and offers a "guaranteed vacation": Any passenger who expresses disappointment, for any reason, before the first port of call will get a prorated refund and a free flight home. Dickinson told me that a minuscule minority—fewer than one-tenth of 1 percent—make use of that offer.

Yet Carnival doesn't think of its business as cruising; instead, Dickinson says, it has a tiny slice, a mere six-tenths of 1 percent, of the 300 million trips taken annually that make up the vacation industry. Assuming that perspective, he says, forces Carnival to avoid complacency and focus on how people choose to spend their leisure time.

Being in the vacation business also means that Carnival's competition is not just other cruise lines but alternative vacations, including the Disney theme parks, Yellowstone Park, Hawaii, resorts like Cancun, and gambling capital Las Vegas, where now the hotels, like Carnival's ships, provide a total entertainment experience for the family: golf, youth activities, shows, meals, and more, in addition to casinos.

Competing in that league, Carnival still sees a huge untapped potential: Only 12 percent of Americans have ever been on a cruise. As the appetite for one-stop shopping and hassle-free fun continues to grow, Carnival is expecting to raise its capacity by nearly 60 percent, expanding its fleet to twenty-one ships.

From the delegator's point of view, AOL operates in its industry—as an Internet service provider—in the same way that Carnival operates in its, as a vacation provider. Each preselects the destinations and puts together a package of offerings that can be bought all at once. For both, after the decision and initial arrangements are made, no further thought or maintenance is required. According to Forrester, a leading market-research firm, four out of every ten people active on the Internet in 1999 were using AOL. Furthermore, AOL retains 97 percent of its customers, the highest rate of any Internet service provider. For all of AOL's blackouts and delays, its slow pop-up ads, and even a short-lived scheme to sell customers' phone numbers, only 3 percent walk away.

Part of the reason for such loyalty comes from the stickiness inherent in delegators: Once a delegator makes a decision, he or she tends to revisit it rarely. But AOL offers other incentives as well. For one, its services simplify chores that are complex and a little scary, which enables its customers to interact with the Web much more than they would without assistance. While it is true that you can surf the Internet without using AOL's browser, and some of its clients do, most are content to stay with the familiar logo. AOL bills your credit card automatically. One has to wonder why magazines still send their subscribers renewal notices, in effect giving customers a chance to discontinue; in contrast to AOL's approach, which leaves the responsibility of terminating the service with the customer, the magazines make it easier to cancel than to renew.

A customer who wants to leave has a hard time figuring out how to disconnect and switch to another provider; she may also worry that the change could mean losing files and changing e-mail identity. All in all, the consensus seems to be that AOL's service is acceptable and the hassle of looking for a new provider isn't worth it. That's why it has more than 21 million customers, each of whom spends an average of thirty-five minutes a day using its services.

Delegators can find help shopping for and selecting merchandise from discount clubs, such as Costco and Wal-Mart's Sam's Club. With sales in the vicinity of $30 billion, each offers its members quality merchandise on better terms than individuals could get for themselves.

These stores have several attractions for delegators, including low prices. But for the middle- and upper-class demographic groups, the perception of value stems from more than their low prices. That the choice of merchandise is limited is viewed as an advantage by delegators, who spend less time and make fewer decisions in these stores, which stock only about four thousand products compared with approximately sixty thousand in traditional stores. Still, the goods are very carefully selected. Beyond a supply of staples, the buying clubs offer special items, including salmon from Norway, perhaps, or ribs from Denmark. And the quality, for the most part, is excellent.

From the consumer's point of view, being a member of one of the clubs is close to having a personal shopper. The stores record customer purchases, analyze the buying patterns, and adjust their procurement decisions and inventory to match demand. Even within a local area, the stores vary their merchandise to cater to the particular preferences of their clients.

The membership clubs lock in customers with an annual fee and issue a membership card with a photo identification of the buyer. Once you have the card, you tend to continue to use it, evidenced in the stores' very high renewal rate of about 80 percent. People complain that loyalty is dead, but it isn't—it has just morphed into habit.

If the buying clubs offer delegators convenience and value, mutual funds provide reassurance and solutions to complex problems in another industry. Investment decisions are intimidating to many consumers; even if we take the time to read annual reports and get advice on investments, we still may not be sure that we've understood it all correctly. Working with Vanguard, Fidelity, Schwab, or the local bank means you are delegating investment decisions to someone with expertise. Obviously, that requires a great deal of trust in the capacity of the funds' managers to perform well and have our interest at heart.

The first strategy of delegation—enlisting help in selecting and purchasing—is mainly for consumers. The three other strategies apply to corporate buyers and are designed in accordance with their varying reasons for wanting to off-load responsibilities.

ENTHRALL YOUR CUSTOMERS
WITH WHAT YOU DO BEST

Market strategy number two is a logical outgrowth of the concept of core competencies, which is the idea that, in a world where specialists increasingly outperform generalists, a business should focus on what it does best and what is essential to its success. All other tasks should be farmed out to people who perform them better. Consistent with that credo, more companies are having components assembled by someone else, as well as delegating chores that include payroll, bookkeeping, manufacturing, even research and development, to specialists who have the scale of operations to perform them efficiently. Allocating as much of what you aren't good at to someone who is better will free your own time and capital to devote to myriad other tasks.

For small businesses, the ideal chore to outsource is the payroll. It is labyrinthine, tedious, and entangled with constantly changing regulations, but it's also a vital part of the operation in which errors could be disastrous. More than 320,000 companies, most of them employing fewer than one hundred workers, rely on Paychex, Inc., to handle their regular payrolls. Many of them also hire Paychex to keep track of their tax payments, pensions, and 401(k) plans, and their workers' compensation insurance.

Paychex, started in 1971 on a shoestring investment of $3,000, has made its founder, Thomas Golisano, a billionaire. In addition, the company has achieved eight straight years of growth rates of 36 percent or more. Golisano claims he was lucky to find a potentially huge and all but untapped market, but in fact, his company's success reflects operating principles shared by most companies that successfully cater to delegators. They are:

Focus on doing one thing supremely well. Golisano decided early on that he would concentrate on the small payroll market and not branch into general accounting of receivables, inventories, and the like. He understood where his clients were in pain and what they really needed. If this seems to be an obvious point, keep in mind that I continuously see companies trying to expand their fields when their customers really need them to maintain their unequaled competence at one thing.

Nurture trust. People who own small businesses tend to be secretive and reluctant to yield control, particularly regarding data and processes in which a mistake could be fatal. Yet Paychex has built a reputation for honesty and reliability, and has persuaded thousands of clients that they could very safely and easily relinquish a complex administrative chore. "It's just one less thing to worry about," says Gene Polisseni, senior vice president for marketing. Even though many clients have never had trouble doing their own payrolls, "it's amazing how many just want the peace of mind."

Build a niche and lock customers in. Golisano believes that his company's tight focus, stress on quality, and competitive pricing are what keep clients on board; and since Paychex performs an essential service, it becomes integral to its customers' lives. Like all delegators, Paychex's clients have little inclination or incentive to change, and in fact, encounter a good deal of bother if they decide to. These factors, plus the formidable software it has accumulated over thirty years, ensure that new rivals will face serious obstacles if they enter this market. For the most part, Paychex and its only national competitor, Automatic Data Processing, have this field to themselves.

Exercise caution in innovating. Customers in the bottom quadrants of our matrix—streamliners and delegators—are far more interested in reliable performance than in having the latest fad. Thus, Paychex has been slow to adapt its operations to electronic cash transfers and posting data on Web sites. "Initially, as a marketing person, I thought, There's a great opportunity here," according to Polisseni. "But it's not the cure-all for everybody. There are security issues, for instance. I don't think companies are ready yet to have that kind of stuff floating around the Internet."

All told, it has been a textbook perfect strategic approach: Along with its steady 36 percent growth rate, Paychex has a profit margin of 22 percent. And since its 320,000 clients make up less than 6 percent of the 5 million employers in the United States, there's plenty of room for expansion.

Depending on their industries, other companies serving delegators use a variety of tactics. In electronics, for instance, the speed of innovation and the brief shelf life of products place a premium on the supplier's flexibility of operations and ability to ramp up output as fast as possible. In the electronics, telephone, and Internet industries, scalability is also a critical issue.

Companies enjoying rapid growth may have their own needs to delegate certain jobs. Amazon.com, for instance, has grown in two or three years to the point that Wal-Mart reached in twenty. If you're Amazon, how do you scale your business rapidly enough to do everything properly? It may be impossible to do that yourself. You need a company that can scale up faster than you; in this case, Amazon delegates its shipping to others. A shortage of capital will also constrain growth. If you are an e-tailer, you would prefer to delegate rather than use the little money you have to build a distribution center or a manufacturing plant. Companies serving delegators make sure they have efficient, scalable operations that work extremely fast and don't require their clients to stake a major capital investment. All this comes as one package.

RUN THE WHOLE SHOW

The third delegation strategy involves more than the second. What we have been talking about so far is the *deep* delegation strategy, that is, off-loading a specific process or activity onto someone that specializes in that task. There is also a *broad* strategy, in which a customer contracts out entire business operations. As in the previous approach, the suppliers' expertise and scale advantages motivate clients to delegate. What distinguishes this strategy is that it places a high premium on the supplier's orchestration skills. The broader the scope and the more critical the nature of the work, the more customers have to trust that the supplier excels in coordinating and juxtaposing various pieces of the puzzle to form a solution and keep it running smoothly.

Responding to this demand, General Electric Power Systems, which builds turnkey power plants for thousands of customers around the world, will even run its customers' plants for them. For the company in need of a power plant, GEPS will take care of everything. In this case, all the delegators have to do is determine the spread between what they plan to charge and what they are willing to pay.

One of Britain's most prominent logistics companies, Hays PLC, manages its clients' entire supply chains. For the large retailers Tesco and Waitrose, Hays provides and runs regional distribution centers. For other large companies, such as Philips Electronics and Shell Oil, Hays offers warehousing and transportation services similar to those rendered by UPS in the United States. For Vodafone, another top 100 company, Hays furnishes what are, essentially, repair centers, as well as logistics-related services. If you have a problem with your cell phone, you don't call Vodafone to have it fixed, you call Hays, which services other clients at the customer center as well. Hays offers warehousing systems, express parts delivery, repair delivery, and technicare services. Undoubtedly, Hays provides a turnkey, one-stop solution for its customers.

In information technology, companies are more frequently looking for turnkey solutions. For suppliers such as EDS, CSC, and IBM, this trend has created a boon. In the past six years, the information services and software companies in my database grew from $73 billion in sales to $220 billion, roughly 50 percent of which I estimate to be delegation-related. For example, in 1993, Xerox signed a ten-year, $3 billion contract that allows EDS to run its IT operations; a few years later, J. P. Morgan signed a seven-year, $2 billion deal to have a consortium of four technology services companies take care of a large portion of its operations; last year, cereal maker Kellogg renewed a multiyear outsourcing contract that arranges for Unisys Corporation to provide it with state-of-the art technology.

In a variation on this theme, information service companies are eagerly catering to customers who are anxious to establish an Internet presence. A manufacturer can allocate entirely the job of arranging a "digital strategy." This means delegating the design, setup, operation, and maintenance of a Web site, which includes keeping the software up to date. The supplier will also oversee your click stream, so that every time someone clicks on to any piece of information on your Web site, the move is recorded and analyzed. With this information, you can figure out which parts of the site are working well, what most customers want to know, and how you can get people to linger longer on the page. What is fascinating is that, now, suppliers are working with their customers at great physical distances. Witness the explosive growth of India's software and information services companies, which emerged from relative obscurity to become a $5 billion industry serving two out of every five Fortune 1,000 companies. By 2008, McKinsey consultants estimate the industry will reach $87 billion, which would most certainly identify it as a veritable delegation success story.

Infosys Technologies is one of the hottest of these Indian companies. Its impressive performance placed it on my top 100 list. Though Infosys Technologies had grown steadily since the early 1980s, it wasn't until the last several years that it really took off. This success accompanied the company's realization that, instead of continuing as a low-cost subcontractor, it could use the Internet to provide an integrated range of technology solutions around the clock and, in so doing, take advantage of India's educated talent, low wages, and geographic location.

For its customers, such as Nestle's, Adidas, Toshiba, Nortel, Amazon.com, Goldman Sachs, and J. P. Morgan, Infosys Technologies provides customized software, maintenance, reengineering services, applications development for manufacturing companies, engineering-related software development, and e-business development. Because its people work while its Western clients sleep, it offers unique advantages in speed—and its prices are 30 to 40 percent below the Western competition.

Today, the Bangalore-based company employs an estimated five thousand people and is always overwhelmed with job applicants. With such strong prospects for growth, it is no wonder that the company's stock price has soared ever since, in March 1999, it became the first Indian company listed on the NASDAQ.

TAKE THE PAIN OUT OF INNOVATION

The fourth strategy aimed at delegators concentrates on a function close to many a company's corporate soul: research and development. Especially in high-tech fields, companies that delegate their innovation are staking their future on the inspiration of people outside the company whose expertise lies in creating new ideas. But to keep R&D in house or outsource it is not an either/or choice. Many companies that have vast R&D capability, such as Microsoft, are also eager to acquire new products developed by others. The trend to delegate is becoming prevalent because companies are feeling more pressure on their resources and time. They have concluded that nearly any activity that can be allocated represents an opportunity for them to do something else.

Some companies have set up separate divisions or units to concentrate solely on product innovation. The distance between these entities and the existing business is useful—the closeness may act to stifle innovation, which Clay Christensen discusses in his book *The Innovator's Dilemma*. To a certain extent, the creative process from which breakthrough products and services are developed conflicts with operations-driven cultures, which explains why, over the years, most of McDonald's new products have originated in the field. One franchisee experiments with a new idea and finds that customers love it. For example, its new fast-cooking technology was developed by an outsider, not by a McDonald's employee. Even companies driven by innovation, such as Sony, Cisco, and Pfizer, need outside stimuli for fresh ideas.

The big pharmaceutical companies, for instance, have their hands full making sure that their products are produced, distributed, and sold properly. Since they can't always keep abreast of the constantly shifting developments in biotechnology and genetic engineering, they engage contract research organizations

(CROs) to supplement their own R&D activities. The more than twelve hundred CROs worldwide, including Quintiles Transnational, Parexel, and Covance, now account for about 20 percent of all the drug development expenditures in the pharmaceutical industry.

An interesting variation on the CRO is Millennium Pharmaceuticals, based in Cambridge, Massachusetts. Millennium is developing a variety of drugs and applications in genetic engineering, but marketing them with a twist. Instead of selling its results and expertise in the usual way, Millennium asks the pharmaceutical companies to take an equity stake in the company. Pfizer, Eli Lilly, and Bayer have all made sizable investments in Millennium to guarantee themselves access to its R&D resources. Bayer alone recently put close to $100 million into the company, buying about 14 percent of it.

Building on the basic R&D findings, different customers develop different applications.

In the telecommunications industry, QUALCOMM exemplifies a company that is furnishing innovation to delegators. QUALCOMM'S business is to achieve and sell intellectual breakthroughs. Indeed, it is a leader in developing a revolutionary technology called CDMA, which applies to cell phones.

Though it used to manufacture cell phones, QUALCOMM's managers recognized that others did this better and cheaper, but where their company really excelled was in research and development. In preparation for changing its focus to R&D, QUALCOMM has recently spun off or closed down its manufacturing facilities. Now it aims to become the brain trust of CDMA technology, outsourcing research to telephone giants such as Nokia and Ericsson.

However, QUALCOMM is not universally admired in its industry; some of its current and prospective clients view its licensing fees as akin to highway robbery. But the disdain and fear it incites is nowhere near that provoked by a little-known company called Gemstar, which recently merged with *TV Guide* and threatens to become a giant power in the media and entertainment field.

Gemstar gained a foothold in 1989 when its founder, Henry Yuen, frustrated in his attempts to record a baseball game on his VCR, set out to simplify the process. He and a partner, Daniel Kwoh, invented the technology that assigns a simple code to every television program, then allows viewers to program their VCRs by punching in that code. They licensed the technology to VCR makers and persuaded newspapers to run the codes in their program guides; the result is a business now worth in the vicinity of $80 million a year.

That was just the beginning for Gemstar, which went on to pioneer interactive program guides equipped with technology that enables viewers to search and browse through on-screen listings and surf programs. It has already licensed this know-how to producers including Sony, Zenith, and Sharp, and Microsoft has paid $45 million to use Gemstar's process in its WebTV program guide.

This technology's potential is awesome. In an era that will soon have five hundred television channels, viewers will be lost without some kind of electronic program guide, and the guide itself will be, like the AOL front page, a beacon for advertisers. Some analysts predict that the bulk of television advertising will gravitate away from the programs and toward the guide itself, since many more viewers will actually see the ads there.

With more than ninety patents covering its technology, Gemstar is in a commanding position. Not shy about fending off rivals, the company has filed more than a dozen lawsuits charging infringement and earning the sobriquet of "patent terrorist." Thus far, it has won an $18 million judgment against General Instrument, and is headed for a showdown with Time Warner, which told its cable systems in California, Maine, and North Carolina to strip Gemstar's programming data from the signals they transmit. Aiming to sell its own interactive guide, Time

Warner maintains that it is not obliged to distribute Gemstar's free version.

The *TV Guide* merger gives Gemstar access to 34 million readers and 50 million homes that now receive or buy the *TV Guide* on-screen listings. Some in the industry already view Gemstar as a potential monopoly that could bypass licensing altogether. Time Warner's set-top box supplier, Scientific-Atlanta, has filed a federal antitrust complaint against Gemstar, accusing it of "a calculated plan to monopolize the U.S. market for the licensing of interactive electronic program guide technology."

Yuen, a lawyer, says his company is simply being pragmatic; his executive vice president, Stephen A. Weisswasser, told an interviewer that Gemstar's infringement suits are only to be expected. "Patents are our life blood," he said, and "you have to protect your assets."

In most industries, the established companies welcome the trend toward delegating R&D and product development. Ford Motor, DaimlerChrysler, and Toyota have long relied on contractors, such as Textron and Johnson Controls, to supply entire subassemblies for their cars. Now the automakers are advancing delegation. Concluding that they can't spend time assessing all of the latest innovations and technological breakthroughs for every detail of what comprises a car, they asked Johnson Controls, which already provides entire auto seat assemblies, to conduct the research required to design an improved, more comfortable seat.

These four market strategies play into delegators' collective desire to farm out whatever they'd rather not do themselves, then to think about it as little as possible. Importantly, delegators who are simplifying their lives are relying on suppliers to perform a crucial function, a position that places the client at risk for both small, transient problems, such as a spoiled vacation, and serious, permanent failure, such as bankruptcy due to inadequate R&D.

Thus, any company that chooses to cater to the delegation market must first dedicate itself to quality and total reliability, and must be able to nurture trust so that its customers have peace of mind.

As the world grows more inextricable, the need for deeper specialization grows in proportion, which makes it likely that companies providing delegation services will thrive. For a close-up of how one company exploits this trend, we turn next to Solectron.

CHAPTER 11

Case in Point—Solectron

Two events marked Friday, December 19, 1997, as a unique day for Solectron Corporation. The first was a White House ceremony in which President Clinton presented Solectron with the 1997 Malcolm Baldrige National Quality Award, making it the first two-time winner of the notoriously demanding award for manufacturing. The same day, Solectron and computer maker NCR Corporation announced plans for Solectron to acquire three NCR manufacturing plants, then for NCR to outsource much of its manufacturing to Solectron. Some twelve hundred NCR employees would shift employer, but nothing else, even continuing to work in the same facilities. As Susan Wang, Solectron's chief financial officer, later observed: "This will make NCR one of Solectron's top five or ten customers."

To companies considering delegating their manufacturing, these two events speak volumes about a supplier's performance and commitment. After all, the only reason Solectron would undertake the rigorous Baldrige examinations four times is that it is obsessed with continuous improvement and being the best of the best. Also, Solectron would not take over NCR's plants and employees unless it felt confident that it could improve their productivity dramatically. The implication to prospective customers is, if Solectron could make such a difference for NCR, it is likely to do the same for others.

Though the company has been a favorite on Wall Street for several years, Solectron is hardly a household name. In fact, many people are not even aware of the industry it leads: electronics manufacturing services (EMS), the business of actually producing many of the devices, from printed circuit boards and routers to cell phones and whole computers, that are sold under more familiar nameplates. In accelerating numbers, electronics companies, including Cisco Systems, Ericsson, IBM, and Nortel, are recognizing that the responsibilities of manufacturing are not among their core capabilities. So, they delegate that crucial function to Solectron and its competitors, including Flextronics, Jabil Circuits, Sanmina, and SCI. In so doing, the electronics companies are free to focus on what they do best, which is usually designing and marketing.

This is hardly a casual decision. All customers who delegate vital facets of their businesses must trust their suppliers. While a home computer user can assume that America Online will handle her e-mail, a company that delegates its production process places its very fate in its supplier's hands. The customer must feel certain that the supplier can produce goods matching the quality of the brand name, at low cost, on a schedule that is both firm and fast, but flexible enough to accommodate a crisis. Simply put, the delegating customer wants the best, and the supplier must inspire confidence that it is the best.

Solectron has done this well enough to earn revenues of $8.4 billion in 1999, and it expects $14.1 billion in 2000, maintaining its dizzying growth rate of 45 percent. The company is in a position to pick and choose its customers, which now number 200, and it is expanding its services across the supply chain, from simple manufacturing to higher-margin involvement in design, materials handling, sourcing of components, and servicing finished goods. In May 2000, Wall Street assigned it a market capitalization of $20 billion—far higher than the market value of such well-known fliers as Apple Computer and 3Com.

Solectron is riding a rising tide: In electronics, more than in most other industries, delegation in the form of outsourcing is rapidly becoming a way of life. In 1998, the EMS companies held, perhaps, 10 percent of the industry's $610 billion hardware business. But while that total business has been growing at about 9 percent a year, the EMS share has climbed by three times that figure. In ten years, according to a number of estimates, half of all electronics hardware will be produced via EMS. Moreover, there are signs that Solectron and a handful of its established rivals are now firmly positioned in the first tier of EMS, which leaves lesser players scrambling for scraps. "The big will get bigger," Susan Wang, Solectron's chief financial officer, told me. "The more we do, the more we get to do." Wang was pointing out the inherent advantage that leading companies, such as hers, have. The larger they get, the less vulnerable they are to customer scarcity, as long as they sustain their customer value superiority.

It is not difficult to understand why outsourcing, as a particular form of delegation, appeals to the big electronics companies, also referred to as original equipment makers, or OEMs. One reason is a simple, fundamental requisite in any industry where delegation is practiced: The servicers who concentrate solely on manufacturing are extremely good at it; they have perfected their techniques.

Because they work for several customers, the servicers can also operate their plants more efficiently, at higher rates of capacity utilization, than any single client can do; and they are in a better position to bargain for economies of scale on materials and components. This means that both parties come out ahead—a sine qua non in any delegating relationship. All told, Solectron can deliver products at a cost that is 10 to 20 percent lower than what its big clients incur in their own plants. Since Solectron's profit margin is a razor-thin 3 to 4 percent, the clients still get their goods at a considerable discount.

Speed is another significant benefit for OEMs that delegate. As the life cycle of electronics products shortens, the cost of components shrinks—on average, by roughly 1 percent every week. Dell builds computers to order in two days; if you make one that sits in inventory for six weeks, Dell will beat your price by 6 percent. In fact, electronics products are a bit like fish: spoiled in two days, rotten in three, and unapproachable in four. Getting them to market quickly is critical.

With forty-eight factories around the world replete with facilities standardized enough to make jobs interchangeable, Solectron can be responsive to any customer's local marketing need. Its whole system is geared to methodically exploiting the supply chain for maximum speed to market, while reacting flexibly to whatever occurs. Furthermore, by outsourcing manufacturing, delegating customers free up their own capital to devote to research, product design, and marketing what would otherwise be tied up in plant facilities and equipment. This can be especially crucial for start-up companies and others that are cut off from Wall Street's venture capital spigot.

None of these motives for outsourcing could make it happen in the absence of genuine trust—the essential lubricant for all delegation. Solectron has been developing and, more important, maintaining trustworthy customer relationships for two decades.

After Solectron's faltering beginning as a maker of solar energy products during the energy crisis in the 1970s, its leaders sensed opportunity in the electronics boom in Silicon Valley. "We hopped on the outsourcing bandwagon," its first chief executive officer, Winston Chen, has recalled. Formerly an IBM executive, Chen imbued IBM's creed—customers' needs come first—into Solectron. He held his reins loosely, allowing employees and managers the freedom to act on their own initiative. His dedication to his customers was genuine; in fact, he organized a system to measure and ensure customer satisfaction that still works.

On a weekly basis, each customer gives Solectron a grade—A to D—on five aspects of its business: quality, delivery, communication, service, and overall performance. The results are posted on every assembly line, and any grade lower than B triggers an intense internal inquiry aimed at improving matters within seventy-two hours.

Chen's successor, Koichi Nishimura, was every bit as dedicated to his customers. A Japanese-American who spent years in internment camps in the United States during World War II, Nishimura learned from his grandmother the concept of *kyosei*—mutually beneficial coexistence. That turned out to be prescient: Without *kyosei*, business delegation could not exist. Both partners must be able to say they are enhanced by their relationship.

Known as Ko, Nishimura went even further than Chen to invite outside scrutiny and evaluation of his company. He persuaded Solectron's managers to apply for the prestigious Malcolm Baldrige National Quality Award in 1989.

What he gained, Nishimura said later, was "free consulting"—a report from the Baldrige evaluators advising Solectron to pay even closer attention to its customers, and particularly to its long-range planning for customer needs. Nishimura promptly installed one- and three-year strategic plans, using a Japanese communications technique called *hoshin kanri* that remains in Solectron's repertoire of management methods. The next year's entry brought more advice for improvements, which Nishimura followed again.

Nishimura claimed that he never intended to win the award, just to improve his company. But in 1991, Baldrige evaluators were impressed enough by Solectron's application to send a team to visit the plant in Milpitas—and that fall, at a White House ceremony, Solectron won the prize. It was the first time the Baldrige was given to any company in the outsourcing business. And Solectron won it again in 1997, becoming the first repeat winner in the award's twelve-year history.

The company's focus on its customers may appear obsessive to a traditional manager, but it should be a matter of course to one who wants delegated business, and thus aims to become inseparable from his or her customer's operations. "It is our objective to form partnerships with all of our customers," proclaims the mission statement, and that attitude prevails from Nishimura's office to the assembly lines. When Baldrige examiners visited, according to Susan Wang, they found that workers on a line handling an IBM job would say they were working for IBM; on a Cisco Systems line, the workers identified themselves as Cisco people. The examiners concluded, she said, that "our customer culture is so deeply ingrained that our people actually believe they work for the customer."

Since the customer relationship relies on trust, Solectron's sales pitch to a new client is long and arduous. An order is discussed thoroughly; at every level of both companies, from chief executive officer to production foreman, the counterparts meet and talk. A small prototype order may be run off, to test not only the capabilities but the relationship as well.

As Wang told me: "The customers need to really feel comfortable that they can call anyone anytime and get the right kind of response, as if we were part of their own company. . . . When customers come in to observe the production, they have full access to the production floor assembler. . . . On an ongoing basis, customers are constantly in our factory, looking at things and peeking under the covers anytime they feel like it."

Delegating customers, in short, have a license to be demanding. But from its earliest days in the outsourcing business, Solectron has been smart enough to learn the business from its demanding customers and, as a result, improve its own performance. When Susan Wang joined the company in 1984, IBM was its biggest customer, and in her words: "Our actual understanding of manufacturing process control and quality control was not as good as IBM's. IBM . . . required us to implement statistical process control and other quality control measures. At their insistence, and also because we were very hungry for knowledge and improvement, we very willingly engaged in these improvement programs to learn, as quickly as possible, to . . . be as good as our customers . . . and exceeded their expectations."

Working with customers such as Sun Microsystems and Silicon Graphics, Solectron learned enough about new interconnect technology processes to perfect its own technology for making printed circuit boards and, in the end, to become better than its customers at making the goods they design. Wang points out that because the client companies needed "to go to the next level of capability, . . . we have become experts today. . . . Our early experimentation with them, our investment to continue the development, and our ability to deploy the technology more broadly . . . have made us a world-renowned expert in interconnect process." Solectron's reputation grew, and by the time Ericsson approached with a contract for cellular telephones in 1999, Ericsson took it for granted "that [Solectron's] expertise was far superior to theirs."

Certain customers may have special privileges granted to cement the delegating relationship. For Cisco Systems, its biggest customer, Solectron has tailored its business so closely to Cisco's that when an order comes from one of Cisco's customers—say, for a router—that order is switched to Solectron in the same instant it is received at Cisco. With no further instructions, Solectron produces and ships the device (in a Cisco carton), and the paperwork is done later. The customer never knows that Cisco didn't manufacture its router. Solectron tailors its processes to Cisco's requirements similarly all along the supply chain.

Such customization is not terribly difficult. "The manufacturing process is fundamentally a generic one," Wang explains, and production lines can fairly easily be converted from one customer's job to the next. And the cooperation works both ways. Solectron is free to suggest design changes that will make production simpler and faster, and frequently they are accepted. Here is Wang again: "The real customization is in the customer relations . . . how the customer releases products for production. Rapidly growing companies, for example . . . introduce products to manufacturing before the product is completed in its design. So, they . . . come in on the fly and request or demand engineering change. We have to understand that this is that customer's characteristic, and be very prepared to make those adjustments."

Customization reinforces another characteristic of all delegating customers: the habitual reluctance to make any changes in his or her life. Customized service binds the customer to the supplier. Once the systems are in place, it would entail an enormous amount of work for, say, Cisco to take its business away from Solectron. (Of course, this does not mean that the customer has no other choices. It is useful to remember that although Solectron is Cisco's primary servicer, Cisco also outsources to three others, thus retaining alternatives.)

Some customers become so pleased with outsourcing that they no longer use their own factories—in fact, many of Solectron's manufacturing sites have actually been purchased from its customers, such as Ericsson, Hewlett-Packard, IBM, and as noted earlier, NCR.

Integrating a new facility into Solectron's system is a challenge, says a company spokesperson. The plant's workers usually feel cast off and betrayed, but most rebound as soon as they realize that Solectron genuinely values manufacturing, wants to do it as well as possible, and treats its employees with respect.

For example, when Solectron bought NCR's retail systems plant near Atlanta, Georgia, in 1997, it encouraged the plant managers to make decisions on their own. While a tiny proportion of the seven hundred workers quit in reaction to Solectron's tough performance standards, and some were let go, the rest were motivated by their new company's variable pay system, which allowed workers to earn quarterly bonuses based on their production results, the customer satisfaction surveys, and reports from peer review quality committees. Morale, which had been down, began to rise. "For a person who takes pride in manufacturing, engineering, or materials management," says the spokesperson, "there's no better place to be" than Solectron.

Since Solectron can select its customers, managers are careful to maintain the right balance of stretch customers with the bread-and-butter clients who keep profits flowing. And Solectron can avoid clients who simply don't fit its needs or culture. Thus, a self-reinforcing cycle operates here: By avoiding disruptive or simply wrong clients, Solectron can keep constantly focused on its core strengths.

In practice, says the spokesperson, "We don't want to be everything to everybody. We want to have a balanced portfolio of industry segments . . . we serve, so that we aren't overly dependent on any one sector." Solectron focuses on jobs in computing, communications, and industrial manufacturing, with specific areas of concentration—routers, switches, and cell phones in communications, for instance, and medical devices and avionics equipment in industrial manufacturing.

Solectron has built its customer base in such a way that it has greatly reduced its vulnerability to the ups and downs of any one business or sector. This is crucial when you have capital-intensive operations and investments that you want to run at a steady, predictable level. In contrast to Solectron, airlines are an example of an industry that does not run evenly. If too little demand leaves planes underutilized, during which times enormous amounts of money are lost because fixed costs don't change, then high demand at peak travel times, such as Thanksgiving, creates operational crises when the demand can't be met and customers are distraught. Ideally, a company operates at a steady level throughout the year. Solectron's balanced utilization of its facilities can be more efficient than the operations of any single organization, such as IBM. Far more susceptible to ups and downs, IBM doesn't have the capacity that Solectron has to quickly reestablish its equilibrium.

Solectron's role has certainly expanded from its former image of a hired-gun manufacturer. Recently, Nishimura said that ten years ago, "we were a pair of hands. We were assemblers." Now the company's Web site describes it as "a global supply chain facilitator."

Like any company in the delegation business, Solectron constantly tries to expand its role in its customers' lives, to the point where it becomes indispensable. Customers delegate entire chunks of their businesses to Solectron, whose job now includes speeding up the whole process of filling orders, as well as producing, testing, and shipping goods.

Solectron's managers are acquiring materials and components for their customers, since the enormousness of the company's production gives it bargaining power. And that, in turn, makes Solectron the de facto power in choosing suppliers. Often a new client comes with its own list of contractors but is gradually persuaded that Solectron's favored suppliers can do the job better. Thus, says Susan Wang, "We create value not only for our customers but for our suppliers, who get more business." However, since Solectron's expertise in sourcing is now recognized, some new clients ask for recommendations right away. It is another way in which delegators give up a degree of control over their businesses—and don't mind it.

Solectron's expanded role also includes controlling the logistics of shipping and shifting work among its various plants to make sure that all of its factories are operating at 75 to 80 percent of capacity as well as to speed up delivery times. Additionally, it is getting more involved in its customers' research and development to help design products that can be produced efficiently. Now

clients don't have to worry about the intricacies of design specifications—and Solectron has assumed another piece of the customer's work.

In fact, according to Wang, Solectron's job has evolved into
nothing short of managing the total supply chain to make the entire business operate as smoothly as possible. Some of what this
means is involvement with design, in part to anticipate and head
off problems; managing the suppliers, keeping them informed of
probable new orders, and helping balance their flow of work and
materials; and controlling shipping logistics and coordinating communications, keeping information as transparent as possible and
available to everyone in the chain. And above all, it requires flexibility. The chain must have the capacity to respond to demand
shifts or unforeseen events and still get goods to market as quickly
as possible. "We don't take a problem and push it downstream,"
Susan Wang tells me. "We try to eliminate it."

Everything is connected. But as in all delegation, the process
can work only if the watchword is total quality. And that, in the
end, is Solectron's edge. You don't win two Baldrige awards unless you're not far from perfect.

CHAPTER 12

Team Up with the Collaborators

R emember one of the most talked-about business events of the late 1990s—the year 2000, or Y2K, scare? Companies and governments scrambled to prevent outdated computer code from crippling their information systems. Bracing themselves for power outages or actual disasters that were expected to mark the end of the twentieth century, untold numbers of consumers stockpiled staples, candles, and water. Then, at the stroke of midnight on December 31, 1999, the Y2K scare fizzled like a burned comet. All but forgotten in a matter of months, it was overshadowed by weightier pressures such as coming to grips with the Internet and the bobbing stock market.

Some critics called the scare a blatant marketing ploy, fanned by consultants, technology providers, and litigation lawyers planning to intimidate gullible managers into parting with half a *trillion* dollars worldwide. Even though that is a staggering number—it is more than five times what the United States spent in the Gulf War from 1988 to 1990 to fight another menace, Saddam Hussein—the financial toll of Y2K was not excessive. I estimate that Y2K expenditures accounted for less than 8 percent of the total spending on technology by the 5,009 companies in my research. A more realistic view of this extremely hyped commotion is that most of the money was spent wisely and that many companies—including IBM, which spent $600 million over several years to address its own Y2K problems—used the threat as a timely excuse to revamp and, in many instances, totally upgrade their systems. They turned complexity into opportunity.

No matter how we look at Y2K, we see that it underlines how technology advances can shake up the status quo. If the new millennium had arrived when our technology was at the stage that it was at, say, twenty years earlier, Y2K would have been far less significant. Then, computer systems and software were much simpler and less intertwined than they are now. Finding bug-infested code would have been a snap or, if undetected, would not have set off a chain reaction that threatened to immobilize electric power grids, air control systems, and financial markets. Likewise, five or ten years ago it would have been unimaginable to see the so-called Love Bug computer virus wreak havoc on the Web-connected e-mail systems of millions of people around the world, as it did in a matter of hours in May 2000.

That technology can save time and enhance performance is undeniable, yet at the same time, it adds layers of complexity to our lives, forces us to be more dependent on one another, and confronts us with unforeseen risks. In fact, computer systems and the processes they govern have become so intricate, software so esoteric, that they easily baffle managers.

Technology isn't the only confounding development. We all know that the financial world is in flux. Globalization and deregulation disrupt the coziness and familiarity of many companies that now have to deal with cross-industry alliances and customers who also occupy the role of competitors. Ongoing scientific discoveries further fuel the restless transformation of entire industries. Undoubtedly, complexity and change are interwoven into every aspect of our business lives and are forces to be reckoned with.

Some customers, for whom the technological challenges posed by Y2K were unwelcome disruptions, addressed their concerns the way they would a long-decayed tooth: Do what has to be done, get it over with, and hope the whole issue never surfaces again. Other customers recognized complexity as a source of progress, and its mastery as a way of distinguishing themselves. They saw Y2K not only as a problem to fix, but as an occasion to upgrade their systems for the future. For these companies and their suppliers, flux and turbulence offer opportunities. Realizing their own limitations, these customers have developed a heightened level of interest in suppliers that can help them succeed. I refer to these customers as collaborators, since they are actively seeking to team up with suppliers that have skills and expertise that they themselves are lacking.

What collaborators value above all else are their suppliers' skills as consultants and expertise in project management. That explains why demand has surged for all kinds of advisory services, for instance, the offerings of the Big Five accounting-cum-consulting firms, and the likes of EDS and CSC. Outpacing them all on the basis of growth is IBM, which for decades has been portraying itself as a total-solutions provider. About 60 percent of its growth over the past six years was derived from value-added services, not products. With an army of 130,000 people working to ensure that customers glean the maximum benefit from technology and its complexities, IBM generated $32 billion in service revenues during 1999. Working with collaborators accounted for roughly half of that; outsourcing and related services provided to delegators accounted for the other half.

The trend toward embellishing offerings with value-added support has escaped neither other technology companies nor other industries. Witness Compaq's acquisition of DEC, primarily for the latter's strong service capabilities; another example was the announcement in September 2000 that Hewlett-Packard was negotiating with PricewaterhouseCoopers to buy its management consulting division so as to bolster its own service activities.

In another industry, which we'll discuss in a later chapter, UPS has been busy transforming itself from a unidimensional delivery company to a custom services provider by teaming with key customers to exploit the intricacies of logistics in the Internet age.

Du Pont, too, recognizes that the real promise of chemistry (hence its customers' futures) lies in finding applications that will either add new value or reduce operating costs, and not just by lowering the prices of commoditylike products. Chad Halliday, chief executive officer and chairman of Du Pont, thinks the company should change from a fuel-based chemical company to a knowledge-intensive business that is willing to take on extremely complex and sometimes controversial projects. For example, in its agriproducts business, Du Pont's intent is to increase the amount of nutrition contained in the world's food supply. With its new company, Pioneer Hybrid, it is methodically approaching the problem by gathering a wide spectrum of data. It is not assuming a chemical solution, which is an enormous paradigm change for Du Pont. (Not incidentally, Du Pont has an excellent Web site detailing the company's position on such sensitive and daunting issues as genetically engineered crops.)

Halliday expresses his aim this way: "We want to be paid for what we know, not for what we make." In other words, he wants customers to benefit from the collective knowledge within his company's operating divisions and laboratories, and not simply, or even primarily, through Du Pont's products.

Evident in each of these cases is a shift from arm's-length, often anonymous contact between customer and supplier to closer and more personal interactions. Paralleling this is a move among customers to reduce their supplier base to a select few. Supplier rationalization, as the practice is called, has led companies such as

Xerox to shed 90 percent of its supplier base, and it is a widespread, ongoing development in the automotive sector. A survey by *Industry Week* and Price Waterhouse reported that 69 percent of a cross section of U.S. manufacturing plants have adopted some version of this practice. By dividing their purchases among as few suppliers as possible, the collaborators gain purchasing power and simplify their procurement operations as well. Paring down the supplier base also facilitates more-productive partnerships with the remaining suppliers, which is the essence of what collaborators seek.

Fruitful teaming between collaborators and suppliers assumes that both parties will appreciate and build upon the unique strengths and requirements of the other. Also, the relationship must foster a very high level of mutual trust to facilitate the two companies' working side by side. Furthermore, teaming presumes that the supplier and the customer share the perception that their interests are entwined: Each benefits when one motivates the other to enhance its areas of excellence. If that sounds like a major departure from the contentiousness typical of traditional supplier-customer relations, it is. In the final analysis, the new market leaders' success with collaborators transcends leveraging superior knowledge and expertise. It is rooted in the way they enable their teams to work.

In this chapter, I outline four market strategies, all of which are aimed at turning complexity into opportunity and, in appropriate circumstances, are exploited by the new market leaders in their teamwork with collaborators. The first two, based on particular projects lasting anywhere from weeks to years, address specific issues and complexities, such as the installation of a corporate-wide software system or the assessment of a new business opportunity. The last two entail much longer involvements between the customer and supplier, in which the latter functions either in the role of adviser or as an integral part of the customer's operations.

GET CUSTOMERS UP AND RUNNING

The first winning strategy, seen from the suppliers' perspective, is to get the clients with whom they are collaborating up and running. This strategy addresses the problems customers find most vexing when they change or upgrade their technical (and other) products, including the compatibility between the new and existing products and the effects that the new products will have on established practices and work habits.

Buying a stand-alone product (such as a new software application for personal use or a new power tool) may involve a tricky installation and can take time to master, but the aggravation is almost always temporary. Regrettably, this is not the case when we acquire products that need to be integrated into existing systems, or that mandate a serious overhaul not only of our technology, which would be complicated enough, but of how we operate our businesses or run our lives.

Any company that has installed an enterprise resource planning (ERP) system or a customer relationship management (CRM) solution knows that the software component is a minor concern. The most daunting tasks include redesigning the organization's business processes in their entirety, as well as reconstructing specific tasks; integrating the new systems with the jumble of existing ones; implementing the transition from old to new while, simultaneously, ensuring that everyone affected by the change is as prepared as possible for a dramatically altered workplace. Unsurprisingly, adopting a solution of this sort is usually invasive, takes months to complete, and requires many implementation specialists, also known as consultants and project management experts, who earn their keep by bringing this all about with expedience.

The leading providers of technology solutions have become

adept at helping customers endure the ordeals of implementation. Software giant Oracle, for instance, knows that teaming up with customers is good business: Approximately 58 percent of its $10 billion revenue in 1999 came from services and consulting, not from software sales. With fifteen thousand consultants, Oracle strives to ensure that its software is properly applied. The company has successfully shepherded customers through five thousand or so changeovers to its solutions. Clients know that with Oracle software come implementation tools and support to get things up and running in a set time—anywhere from thirty to ninety days.

Taking a somewhat different tack is SAP, the ERP software pioneer. In 1993, SAP was riding the business reengineering wave with its R/3 software, essentially a prepackaged set of best-practice solutions that replaced customers' outmoded processes. Choosing not to offer consulting support, SAP instead formed partnerships with Arthur Andersen, EDS, Cap Gemini, Siemens Nixdorf, and a dozen other firms that handled the task of implementing its software and making sure that it fit customers' unique requirements. For every dollar customers spent on SAP software, they could easily spend five on advice and services pertaining to running it. In an effort to garner a share of the dollars being paid to consultants, and to help develop closer collaborative relations with its customers, the company decided to shift gears.

SAP now provides a kind of Lego-block approach to the connected processes of purchasing and installing its software. Less concerned with managing all aspects of the transition, this approach concentrates on helping customers find the configuration of blocks—or modules—that best fits their company's particular needs.

The modules are designed to work in twenty-two different industries, including chemicals, automobiles, and financial services. For these industries, SAP offers 120 of what it calls "collaborative business process scenarios"; this means that there are 120 ways to configure specific business processes, say logistics flows or procurement. Finally, it designed three hundred different modules that arrange or define myriad ways of completing a specific task.

SAP's shift has proven worthwhile. Helping customers get their software operational has boosted its earnings from advisory services to 38 percent of 1999 revenues, up from just 15 percent in 1993.

HELP CUSTOMERS BREAK NEW GROUND

The second strategy focuses on solutions that address the specific circumstances of individual clients who are eager to break new ground. In other words, this approach concentrates on exploiting new opportunities and resolving ad hoc problems.

Traditionally, this has been the strong suit of strategy and operations consultants, whose depth of knowledge and years of experience give them a well-honed capacity to solve knotty problems. For a critical perspective and fresh thinking, customers call on McKinsey, A. T. Kearny, BCG, or A. D. Little—to name a few of the larger firms—or any of multiple smaller specialists.

Today, often at the urging of collaboration-oriented customers craving insightful viewpoints and better performance, suppliers are entering the fray. As customers tap their expertise, suppliers realize that they complement and often can substitute for consultants. To extract the most value from their know-how, suppliers are redesigning their selling and marketing processes and developing consulting skills that they emphasize over their ability to take orders, which, of course, they continue to do. They engage the customers' organizations at multiple levels to gain a detailed view of their needs, then assign a cross-functional team to devise individualized solutions, and this is all taking place in collaboration with the customer.

To uncover opportunities with potential, some suppliers initiate pilot projects with selected customers to jointly examine possible areas for process improvement or product breakthroughs. In fact, according to Craig Naylor, group vice president and general manager at Du Pont, his company pursues this method to strengthen its bonds with demanding customers, such as Delphi Automotive and Robert Bosch, two of the world's largest automotive parts makers.

On a grander scale, the new market leaders establish consulting divisions, that is, think tanks or business-development units for the purpose of helping customers break new ground. IBM, which employs multiple strategies to appeal to collaborators, as do UPS and other market leaders, exemplifies this point. IBM's business innovation services division pursues our second strategy by teaching customers how to develop unique e-business strategies, new ventures, Web applications, customer relationship management solutions, and the like.

One innovative company that is worth watching in this context is Ariba, which was founded in 1996 and is one of the youngest organizations in my top 100. Ariba and its major rival, Commerce One, have quickly become the leading pioneers in the highly competitive and swiftly expanding field of business-to-business e-commerce. Ariba broke new ground by establishing and managing, as of now, well over one hundred Internet-based marketplaces that allow participating sellers and corporate buyers to transact business with efficiency and speed. The company's plans are to build thousands of such exchanges in all segments of the economy and the world. Ariba's marketplaces focus on transactions that involve so-called operating resources, such as technology and office equipment, maintenance and repair items, and many other goods and services required to operate a business. In a typical company, these transactions represent the largest segment of corporate expenditures yet are often carried out with paper-based or semiautomated procedures that are inefficient for both buyer and seller. Ariba automates their processes and brings the parties together through its Internet-based network.

Keith Krach, Ariba's chairman, chief executive officer, and co-founder, told me that to launch the company, he focused on signing up a few large companies with nearly unlimited buying power. After attracting Cisco, FedEx, Bristol-Myers, Chevron, Hewlett-Packard, IBM, and companies of similar ilk, it wasn't long before more than twenty thousand sellers registered to make their product lines available through Ariba's network.

The collaboration with Cisco began even before Ariba had a finished product. Krach recalls, "They were about ready to develop their own [network, but when] we blindly exchanged product specifications, there was a ninety-five percent overlap. Then we had them meet our people . . . [who] wanted to review our quality assurance process, wanted to see all our product development schedules." That initial effort eventually resulted in Cisco transacting $1.5 billion annually across the Ariba network.

For other customers, one of Ariba's many innovative ideas was to standardize the size of the information displays in the sellers' product catalog so that buyers could easily make side-by-side comparisons. Additional features that please both buyers and sellers include Ariba's highly expedient and information-rich order management routines. Triggering many of these innovations was the company's practical way of gathering input from collaboration-oriented customers. First, Ariba held dozens of individual conversations with buyers and sellers, each of whom was asked to identify and clarify the issues significant to him or her. Then the company formed an advisory council that brought most of the participants together and invited each member to present to the others his or her idea of an ideal solution. Twenty-five hundred people participated in the council's most recent, its fifteenth, session. Krach is considering splitting up future sessions so they can focus on collaborative opportunities within specific jobs and industries.

The value Ariba delivers to its clientele transcends its efficient transaction network. In Krach's words, "We help [our customers] with their overall business strategies. Should they form a separate business unit, or a new company, to benefit from Ariba's e-commerce platform? If so, what's the revenue model? Or what are the value-added services our customers could provide to their customers? How should they divide up equity if they set up a new company?" Furthermore, Ariba leverages its expertise by working with customers to discover new applications for its business. For example, after signing American Express and Bank of America, the company developed an electronic payment utility. And it has created an interface that allows customers to connect their own electronic hubs to Ariba's network, and to do so seamlessly. With skill and finesse that will be difficult to mimic, Ariba has exploited complexity successfully to break new ground.

Commenting on partnerships and alliances, Krach concludes: "I think people who believe that they can go it alone in B-to-B e-commerce are naive. I think a key critical success factor is your ability to partner and create an ecosystem. I think that's clearly been one of the keys to our success. . . . [You] strive for a sixty/sixty deal where both parties . . . believe that they're getting the best part of the deal, because that's the only way that you're going to be able to have a long-term, sustaining relationship. If it's fifty-one/forty-nine, one of the guys feels that he's getting ripped off and it will never last."

On that note, let's move on to the next strategy to win with collaborators.

BECOME THE CUSTOMER'S TRUSTED COMPANION

So far, we have talked about projects that may take as little time to complete as a week or as much as several years. When a client replaces its computer systems or sets up a business-to-business exchange, the involvement, though lengthy, is finite with a specific beginning and end.

Here we focus on providing ongoing coaching and value-adding services to collaborators for as long as they are needed or wanted. The market leaders that excel at offering them stand out as much for their insight and knowledge as for their clear understanding of customers' specific and evolving needs. At the root of their success is the capacity to form genuinely respectful, trusting, close relationships with their clients. Not unlike the relationships that doctors, clerics, lawyers, and other confidants form with their patients and clients, these suppliers get to know and understand their customers, hence are far more able to guide and advise them on myriad circumstances.

Let's consider Charles Schwab, the investment company, which began with the goal of winning customers by making their stock transactions fast, easy, and inexpensive. Though Schwab provided a useful service, its clients' needs changed over time. Many had more money, more complex lives, and greater concerns about retirement and trust planning. They wanted a wider range of investment services, including personalized advice. In a word, they wanted a trusted partner to rely upon.

With its core business continuing to focus on the needs of streamline-oriented customers (as we discussed in an earlier chapter), Schwab initiated a separate effort to cater to its clients who were craving collaboration. It established AdvisorSource, which is, in essence, a referral network of independent financial service providers that have been screened by Charles Schwab. Approximately 450 of Schwab's 5,500 independent advisers participate in AdvisorSource. Moreover, in early 2000, Schwab merged with U.S. Trust, an organization that provides financial planning and trust services, including ongoing counseling, to affluent investors.

Of course, Charles Schwab's customers are not atypical. It has been apparent to successful financial services providers for a long time that personal advice and trust cement relationships with customers and gain their long-lasting patronage as much as, if not more than, handling their funds efficiently. That Internet trading and electronic banking are lavished with publicity does not mean that self-help has replaced traditional relationships based on trust. Fortunately, the choice doesn't have to be made. Market-leading financial institutions provide sophisticated timesaving technology without compromising personal contact.

When the issues are complicated and the particular segment of the marketplace in constant flux, as in the financial field, collaboration is extremely important. In such circumstances, customers value having access to suppliers they trust, who are aware of their particular circumstances. This applies equally to business customers. I am no longer surprised when I enter companies to find people other than employees settled into offices. They are, in fact, steadfast suppliers (and not infrequently, consultants) who permanently reside at the client company, acting as virtual employees.

Exemplifying this is a little-noted company, Amdocs, Ltd., which is ranked 88 on my top 100 list. In the last six years, Amdocs's sales grew tenfold, with 2000 revenues expected to top $1 billion. Its success rests on its formidable skill in building long-term strategic relationships with customers in the communications industry. Amdocs offers companies such as the baby Bells, Sprint, Deutsche Telekom, and Vodafone ongoing guidance in an area that now differentiates phone companies: customer care.

The company began two decades ago as a publisher of Yellow Pages in rural Missouri, but in the early 1990s expanded into innovative software products and services to help communications companies handle their ordering, billing, and customer relationship management tasks. In a rapidly evolving industry, such tasks are critically important to boost customer retention and satisfaction, making a customized approach for each communications company a necessity. Distinguishing itself from systems integrators and other project-oriented suppliers that move on as soon as a solution is in place, Amdocs's strategy is to stay deeply involved in its clients' companies, even to be on call to address new developments immediately. It's no wonder that it derives 88 percent of its revenues from ongoing servicing fees, rather than from licensing or selling its software.

INTERLOCK YOUR OPERATIONS—AND FORTUNES

When your largest customer dominates its industry, you can expect to share in its good fortune. This is self-evident to the executives at Keystone Foods and J. R. Simplot, two privately held (hence unranked) companies that supply McDonald's restaurants in the United States with, respectively, meat and potatoes. They are among the many suppliers whose fruitful collaborations with the fast food chain have lasted decades, after starting with nothing but a handshake agreement.

When customer and supplier interests are so intricately entwined, the concept of teaming up with customers assumes another dimension in addition to those we have discussed thus far. As a result, my fourth strategy for winning collaborator customers calls for more than specialized expertise and a close relationship. It entails a radical commitment—not easily reversed—to joint success. Here the primary emphasis changes to the physical and strategic interlocking of the supplier's and customer's businesses.

That extensive collaboration can contribute to the fortunes of both parties is clear from the now well known pact made between Wal-Mart and Procter & Gamble in 1985. With their contentious pasts behind them, they integrated their logistics and order management processes into a highly intricate, extremely streamlined, efficient whole. In so doing, they learned how to enact similar collaborations with other suppliers and customers.

Through the lens of the buyer, Toyota's style of cultivating its supplier base reflects how such collaborations come about. Though it had been selling cars in the United States since 1957, Toyota did not manufacture them here until 1984, when it formed a joint venture with General Motors. Today, annual production of Toyotas in its four North American plants exceeds 1 million vehicles.

As Dennis Cuneo, senior vice president of Toyota Motors North America, recalls, the Japanese company's first task was to ask GM for a list of the best suppliers of various components. Selections were not based on who provided the initial lowest cost; instead, Toyota was looking for three nonnegotiable characteristics: management attitude, technical capability, and the willingness to meet its stringent standards and adapt to the Toyota production system. That production system, vaunted for its quality, efficiency, and responsiveness to customer demand, was far from easy to master. Toyota gave the selected suppliers as much coaching and encouragement as they needed to ease the stress of reorganizing. Indeed, it seemed that the supplier companies were adopted by Toyota and became an extension of its production line.

Against predictable resistance, Toyota asked the vendors for their cost data. Cuneo explained, "We want to know exactly what their costs are on a particular part. Then we'll look for a way, together with them, to reduce the cost of the part and then we'll share that cost savings." In addition, the company had to assure its suppliers that it was committed to long-term relationships and had no intention of bidding out the business to the lowest-cost supplier every year.

Similar to the arrangements McDonald's made with its suppliers, Toyota did not draw up any formal long-term contracts, yet fifteen years later, most of the initial suppliers are also the current ones.

Toyota hosts an annual business meeting for its suppliers to thank them and award star performers. At the event, it also shares how the challenges that lie ahead will translate into even higher expectations for improvement. What remains unspoken, but realized by everyone present at Toyota's events or comparable meetings at other collaborating companies, is that winning once and maintaining that status are not the same thing. As we know, if you want to stay in the spotlight, you must continue to win. And that demands a concerted effort that stretches everyone involved.

The contemporary industrial world lends itself to new collaborative approaches that involve interlocking operations of one sort or another. Enterprise resource planning, focused on automating a company's internal operations, is giving way to extended enterprise systems (EES) and similar-sounding acronyms, all aimed at coordinating and synchronizing the operations of buyers, sellers, and their business partners.

Entirely new forms of collaboration are emerging. While most are still at an embryonic stage, some will undoubtedly come to dominate the business agenda in the future. In many instances, the distinctions between these strategies and those previously discussed are blurring, and some collaborations may at first glance look askew. Think of IBM teaming up with Dell to provide maintenance and coaching services to the latter's customers and, in so doing, adding sufficient value to Dell's computer systems to make them a much more formidable rival to IBM's own systems. Could their next move be to have Dell sell IBM's computers, thus truly interlocking the two companies' fortunes in the personal computer market?

More than other buying patterns, the various forms of collaboration will continue to mutate, attributable in large measure to the fact that collaboration feeds on complexity, which then spawns a new generation of more-elaborate complexity. The suppliers who recognize this and, in turn, understand how to provide the wedge between the level of complexity with which collaborators are comfortable and the next level, which will cause anxiety, will be the market leaders of the future.

CHAPTER 13

Case in Point—UPS

Mention United Parcel Service, and most people immediately picture a clunky-looking chocolate brown truck with a brown-uniformed driver, faithfully picking up and delivering packages. And that's still a large part of what UPS is. But over the past decade, the company has also transformed itself into a high-tech, customer-oriented powerhouse whose purpose is not just distributing goods but enabling global commerce. That means providing custom-tailored solutions, advice, and ongoing coaching to help companies around the world master the New Economy. It all adds up to a fine example of collaboration in action.

The story of UPS's metamorphosis is remarkable—as are the efforts it will make to help its customers, big and small alike. With one hand, UPS teams up with Ford to cut the delivery time of cars to Ford's dealers by 40 percent. With the other, it helps a San Francisco bakery tune up its computer system for more efficient holiday deliveries of sourdough bread. UPS advises clients on incubating new e-commerce ventures, puts up capital so that a Malaysian fabric maker can do business without a letter of credit, and takes over key parts of other customers' manufacturing operations. That's some delivery service.

The remaking of UPS began more than a decade ago, when some of its key executives took a long look at the business and sensed trouble ahead. From its beginnings in Seattle nearly a century ago, UPS had been a model of operational excellence, with reliability and efficiency as twin corporate grails. Its customers' preferences were decidedly secondary: UPS drivers were trained to tell customers why it was in their interest to run their operations to fit the UPS schedule. As Dale Hayes, vice president of business development, told me: "We ran the tightest ship in the shipping industry, and you did it our way."

But the world was changing. Deregulation in the early 1980s had spawned vigorous competition, and by the end of the decade, profits were declining. UPS executives led by Kent "Oz" Nelson, who was to become the company's chief executive officer, mounted a charge for change. It became a threefold effort: UPS resolved on a major investment in technology, ultimately spending more than $11 billion during the 1990s. It empowered its employees to take initiatives and risks in the service of customers. And it leveraged its brand onto the global stage with a series of acquisitions and partnerships. But the key change was in the corporate mind-set. It seemed revolutionary, Nelson recalled. "We had to say, 'We have to serve customers the way they want to be served.'"

This meant, for instance, that a driver's route was no longer carved in stone. If a customer called for a pickup after the truck had already been there, the driver would double back. Drivers could suggest new route patterns. When customers wanted next-day delivery, the company found ways to arrange earlier pickups and new sorting procedures—and to UPS's astonishment, the faster service turned out to be more efficient than the old way, actually saving money.

A symbolic turning point was the acknowledgment that customers wanted to be able to track their packages in the delivery process. UPS had never bothered: If the thing got there, why waste money finding out how? But that was what the customers wanted, and one day Nelson found himself telling then CEO Jack Rogers that UPS had to start spending thirty-five cents per package for tracking data. "He almost had a heart attack," Nelson explained. Little wonder: With 12 million packages a day going through UPS, tracking at that price would add more than $800 million a year to costs, just to get information that the company saw as useless.

Still, Rogers consented. Some of the staggering billion-dollar annual budget for technology went to develop the DIAD, or delivery information acquisition device, a handheld computer with which drivers and handlers can follow each package. It has turned UPS into the world's largest user of mobile communications technology. Now in its third generation, the DIAD has cut UPS's cost of tracking to less than ten cents per package. It lets drivers communicate with operations by satellite transmission, two-way radio, cell phone, or landlines. When the driver punches in data on a package, it takes just three-tenths of a second to get into the system—which tracks the package continuously until another driver collects the digital signature of the person accepting delivery. All of this information is instantaneously fed to UPS's massive data centers in New Jersey and Atlanta, making it immediately available internally to UPS and externally to customers.

And the information itself, far from being worthless, turned into a valuable asset. For one thing, the new detailed data allowed UPS to fine-tune its rates and improve its system. More important, it helps customers cut their inventories, manage their systems, and keep their receivables and late payments under control.

One technology products company, for instance, set up its computers so that the DIAD's signal that a package has been delivered automatically triggers an invoice for the goods—which goes out with a copy of the digital signature proving that delivery has been made. That has short-circuited so many long-drawn-out billing hassles that the company cut its receivables enough to free up $4.6 million a year in cash flow. Other clients have simply used the digital signature to speed up resolution of billing disputes.

Tracking information also played a key part in the evolution of UPS's own business. As they came to know more about their customers, UPS engineers who understood shipping efficiency could analyze distribution patterns and teach the customers how to improve procedures, offer alternative services, locate and set up warehouses, and generally cut costs. Marketing and sales people started getting similarly involved. UPS was becoming a kind of consultant.

While all this was happening, the Internet had become a growing force in business, and UPS's new chairman, Jim Kelly, was pondering how to respond to it. As he sees it, e-commerce has turned traditional business on its head: While manufacturers formerly pushed their goods at customers, customers now pull what they want from the system—a role reversal that is changing business at every level. UPS, said Kelly, has always been a driver for commerce. But with the rise of the Web, it was like driving down a superhighway and suddenly seeing the traffic coming at you. "Rather than crash, we decided to turn around," he noted dryly. In speeches and articles, Kelly began preaching a new mantra: In the New Economy, "the adage 'If it ain't broke, don't fix it' no longer applies. Complacency destroys." It was time for aggressive change, starting at home.

Kelly also realized that it wouldn't be enough for UPS to adapt to the New Economy if its customers didn't change as well. So UPS set up a Web site to help educate them—www.ec.ups.com. It began by providing basic information on the Internet, e-commerce, and what UPS could do to help customers get started. These days the site is vastly expanded and interactive, so that customers can explore UPS services in detail and view backend technology through simulated and actual purchases.

And in 1997, the company began offering what it called UPS Online Tools—technology that its clients could download and use in their businesses. Analyzing its shipping system, for instance, UPS saw that it was actually thirty-two different processes or services that clients could use—anywhere from providing their on-line shopper with up-to-the-minute shipping reports, to validating that shopper-entered shipping addresses are correct at the time of order, to a service that lets shoppers choose the best shipping service by viewing a color-coded map showing a package's transit time. The new tools "allowed our customers to work with us to change the way they do business, to become more efficient, to reduce costs, and then to improve their customer service," said Dale Hayes.

What truly spurs on the transformation of UPS is its strategy for teaming up with collaborators: the customers at the leading edge of change.

While UPS serves 98 percent of all U.S. businesses, according to Mark Rhoney, president of the new E-Ventures division, it's the 5 percent of clients who are on the leading edge that push the company to develop solutions that it will ultimately sell to the rest. Those stretch customers, Hayes told me, "are going to be very hands-on, very involved with you. We love that kind of customer, because at that point we're still learning ourselves. It's a win-win proposition, and we both learn."

A prototypical stretch customer was Marshall Industries, a maker of electronic components that first pushed UPS to develop package-tracking capabilities on Marshall's transactional Web site. UPS liked the idea. It connected the Marshall system to its own tracking service, provided logos to identify the service as coming from UPS, and Marshall's customers could track shipments to them on Marshall's Web site.

UPS went on to develop tracking as the first UPS Online Tool. With a click-and-agree contract, any company could download package tracking for its own Web site. So far, about fifty-five thousand customers have clicked on the service, and more than 40 percent of UPS's tracking requests originate on customers' Web sites. That success, Rhoney explained, inspired the UPS strategy of integrating its processes in its customers' operations—which gives the clients more reasons to stay with UPS and also makes it more difficult for them to leave.

UPS itself is still exploring the Internet and its implications. There are monthly meetings of the Information Technology Steering Committee, which was set up with senior managers from every part of the company to explore the new business world and the way it was affecting UPS. These days, the committee hears outside speakers—scholars or potential partners and customers—who can provide fresh views of the state of the art of e-commerce.

None of this has been easy, and some of the old-guard UPS managers were slow to climb aboard. It took a while, for instance, to swallow the idea that many customers simply preferred to pay by credit card—and American Express would have to get its percentage.

But Rhoney recalled that a turning point came when it began to dawn on management how much UPS itself was benefiting from the power of the Web and the data it provided. In bill preparation and correction alone, UPS was saving $200 million a year. "As a marketing group, we said, 'Let's take that to our customers,'" Rhoney said. "If we integrated our information with their business processes, how much cost could we whack out of their businesses? That was the big 'Aha!'"

Soon, more than half of UPS's annual $1 billion technology investment was going for what are now known as customer-facing applications. UPS learned, for example, to cut a customer's cost for a telephoned order from $2.50 to ten cents. The cost of a second invoice could be reduced from $5 to twenty-five cents. More important, entire procedural steps could be bypassed. With benefits like that, salespeople didn't even have to tell clients how much they could save. "When you say, 'I can cut out twenty-five percent of your phone calls,' they just want to know how fast you can do it and what it will cost," Rhoney noted.

Almost imperceptibly, the process led from helping the leading-edge, collaborative customers solve problems to selling others the solutions, and then to taking over entire parts of other clients' businesses. UPS Logistics Group has become the fastest-growing part of the company, up 70 percent in revenue in just two years. Logistics will perform chores ranging from inventory control to repair services. At a huge facility near its hub in Louisville, Kentucky, for instance, UPS repairs computer monitors and laptops for a host of PC manufacturers. In a five-year, $150 million deal, UPS will redesign and manage National Semiconductor's global distribution network. And when Ford Motor Company needed advice on how to reengineer its transportation network and speed up the daily delivery of 18,500 vehicles from twenty-one manufacturing plants to six thousand dealers, who did it call? Who else? UPS.

The company also handles e-commerce for clients, taking orders for Nike.com at a call center in San Antonio and fulfilling them from the Louisville warehouse. With a Web site and a customer's product in hand, explained Rhoney, "I'll do the rest. I will take care of everything—inbound orders, warehousing, picking and packing, shipping, returns, customer care, invoicing, payments—the whole nine yards."

Strictly speaking, Rhoney said, all this isn't really e-commerce. But it is made possible by the capabilities of e-commerce, and also by the full visibility permitted by all the information that is now available.

Such activities as billing, distribution, and quality control are "the lifeblood of your business," he said. "Without real-time, near-perfect information, you wouldn't trust that to a soul." Now, however, clients can watch every step of what UPS does for them—and with transparency comes trust. While clients give up the actual work, "It's not as if they lose control. They actually gain control."

Trust is a commodity UPS has earned over the years. Each day, its 157,000 brown trucks make pickups from 2 million locations and deliver to 7 million; its drivers, who had ownership shares in the company even before the $5.5 billion public offering of 1999, are legendary for their reliability and integrity. And the company has honed its reputation partly out of necessity. Picking up, repeatedly sorting, handling, and delivering 12 million packages a day provides at least 36 million chances every day to make a mistake. As former CEO Nelson drummed into his troops, an error-free standard of 99.9 percent is the minimum acceptable.

Trust in the UPS reputation and familiar presence also bolster the new UPS Capital division, an effort to embed the company even further in its customers' operations by providing financial services. UPS Capital will pay shippers in advance for cash-on-delivery parcels, guarantee credit, extend loans for accounts receivable, and lease tools ranging from computers to warehouse equipment. It aims to ease the cash flow problems particularly of smaller businesses that lack the resources to handle delays in payment. And trust is equally vital to UPS Dossier, an ongoing effort to develop an encryption system for secure electronic delivery of confidential documents.

All told, UPS has become a somewhat schizoid global giant. In its core business, its brown trucks and its fleet of nearly six hundred cargo planes take in $28 billion a year in the traditional trade of moving goods from one spot to another. In the United States alone, 6 percent of the gross domestic product is physically moved by UPS. And its headquarters in Atlanta reflect classic management values. Kelly, an up-from-the-ranks onetime driver like Nelson before him, insists that all his executives keep shoe-shine kits in their offices, clean off their desks every night before leaving, and spend several days a year delivering packages and meeting customers. Drivers show up every morning for a three-minute inspection and lecture on the management topic of the day. They are also trained in *Modern Times* efficiency techniques: On leaving the truck, keep the ignition key on your pinkie finger so you don't waste time fumbling in your pockets for it; when you get back in, your left hand fastens the seat belt while the right inserts the key.

Yet UPS is also thoroughly up-to-date. The goods it moves include 55 percent of all e-commerce in the United States (versus 8 percent for FedEx), and 1.7 million customers use its services around the world. Its telecommunications link nine hundred thousand users in one hundred countries, and its Web site gets nearly 40 million hits every day. What sets UPS apart from the competition, explained Dale Hayes of business development, is "the integration of e-commerce in technology and information. A lot of companies pick up stuff and move it from one place to another, but they simply do not provide the same level of information, connectivity, and technology products."

And UPS customers always want more. "They're always challenging us," said Hayes. "The speed of the Internet has increased the speed at which people want solutions." That velocity also makes it necessary for UPS to understand not just its customers, but their customers too, to help the search for solutions that will stay ahead of the ultimate pull of consumer demand. These days, UPS salespeople call on the vice president of marketing, who knows what his customers want, as often as they talk to the shipping manager. In some cases, UPS has even commissioned its own consumer research.

UPS will go to astonishing lengths to help its clients—large, small, or even potential. Hayes recalls a would-be Internet entrepreneur who wanted to run auctions that would preserve the anonymity of both buyer and seller. The challenge was to arrange shipping and payment systems without identifying either party. Hayes and several of his colleagues spent most of a day working out a model for blind shipping and payment through a UPS subsidiary. But the scheme fell through because the client's business model had assumed that the transaction would cost only $5—a fifth of the best price Hayes could come up with. Frustrated, the client threatened to go to the competition. Hayes told him to go ahead. "I was even willing to give him the phone numbers," he explained, "because I knew we had created the best solution. What he was looking for just wasn't there at the price he wanted."

In finding solutions, said Hayes, "we prefer to be involved early on. It gives us time to be more creative and explore all the options. But even at the eleventh hour, we will jump through hoops to help. Unfortunately, it doesn't always work out." The auctioneer's business never got launched.

It's almost as astonishing that UPS doesn't want to be paid for such efforts. Very early on, said Rhoney, there was a major internal debate over how UPS would profit from its new role. Some in the old guard were aghast at the expense of the new technology and wanted UPS to be directly reimbursed; others believed, in the spirit of the young Internet, that added service would be repaid by more business from repeat customers.

A turning point came over package tracking. For more than four years, UPS charged customers for the tracking information they received. Finally, Rhoney said, "I had to go to the vice chairman and say, 'We can't keep charging for that. It's part of the deal now. It's the minimum acceptable requirements of a good package carrier to provide tracking information for free.'" By then, however, tracking was bringing in revenues of $62 million a year. When the vice chairman asked how those funds would be replaced, Rhoney could only repeat the hope that the business would grow. But he could make no promises, and warned that proof would never come: "If we grow 3.1 percent next year instead of three percent, you're going to have to trust me that I got you that tenth of a percent, and that covered your $62 million."

In the end, UPS took the leap of faith. Since then, he said, the benefits of collaborating with customers have been increasingly plain: "Our growth rate has accelerated, and we've had better customer retention—which in turn accelerated growth, which lowered overall unit costs." And even though UPS rate increases have been comparatively minor, profits rose.

What UPS sells is not shipping but solutions. Its rates aren't the lowest in the business, said Hayes, but they don't have to be. It's a question of the total value the customer gets. "If my price is twenty or thirty percent more than the cheapest competitor's, but I can save you money by reducing your inventory, improving your information, improving your customer service, and reducing your cash flow, all that has real value to you. After all, if you're charged with growing the business and I can give you access to new markets and open up the doors for you, what's the value of that?"

In sum, UPS has completely reversed the mind-set of twenty years ago. From telling customers how to run their businesses, it has customized all of its services to suit the demands of any client. It has moved aggressively to expand its overseas operations to take advantage of the higher margins available there, especially in Europe. The company's highly successful $5.5 billion public offering was meant to provide currency for mergers and acquisitions.

And UPS continues to look for whole new fields to move into—including what Rhoney called "the next level of home delivery." Nobody is sure what this may mean—in fact, UPS has hired anthropologists to study consumer behavior in an effort to figure it out. But the company is sure the New Economy will need new services, whether they are grocery deliveries in refrigerated brown trucks or pickup centers where customers can drive to get the goods they have bought on-line.

The one sure thing for UPS is that change isn't finished. "We must change at the speed of the market to meet the customers' needs," Hayes told me. "You have to listen to your customers. Listen to their problems, listen to their complaints, listen to what no one else is able to solve." Then you team up with the customers to find the solutions that will keep them on top in the New Economy. That's a credo for collaborators.

CHAPTER 14

Take and Keep the Lead

The pursuit of marketplace victory is an emotionally charged topic. As the competition intensifies, so do the excitement and apprehension in those participating and watching. Top performers and winning teams evoke feelings of ecstasy and admiration in some, but agony and envy in others. Likewise, when the results of the battle over customers are tallied, some managers are electrified, while others are filled with dread.

Invariably, the managers most conflicted are those who had been within striking distance of winning, only to watch victory slip from their hands. They pursued strategies very similar to those employed by the leaders, but not with the same results. In fact, most of what this book addresses would apply to them—if only they could notch up their performances.

"What's missing?" they ask in frustration. "We do everything our toughest competitors do, if not more. It isn't possible to work harder than we do, and still, we aren't breaking through." Adding insult to injury, Wall Street and the business press ignore their not insignificant accomplishments, charmed instead by flashier performers and upstarts despite the fact that these companies are yet to see a profit. As the "almost winning" managers will attest, there's an elusive quality surrounding market leadership that deserves further comment in this final chapter.

To understand more clearly that fine but critical line between near victory and victory, I discussed the issue with numerous executives who had experienced both sides of it. As diverse as their viewpoints are, they concur that establishing a market presence, boldness, capitalizing on customers' shifting priorities, and a healthy dose of fearlessness determine the battle for customers. But, they add emphatically, ultimately what gives them the edge—especially when they're in a close contest on an even playing field—is their motivation and method. Permeating the core of each employee as well as the general environment of the organization with the shared ambition and unflagging determination to win in the marketplace is how they describe motivation. Method requires identifying which approach or process works best for the organization, then building momentum by systematically and relentlessly improving upon it—practice, practice, and practice.

Certainly, I do not disagree: Their directives echo those laid out in *The Discipline of Market Leaders* as well as in numerous other books and articles on the topic. Though not revolutionary, they are easily overlooked in the heat of the race. For the purpose of illustration, let's consider how three different managers respond to the successes of others. Their reactions offer clues and reminders of what is missing from their quests for success.

First, think about managers who love to hear memorable stories about the exploits of top performers. They are motivated by the market leaders' bold and imaginative activities, especially when the winners start out against the odds. At the same time, hearing about the leaders induces anxiety and makes them acutely aware of the dangers inherent in falling behind. The resulting ambivalence of inspiration and fear creates a sense of urgency. They feel impatient to initiate some sort of action even though its details have not yet been refined and their troops are not yet prepared.

In market-leading companies populated with like-minded folks, these calls to action find a receptive audience and serve to invigorate the business. Even when directions are sketchy—possibly *because* they are not set in stone, thus leaving room for exploration—these organizations find a way to convert that sketchiness to their advantage. Many have been in this position before; and if not, they're confident, and usually justifiably so, that they will find a way to make the plan work.

Similar calls to action may resonate less well in companies that are lagging in their fields. There, the employees can be leery of undertaking the manager's biddings because, at least in part, the word "challenge" connotes more work. Unconvinced that the extra effort will matter, they don't share the boss's resolve, exuberance, and optimism. Cajoled or coerced into action, they cooperate, but fail to exert themselves. Only staring disaster in the face mobilizes them to scramble, but by then it is usually too late.

What is missing is a common sense of urgency (felt in time to matter) and a reliable road map. Lacking in these companies are clear goals and a well-practiced, organized method of tackling issues. Managers can't articulate an inspiring course to their employees if they don't have one, and many companies (that is, people) are not good at making it up as they go along.

The second type of manager is keen to learn from market leaders. Astute observers, they have a penchant for analysis and methodology. You can visualize them taking copious notes, jotting down ideas, making checklists, and trying to decipher winning formulas. These managers reside equally among market-leading companies and their lagging competitors. Both design insightful strategies and plans for action. Yet the laggards have more trouble getting others within their organizations to adopt their plans. That even seasoned managers aren't immune to this problem is evidenced in the number of well-considered plans and sound proposals that die prematurely because they are stonewalled by other departments, ignored by coworkers, or overshadowed by more prosaic routines. This situation is all too familiar to consultants whose well-crafted recommendations end up collecting dust because their clients were not adequately prepared for the changes the new plans entailed. Additionally, rookie MBAs face a rude awakening the first time their knowledge and bright ideas are not instantly acclaimed.

Whereas earlier the manager's trouble was mobilizing employees, in this instance the obstacle is her or his inability to rally colleagues and bosses around the proposed solutions. If and when they overcome their resistance, excessive amounts of precious energy and time will have been lost. That they may shine methodically is irrelevant in this context because their direction and priorities aren't aligned with those of the other people who have a stake in the outcome. Market leadership doesn't bypass these managers because their plans lack specificity or rigor, but rather because they are not sharing the perspective held by the rest of the organization regarding exactly what needs to be done to win in the marketplace.

The third and largest contingent of managers that I encounter perform strongly and aggressively. Still, when we look very closely we see that most of its members are yoked to the status quo. Of course, they would love to be number one, if only it didn't require so much effort and sacrifice. Though these managers feel a momentary thrill when they observe leaders in action, they can't seem to break away from their habitual routines. They react poorly when the success of a rival, even an indirect one, is discussed. Suddenly, that market leader is viewed with suspicion, disdain, and as a villain. These managers demean the leader's practices, attribute its success to luck, claim that its blemishes were overlooked or its edge built on quicksand.

Trivializing and disparaging another's accomplishments are not hard to do, and these managers show a special knack for it. When they come face-to-face with their own deficiencies, they cope by deflecting responsibility from themselves, hence projecting it onto the winners.

Still, for the most part, the managers' hostility or suspiciousness (which others would name envy) does not hinder their relish, albeit temporary, in a good market-leadership story. Such anecdotes elicit the same pleasure that sports fans experience when they watch the Wimbledon finals or the Ryder Cup; that is, they feel heightened resolve to improve their own games, to try harder, maybe even take a lesson or two. But just as New Year's resolutions trigger an initial stampede to health clubs that tends to subside by February, former business habits are usually back in place by about the same time. It takes more than a vicarious experience—however potent—to motivate a potential winner for the long term. As we've seen in other groups (though I think it is most pronounced in this one), missing are determination, stamina, and a systematic approach to sustain improvement.

All of these examples clarify that motivation and method are powerful and decisive factors in the battle for customers. The question that remains is how to best cultivate these traits. Another way of asking the same question is, how do we translate these factors into a successful strategy? To everyone's chagrin, there is no uniform answer, and a lot depends upon whom you ask. If you speak with market leaders, they will be happy to reveal the "secrets" of the Cisco way, the GE way, the Microsoft way, or whatever signature approach they've cultivated, not just to secure the present but to prepare for what is to come.

Numerous books and articles have been and continue to be written on their business practices, cultures, and management styles, and it adds to the panoply of insights. If you are hungry for more information, seek out management consultants and business school professors, who are usually eager to provide their perspectives. Some will advocate their most favored methodology, while others will help you select an approach most appropriate for your needs (not unlike consultants and professors in any field). Whatever you decide, one problem you will not face is a dearth of knowledge and directions.

———

In closing, let me sum up the most pertinent insights I gained from the market leaders. They should serve as constant reminders to the managers who keep asking, "What's missing?"

- First, securing market leadership is not the result of a series of isolated or episodic efforts. Instead, it grows from *a process of change* that you can never relax. Although your choice of a specific process is important, it is less so than your commitment to practice it relentlessly. Ingraining your current performance is less important than persistently exploring better or new ways to improve it.

- Second, motivation and performance will peak only when channeled toward *shared ambitions and clear goals.* The battle for customers isn't a solo event. It is a team effort that requires the cooperation and commitment of every participant. Open interaction and communication—both inside the company with colleagues and outside it with customers—foster this process.

- Third, you need to *know where you stand*. Salient metrics gauge your progress; feedback mechanisms keep you on track; and frank, honest discussions, which include confronting facts directly, even if they are upsetting, are the only reliable antidotes to delusion and complacency.

If you want to glean the final and, ultimately, most meaningful insight, look again at Yahoo!, EMC, Solectron, UPS, and the other new market leaders featured in this book. Then remember that these organizations surpass their peers by making absolutely certain that what they are not missing is their single most precious asset—customers, customers, and customers.

Appendix One

In my ongoing research on market leadership, I have been tracking the performance of the world's most influential companies since the late 1980s. My original database covered a thousand or so larger organizations. Today, that database has grown fivefold, covering many more medium-sized and up-and-coming companies whose influence in the marketplace outweighs their size. Also in the database is a large group of non-U.S. businesses.

The Database

My research covered 5,009 companies in every imaginable facet of the economy, each of which had revenues of at least $25 million and a market value of $50 million, as of May 31, 2000. Of these, 3,753 are U.S.-based, and every publicly traded company that met the criteria above is included; the second requirement was that reliable sales histories for the six-year period of investigation were available. The 1,256 non-U.S. companies represent a sample of the most prominent businesses traded on major foreign exchanges for which timely data could be found.

Examining such a wide variety of companies presents a challenge. How do you compare the performance of a very large, established player with that of an upstart? I could have composed separate lists of old and new market leaders, but that felt like a superfluous distinction. Given the increasing convergence of the old and new economies, both categories would be competing for the same customers.

I resolved the dilemma by assigning each company to an industry category that most closely matched its dominant sales orientation, or if there were multiple possibilities, the category where it performed the strongest. The categories were defined broadly, so as to include not only immediate competitors but also more extended rivals for the same customers' business. For instance, all financial service firms were grouped into one category, as were all media, whether they were established or new, print or broadcast.

Then I compared each company's performance with that of a peer group, which included the company itself and the twenty others in its category that were closest in size. The size of the peer group did not appear to be critical to the results. Rankings varied only modestly when I used a smaller or larger peer group, especially in homogeneous industry categories.

In practice, managers can get a good idea of a business's relative performance by comparing it with just a half dozen or a dozen of its most immediate rivals.

Sales Growth

I calculated the sales growth of each company by comparing its latest available twelve-month sales, as of May 31, 2000, with the figure from six years earlier. If the company didn't exist six years ago, the number zero was substituted. For non-U.S. companies, sales growth was calculated in the local (or reporting) currency before it was converted into dollars. As it turned out, adjustments for inflation were not needed; their effects on the rankings were immaterial.

To ensure that my analysis would be based on organic sales growth, without being distorted by major mergers, acquisitions, or divestments, I consolidated the sales figures of affected entities. For instance, I arrived at the six-year sales growth of Daimler-Chrysler by comparing the company's latest sales with the combined sales of Daimler and Chrysler six years earlier. Likewise, when a company sold or spun off a major piece of business, I calculated its net sales growth by deducting the six-year sales growth of the spun-off unit. In more than a few cases, companies made several major acquisitions or divestments during the research period, all of which were taken into account in calculating each company's sales growth. If a unit's or a company's exact sales could not be found, I did one of two things: Either I used related data to estimate the number (as with NTT DoCoMo and other recent highfliers) or, if the figures were too ambiguous, I excluded the company from my analyses. This explains why notable companies such as AES Corp. (a utility), CMGI Inc. (an Internet player), and Clear Channel Communications (a media company) do not appear in my research.

For the purposes of this book, I treated pending mergers that were close to completion at the time I was writing, such as the one involving AOL and Time Warner, as if they were consummated.

The Sales-Growth Index

To calculate each company's sales-growth index, I divided its six-year sales growth (in dollars) by the average growth of its peer group. An index of 1.0 means that a company's sales growth matches its peer group average. Higher than 1.0 indicates superior performance; less than 1.0 means a company trails in the race for customers. Because companies' peer groups are different, they end up with different sales-growth indices even when they grow by the same amount.

For example, at Starbucks Corp., the specialty coffee retailer, sales rose by $1.7 billion over the six years of my research, while at the giant department store Nordstrom, Inc., they rose by almost the same amount. The raw numbers reveal nothing about leadership, however, because Nordstrom was far larger than Starbucks at the outset. Nordstrom's peer group included other larger retailers, such as Saks Fifth Avenue, the Gap, Inc., TJX Companies, Inc., and Rite Aid Corp. These were the retailers that had sales closest to Nordstrom's six years ago. Examples of Starbucks's closest peers are Farmers Bros. Co., Duane Reade, Lillian Vernon Corp., and Dollar Tree Stores, Inc.

Nordstrom's sales-growth index emerged at a lackluster 0.4. Starbucks, on the other hand, scored 2.6. That means its sales grew at almost three times the pace of its peer group, a clear sign of the company's enormous appeal to its customers. Of the two, only Starbucks passed my first measure of market leadership.

The Market-Value Index

Arriving at this index was a three-step process. First, I calculated how much investors were willing to pay for one dollar of a company's sales. I got that number, the market-value-to-sales ratio, by dividing the company's market value as of May 31, 2000, by its latest twelve-month sales.

The second step was to calculate that same ratio for the company's peer group: I divided the combined market value of the twenty-one companies in the group by their combined sales.

The third step required figuring each company's market-value index. To obtain it, I divided the first number, the market-value-to-sales ratio, by the second, the peer group average. An index of

1.0 tells me that each dollar of a company's sales is valued as equal to a dollar of the peer group's sales. A number higher than 1.0 tells me the customer franchise is worth more than average, indicating superior prospects.

As an example, take another look at Nordstrom and Starbucks. With Nordstrom's latest sales at $5.1 billion and its market value, as of May 31, 2000, at $3.2 billion, each sales dollar was worth sixty-three cents to investors. The average for the peer group, which includes twenty other retailers with current sales closest to those of Nordstrom, was sixty-eight cents per dollar of sales. Thus, Nordstrom's market-value index is 63 divided by 68, or 0.9, which is a little below average.

Starbucks, on the other hand, ended up with a market-value index of 3.3, placing it comfortably in market-leader territory.

Of course, these numbers don't tell the whole story, since Starbucks's higher net profit margins (6.1 percent versus Nordstrom's 4.0 percent) undoubtedly affected investor decisions. Similarly, Starbucks's future earnings growth (estimated by analysts at 25 percent per year, versus Nordstrom's at 15 percent) made its customer franchise more attractive to investors. Regardless of the reason, what investors were implicitly judging was the future value of a company's most precious asset, its customer base, in relation to that of its peers.

A strong market-value index is tantamount to a vote of confidence from investors, a group not known for its patience with underperformers. The index incorporates their combined judgments about a company's prospects. It reflects a company's capacity to convert sales into profit growth. Starbucks shines on that count; Nordstrom is a little below average; and CHS Electronics, the deceptively hot company I mentioned in the first chapter, didn't even come close to passing that test. It had a market-value index of 0.1 well before it ran into serious difficulties.

Overall Ranking

The two indices made it possible to pare down the field to 640 new market leaders that performed better than their peers in both dimensions. Ranking these 640 companies presented another difficulty—that of comparing leaders with similar scores but operating in different categories. For instance, look at Coca-Cola and Harley-Davidson. Both had very similar sales growth indices (1.2 and 1.3, respectively), which says that they did equally well outpacing their peers. But Coca-Cola's sales grew by $5.8 billion, more than four times Harley-Davidson's growth of $1.4 billion. If we are evaluating which company had more influence, overall, on customers and the marketplace, we conclude that Coca-Cola deserves more credit.

A similar logic applies when comparing companies with almost identical market-value indices, such as Sprint PCS Group and Gillette; the index of both was in the 2.5–2.6 range. Operating in a sphere where all of its peers have sky-high market values, Sprint's number indicated that its customer franchise was valued far higher than Gillette's, and it was important to reflect that fact in any overall ranking involving both companies.

I resolved the issues by calculating a weight for each index. To get a bit more technical, first, I calculated each market leader's sales growth relative to that of all the companies in the database (treating nonfinancial companies and financials separately); then, I figured each company's market-value index relative to the index of the entire database. Finally, I calculated the geometric mean of the four numbers—the two indices and the two weights—and used that mean to rank all 640 leaders. With this method, each leader was credited appropriately, yet within any particular category, the relative standings would be stable. (Using the geometric rather than the arithmetic mean has an added benefit, because it boosts the rankings of companies that showed a balanced performance on both of my measures, while downplaying lopsided performance on just one yardstick.)

Appendix One

Annual Investor Returns

The shareholder returns shown in this book include share price appreciation and dividends. They cover the period from December 31, 1994, to May 31, 2000.

The top 100 new market leaders generated an average annual return of 48.4 percent. In comparison, the hundred largest companies worldwide, based on market value, earned on average 36.9 percent per year for their investors, while the largest hundred companies based on sales returned an average of 21.7 percent per annum.

Data Sources

The scope and duration of the research made it necessary to consult a variety of sources, all publicly available. While data on companies' market value and sales is more readily accessible than ever, its completeness and timeliness, especially going back several years, leaves something to be desired. Some companies (especially those outside the United States) are less prompt in announcing their sales numbers. Moreover, reporting periods vary widely. For instance, in Japan, March is a common fiscal year end; in the United Kingdom, it is September; and in Australia, June is the preference. While some companies issue half-yearly or quarterly updates, others don't. In the end, I used the latest information available for estimating the numbers.

Much effort was expended to verify data, to reconcile discrepancies between various data sources, and to obtain reliable information on companies that are not as well known or have sketchy sales histories. Therefore, the numbers I used for the rankings in this book may deviate from those reported elsewhere. Certainly, they represent my best estimate of each company's status.

With no single source dominating my research, I consulted company reports, presentations, and regulatory filings; numerous

231

business publications, of which *Business Week,* the *Financial Times, Forbes,* and *Fortune* proved to be the most valuable; and a host of Web sites, of which www.corporateinformation.com was the most up-to-date and complete based upon the several resources against which I checked my data. The resulting data used and their analysis represent my interpretation of the available materials. Any omissions, inaccuracies, or errors are solely mine.

Exhibits

Exhibit 1

This four-part exhibit includes key statistics on the top 100 new market leaders (shown in bold type) as well as on the next one hundred leaders, sorted by market category.

Each company's ranking was calculated by comparing its performance with that of its peers of similar size, operating in the same category, anywhere in the world. For instance, Yahoo!'s peer group was composed of similar-sized media and entertainment companies, not just Internet companies; Coca-Cola was compared with peers that included the largest consumer nondurables companies globally.

The Top 200 New Market Leaders (Part 1)

Overall rank	COMPANY (status on May 31, '00)	Market value $M	Sales latest 12 mos. $M	Market value/ sales ratio	Six-year sales growth $M	Annual investor return %	Country	Sales-change index	Market-value index
MEDIA AND ENTERTAINMENT									
5	Yahoo!	61,423	723	85.0	723	NA	USA	3.1	10.6
10	AOL Time Warner	224,012	34,092	6.6	18,051	75	USA	5.0	1.8
54	Viacom	101,020	20,232	5.0	9,267	NA	USA	2.6	1.4
58	Gemstar	20,200	1,439	14.0	1,298	NA	USA	2.8	2.8
62	EchoStar Communications	18,740	1,859	10.1	1,638	NA	USA	3.6	2.1
63	British Sky Broadcasting	34,809	2,687	13.0	1,797	34	UK	1.6	3.1
71	Infinity Broadcasting	33,931	2,764	12.3	1,720	NA	USA	1.5	3.1
76	Comcast	35,210	6,694	5.3	4,040	34	USA	2.9	1.4
87	Walt Disney	87,666	23,737	3.7	8,753	21	USA	2.4	1.0
93	Cox Communications	25,612	2,600	9.9	1,892	35	USA	1.8	2.3
98	At Home	8,141	450	18.1	450	NA	USA	1.9	4.3
119	DoubleClick	6,676	329	20.3	329	NA	USA	1.4	5.4
125	TeleWest	11,982	1,624	7.4	1,499	79	UK	3.4	1.3
149	Canal Plus	23,753	3,052	7.8	1,633	42	France	1.4	2.1
167	United Pan-Europe Comm.	11,100	810	13.7	718	NA	Netherlands	1.8	1.9
192	Univision Communications	10,640	737	14.4	642	NA	USA	1.6	1.8
CONSUMER DURABLES									
30	Sony	80,800	60,053	1.3	26,514	24	Japan	6.8	1.3
91	Philips Electronics	60,102	34,799	1.7	9,964	38	Netherlands	2.6	1.7
160	Harley-Davidson	11,273	2,576	4.4	1,359	36	USA	1.3	4.6
CONSUMER NONDURABLES									
40	Coca-Cola	132,003	19,796	6.7	5,833	15	USA	1.2	4.8
47	L'Oreal	46,112	11,399	4.0	4,881	33	France	3.2	3.0
101	Procter & Gamble	86,934	39,740	2.2	9,331	16	USA	1.9	1.6
137	Gillette	34,950	10,003	3.5	2,850	12	USA	1.7	2.5
140	Heineken	16,010	6,567	2.4	2,774	26	Netherlands	2.3	2.7
144	Nestle	74,285	49,377	1.5	10,992	19	Switzerland	2.3	1.1
157	Royal Numico	6,119	3,061	2.0	2,293	37	Netherlands	3.5	2.2
165	Grupo Modelo	7,171	2,576	2.8	1,910	71	Mexico	1.7	3.7
187	Luxottica	5,188	1,684	3.1	1,388	26	Italy	2.8	2.2
194	Estee Lauder	10,845	4,277	2.5	1,765	NA	USA	1.8	3.1
195	Ryohin Keikaku	4,088	941	4.3	664	NA	Japan	1.5	5.7
RETAIL, INTERMEDIARIES									
6	Home Depot	112,633	40,594	2.8	31,529	34	USA	5.9	3.2
7	Wal-Mart	256,664	166,809	1.5	91,098	37	USA	6.5	1.8
17	Amazon.com	16,902	1,920	8.8	1,920	NA	USA	4.3	8.7
50	Gap	29,840	11,635	2.6	8,368	46	USA	1.9	4.2
61	Hennes & Mauritz	20,902	3,375	6.2	2,217	54	Sweden	1.3	6.9
72	Kohl's	16,979	4,557	3.7	3,269	54	USA	1.8	4.6
78	Priceline.com	6,486	747	8.7	747	NA	USA	1.7	8.0
97	Walgreen	28,590	19,563	1.5	10,888	36	USA	2.1	2.1
103	Lowe's Companies	17,808	16,601	1.1	11,730	20	USA	3.1	1.6
123	Starbucks	6,260	1,930	3.2	1,736	35	USA	2.6	3.3
156	Best Buy	13,002	13,072	1.0	10,296	47	USA	2.7	1.3
159	CDW Computer Centers	5,092	2,886	1.8	2,615	54	USA	4.3	1.8
161	Staples	6,755	9,421	0.7	8,102	22	USA	4.4	1.3
162	Intimate Brands	11,063	4,645	2.4	3,014	NA	USA	1.8	2.7
163	Wal-Mart de Mexico	9,346	6,456	1.4	4,965	18	Mexico	1.4	3.4
171	Bed Bath & Beyond	5,168	1,878	2.8	1,572	34	USA	2.7	2.6
182	Carrefour-Promodes	49,122	55,340	0.9	20,705	30	France	1.5	1.0
185	Pinault-Printemps-Redoute	25,499	20,136	1.3	9,911	47	France	1.2	1.7
HOSPITALITY AND FOOD SERVICE									
45	McDonald's	47,288	13,568	3.5	6,160	18	USA	3.4	2.7
95	Carnival	16,396	3,653	4.5	2,096	19	USA	2.0	3.8
131	Granada	16,565	6,887	2.4	4,257	18	UK	2.3	1.9

The Top 200 New Market Leaders (Part 2)

Overall rank	COMPANY (status on May 31, '00)	Market value $M	Sales latest 12 mos. $M	Market value/ sales ratio	Six-year sales growth $M	Annual investor return %	Country	Sales-change index	Market-value index
TRANSPORTATION AND LOGISTICS									
35	**United Parcel Service**	**69,010**	**27,608**	**2.5**	**9,826**	**NA**	**USA**	**3.2**	**3.4**
110	Hays	9,662	3,060	3.2	2,163	36	UK	2.0	4.3
183	Kansas City Southern Ind.	7,494	2,123	3.5	1,177	42	USA	1.1	6.1
AUTOMOTIVE									
34	**Toyota Motor**	**170,214**	**115,671**	**1.5**	**30,300**	**16**	**Japan**	**1.8**	**3.3**
169	BMW	20,231	36,370	0.6	20,416	22	Germany	2.2	1.2
INDUSTRIALS – DIVERSIFIED									
2	**General Electric**	**520,247**	**117,461**	**4.4**	**57,255**	**41**	**USA**	**10.4**	**2.4**
53	**Tyco Int'l.**	**78,190**	**25,753**	**3.0**	**13,554**	**28**	**USA**	**2.5**	**1.6**
81	**Bombardier**	**18,004**	**9,170**	**2.0**	**6,229**	**49**	**Canada**	**3.2**	**2.2**
134	Johnson Electric	6,888	465	14.8	271	48	Hong Kong	1.1	9.8
150	Emerson Electric	25,430	14,692	1.7	6,302	14	USA	2.2	1.6
158	General Dynamics	11,850	10,128	1.2	6,054	22	USA	4.5	1.1
197	Heidelberger Druckmasch.	5,590	4,747	1.2	3,111	NA	Germany	4.0	1.7
INDUSTRIALS – MATERIALS									
64	**E.I. duPont de Nemours**	**51,318**	**29,520**	**1.7**	**9,955**	**13**	**USA**	**2.8**	**2.4**
117	Reliance Industries	8,001	2,022	4.0	1,451	14	India	2.3	4.0
155	Nan Ya Plastic	10,440	4,231	2.5	2,135	13	Taiwan	1.9	3.6
174	CEMEX	6,120	4,808	1.3	3,862	9	Mexico	3.2	1.9
175	Alcoa	25,230	23,756	1.1	8,190	23	USA	2.3	1.5
180	Vale do Rio Doce	10,056	3,787	2.7	2,133	31	Brazil	1.4	3.6
184	Shin-Etsu Chemical	20,512	6,362	3.2	2,279	20	Japan	1.1	3.4
198	Masco	8,812	6,906	1.3	4,663	13	USA	3.2	1.3
ENERGY – OIL									
70	**Schlumberger**	**41,862**	**8,752**	**4.8**	**2,047**	**24**	**USA**	**1.6**	**6.5**
82	**RoyalDutch/Shell**	**214,667**	**105,366**	**2.0**	**10,213**	**25**	**Netherlands**	**2.8**	**1.4**
113	ExxonMobil	289,998	163,881	1.8	9,480	24	USA	2.6	1.2
130	Petrobras	27,650	16,351	1.7	8,048	39	Brazil	2.5	1.3
BUSINESS SERVICES									
41	**Paychex**	**12,945**	**1,351**	**9.6**	**1,142**	**53**	**USA**	**3.0**	**6.7**
44	**Vivendi**	**64,020**	**42,079**	**1.5**	**18,124**	**33**	**France**	**2.6**	**2.8**
139	Capita	4,850	529	9.2	462	85	UK	1.1	9.2
151	Cardinal Health	18,444	28,206	0.7	18,156	24	USA	2.6	1.2
177	Robert Half Int'l	5,258	2,229	2.4	1,923	45	USA	3.2	2.0
178	Adecco	13,858	12,145	1.1	7,704	31	Switzerland	1.2	2.8
MANAGEMENT AND ADVISORY SERVICES									
100	**Omnicom**	**14,911**	**5,363**	**2.8**	**3,674**	**42**	**USA**	**5.1**	**1.2**
133	Reuters	21,147	5,057	4.2	2,024	15	UK	2.8	1.8
135	Altran Technologies	6,709	719	9.3	624	95	France	1.3	5.9
141	TMP Worldwide	6,008	872	6.9	798	NA	USA	1.7	4.4
154	Interpublic	12,746	4,743	2.7	2,897	31	USA	4.0	1.2
SOFTWARE AND IT SERVICES									
3	**Microsoft**	**326,287**	**22,916**	**14.2**	**18,705**	**49**	**USA**	**5.1**	**2.1**
8	**Oracle**	**204,011**	**10,130**	**20.1**	**8,420**	**68**	**USA**	**2.3**	**3.0**
32	**Softbank**	**50,612**	**4,905**	**10.3**	**4,347**	**56**	**Japan**	**3.3**	**2.1**
38	**i2 Technologies**	**16,802**	**756**	**22.2**	**744**	**NA**	**USA**	**3.8**	**3.7**
42	**Siebel Systems**	**23,300**	**959**	**24.3**	**959**	**NA**	**USA**	**2.1**	**4.1**
49	**SAP**	**48,102**	**5,166**	**9.3**	**4,571**	**38**	**Germany**	**3.0**	**1.4**
68	**Ariba**	**12,291**	**91**	**135.1**	**91**	**NA**	**USA**	**1.0**	**8.5**
77	**Sage Group**	**12,375**	**616**	**20.1**	**540**	**103**	**UK**	**2.2**	**3.6**
83	**Infosys Technologies**	**11,202**	**203**	**55.1**	**197**	**143**	**India**	**2.1**	**3.7**
88	**Amdocs**	**13,640**	**959**	**14.2**	**858**	**NA**	**USA**	**2.7**	**2.3**
104	BEA Systems	13,420	533	25.2	533	NA	USA	1.1	4.1
112	Trend Micro	9,678	121	80.0	120	NA	Japan	1.1	5.1
136	Phone.com	6,853	47	146.7	47	NA	USA	1.0	6.3
173	BMC Software	10,709	1,719	6.2	1,420	40	USA	2.3	1.5
191	Logica	10,886	1,107	9.8	784	85	UK	1.3	2.6

The Top 200 New Market Leaders (Part 3)

Overall rank	COMPANY (status on May 31, '00)	Market value $M	Sales latest 12 mos. $M	Market value/ sales ratio	Six-year sales growth $M	Annual investor return %	Country	Sales-change index	Market-value index
TELECOM SERVICES									
12	NTT DoCoMo	247,200	33,381	7.4	23,182	NA	Japan	2.3	2.2
16	Sprint PCS Group	50,780	3,753	13.5	3,753	NA	USA	5.0	2.6
20	Nextel Communications	37,302	3,741	10.0	3,672	46	USA	6.4	1.9
29	Vodafone AirTouch	280,126	37,065	7.6	15,471	63	UK	1.3	2.2
55	SK Telecom	30,380	3,786	8.0	3,426	59	South Korea	3.2	1.9
142	Global Crossing	21,872	3,834	5.7	2,803	NA	Bermuda	1.9	1.4
164	McLeodUSA	11,550	983	11.7	981	NA	USA	1.4	2.1
193	Mobilcom	6,098	1,518	4.0	1,487	NA	Germany	4.0	1.0
COMMUNICATIONS PRODUCTS									
1	Cisco Systems	395,554	16,819	23.5	16,170	91	USA	4.1	5.5
9	Nokia	244,940	23,770	10.3	19,523	77	Finland	2.2	2.4
19	QUALCOMM	49,190	3,912	12.6	3,717	81	USA	5.8	2.1
26	LM Ericsson	159,282	32,018	5.0	24,381	59	Sweden	2.8	1.2
28	Network Appliance	19,664	579	33.9	578	NA	USA	2.8	5.9
33	Nortel Networks	155,476	24,467	6.4	16,402	64	Canada	1.9	1.5
37	Lucent Technologies	183,341	40,051	4.6	20,871	NA	USA	2.4	1.1
39	CIENA	16,750	608	27.5	608	NA	USA	2.9	4.8
118	Comverse Technology	14,422	872	16.5	734	80	USA	1.7	2.5
152	Tellabs	26,412	2,489	10.6	2,159	51	USA	1.4	1.2
COMPUTERS, PERIPHERALS									
14	Dell Computer	111,554	25,265	4.4	22,463	118	USA	3.8	2.1
15	EMC	126,194	7,109	17.8	5,270	80	USA	1.4	6.0
25	Sun Microsystems	120,668	14,219	8.5	9,720	93	USA	1.2	4.1
31	Hewlett-Packard	120,143	45,381	2.6	28,273	34	USA	3.3	1.3
36	Palm	12,984	1,058	12.3	1,058	NA	USA	6.6	3.0
59	IBM	190,248	86,579	2.2	21,547	39	USA	2.5	1.1
SEMICONDUCTORS									
4	Intel	416,710	30,279	13.8	21,305	66	USA	6.4	1.5
11	JDS Uniphase	82,325	1,599	51.5	1,385	NA	USA	3.0	4.4
23	Broadcom	27,987	610	45.9	595	NA	USA	4.3	3.5
51	Taiwan Semiconductor	50,034	2,862	17.5	2,472	43	Taiwan	2.1	1.9
65	PMC-Sierra	22,312	315	70.8	223	128	USA	1.1	6.6
74	Applied Materials	66,924	7,126	9.4	5,665	70	USA	1.7	1.0
120	RF Micro Devices	8,440	289	29.2	288	NA	USA	2.3	2.5
145	Xilinx	24,458	1,021	24.0	764	66	USA	1.2	1.8
146	Altera	17,095	923	18.5	774	68	USA	2.1	1.3
147	Vitesse Semiconductor	8,334	343	24.3	324	114	USA	2.1	2.3
153	Maxim Integrated Products	17,890	768	23.3	642	65	USA	1.8	1.4
TECHNOLOGY – OTHER									
60	Murata Manufacturing	41,440	4,303	9.6	1,848	40	Japan	1.4	5.1
66	Solectron	19,665	10,173	1.9	8,904	54	USA	5.3	1.2
67	Agilent Technologies	33,280	9,266	3.6	3,720	NA	USA	3.6	2.3
84	Flextronics International	9,527	5,740	1.7	5,495	70	Singapore	8.7	1.0
116	TDK	16,487	9,262	1.8	5,241	19	Japan	5.1	1.1
124	Sawtek	3,178	124	25.7	108	NA	USA	2.0	8.8
126	Aixtron	4,320	90	48.2	90	NA	Germany	1.1	9.8
148	Jabil Circuit	6,440	2,586	2.5	2,238	124	USA	3.5	2.0
199	Sanmina	8,202	1,673	4.9	1,391	75	USA	1.8	1.9
PHARMACEUTICALS AND MEDICAL SUPPLIES									
13	Pfizer	277,438	29,922	9.3	16,967	47	USA	2.9	1.8
21	Amgen	65,977	3,409	19.4	2,035	49	USA	2.2	5.2
27	Medtronic	60,600	5,015	12.1	3,339	45	USA	3.8	2.4
46	Medimmune	10,807	446	24.2	431	133	USA	3.4	5.4
69	Eli Lilly	83,016	10,198	8.1	5,794	34	USA	1.3	1.7
75	Genentech	28,210	1,485	19.0	835	34	USA	1.2	4.5
79	Schering-Plough	71,067	9,396	7.6	5,167	37	USA	1.4	1.6
90	Bristol-Myers Squibb	108,796	20,601	5.3	9,188	29	USA	1.6	1.0

The Top 200 New Market Leaders (Part 4)

Overall rank	COMPANY (status on May 31, '00)	Market value $M	Sales latest 12 mos. $M	Market value/ sales ratio	Six-year sales growth $M	Annual investor return %	Country	Sales-change index	Market-value index
PHARMACEUTICALS AND MEDICAL SUPPLIES (CONT'D)									
102	Elan	11,420	1,098	10.4	991	31	Ireland	3.3	1.8
105	Immunex	12,952	623	20.8	500	76	USA	1.3	4.4
106	Millennium Pharmaceutical	7,650	206	37.1	196	NA	USA	1.9	4.3
111	Guidant	15,524	2,387	6.5	1,592	41	USA	1.9	2.8
168	King Pharmaceuticals	3,403	382	8.9	350	NA	USA	3.9	2.7
181	Biogen	8,226	840	9.8	703	36	USA	1.9	2.2
188	Andrx	3,795	514	7.4	503	NA	USA	4.4	1.6
200	Qiagen	5,630	144	39.1	129	NA	Netherlands	1.2	3.7
HEALTH CARE SERVICES									
99	**UnitedHealth**	**12,120**	**19,852**	**0.6**	**16,737**	**9**	**USA**	**4.8**	**1.3**
FINANCIAL SERVICES									
18	**Citigroup**	**209,864**	**85,192**	**2.5**	**39,702**	**24**	**USA**	**3.5**	**2.0**
24	**American Int'l Group**	**173,501**	**38,680**	**4.5**	**20,407**	**34**	**USA**	**1.4**	**3.5**
43	**Morgan Stanley**	**81,437**	**36,866**	**2.2**	**22,342**	**49**	**USA**	**2.9**	**1.6**
48	**Berkshire Hathaway**	**78,612**	**25,056**	**3.1**	**15,012**	**19**	**USA**	**2.2**	**2.1**
52	**Charles Schwab**	**42,295**	**4,803**	**8.8**	**3,392**	**73**	**USA**	**2.5**	**2.6**
56	**Wells Fargo**	**73,541**	**21,795**	**3.4**	**11,664**	**30**	**USA**	**2.2**	**2.1**
57	**Bank of America**	**92,646**	**59,188**	**1.6**	**32,729**	**20**	**USA**	**2.7**	**1.3**
73	**MBNA**	**22,350**	**6,470**	**3.5**	**5,077**	**40**	**USA**	**3.4**	**1.8**
80	**Fannie Mae**	**61,312**	**37,184**	**1.6**	**22,351**	**26**	**USA**	**2.2**	**1.2**
85	**Allianz**	**89,018**	**70,305**	**1.3**	**28,754**	**24**	**Germany**	**2.5**	**1.0**
86	**Marsh & McLennan**	**29,612**	**9,471**	**3.1**	**6,308**	**32**	**USA**	**1.9**	**2.4**
89	**Lloyds TSB**	**59,408**	**22,672**	**2.6**	**11,853**	**28**	**UK**	**1.6**	**1.8**
92	**E*Trade**	**4,540**	**944**	**4.8**	**922**	**NA**	**USA**	**10.2**	**1.9**
94	**Skandia Forsakring**	**26,138**	**16,009**	**1.6**	**9,852**	**70**	**Sweden**	**2.8**	**1.9**
96	**Firstar**	**24,780**	**6,424**	**3.9**	**4,520**	**42**	**USA**	**2.3**	**2.0**
107	Banco Santander Central	39,980	24,275	1.6	15,281	28	Spain	2.4	1.1
108	3i	11,272	531	21.2	354	28	UK	1.5	5.9
109	HSBC Holdings	93,703	39,348	2.4	12,233	25	UK	1.2	1.9
114	American Express	71,724	21,964	3.3	7,791	37	USA	1.2	2.1
121	First Union	34,750	22,084	1.6	14,095	14	USA	2.5	1.0
122	Groupe Bruxelles Lambert	5,850	1,710	3.4	1,583	15	Belgium	5.6	1.9
128	Chase Manhattan	61,580	34,475	1.8	17,581	33	USA	1.4	1.2
129	Concord EFS	5,148	918	5.6	842	45	USA	5.6	2.0
143	Unicredito Italiano	22,130	12,978	1.7	7,547	37	Italy	2.2	1.7
166	Associates First Capital	19,984	12,244	1.6	8,129	NA	USA	2.1	1.3
172	Munchener Ruckvers	51,859	33,444	1.6	17,048	33	Germany	1.2	1.1
179	Goldman Sachs	39,001	27,471	1.4	12,671	NA	USA	1.5	1.2
186	State Street	17,904	4,749	3.8	3,217	47	USA	2.4	1.0
190	Fifth Third Bancorp	21,030	3,615	5.8	2,355	35	USA	1.4	1.6
UTILITIES									
22	**Enron**	**53,243**	**45,625**	**1.2**	**37,058**	**35**	**USA**	**6.9**	**1.5**
115	Endesa	21,940	13,990	1.6	9,259	16	Spain	2.0	1.9
127	Duke Energy	21,405	24,800	0.9	16,032	12	USA	3.1	1.1
132	Scottish & Southern Energy	6,887	4,815	1.4	3,533	13	UK	5.5	1.6
138	Devon Energy	5,178	995	5.2	896	27	USA	2.8	3.2
170	El Paso Energy	11,804	11,410	1.0	8,760	27	USA	2.9	1.2
176	Scottish Power	14,518	6,501	2.2	3,962	12	UK	1.7	1.9
189	Tenaga Nasional Berhad	11,100	3,185	3.5	1,866	6	Malaysia	1.7	2.4
196	Gas Natural SDG	7,902	3,205	2.5	1,906	24	Spain	3.1	1.7
TOTALS:									
	Top 100 market leaders	**8,658,778**	**2,087,382**	**4.1**	**1,080,994**	**48**		**3.1**	**3.0**
	Top 200 market leaders	**10,640,450**	**3,057,375**	**2.8**	**1,511,197**	**43**		**2.7**	**2.8**
	All 640 market leaders	**12,702,003**	**4,397,556**	**2.4**	**2,154,144**	**30**		**2.0**	**2.1**
	All 5,009 companies	**27,875,175**	**17,163,000**	**1.6**	**6,409,408**	**14**		**1.0**	**1.0**

Exhibit 2

My research found 640 new market leaders worldwide, 226 of which are headquartered outside the U.S. In all, twenty-five of the 226 appear on the book's top 100 list.

This exhibit shows these twenty-five top-ranked leaders (in bold type) together with all other non-U.S. market leaders, sorted by region. Please note that while the research covered 1,256 of the more prominent companies outside the U.S., many others were omitted because the required data was missing or ambiguous.

The Non-U.S. Market Leaders (Part 1)

Rank by region	COMPANY (status on May 31, '00)	Market value $M	Sales latest 12 mos. $M	Market value/ sales ratio	Six-year sales growth $M	Category	Country	Sales-change index	Market-value index
AUSTRALIA									
1	Nat'l Australia Bank	22,255	12,487	1.8	5,748	Financial Services	Australia	1.2	1.7
2	Broken Hill Proprietary	18,008	14,450	1.2	3,922	Industrial–Materials	Australia	1.6	2.0
3	Lend Lease	5,807	2,378	2.4	1,624	Financial Services	Australia	1.5	1.1
4	Coca-Cola Amatil	1,944	2,488	0.8	1,228	Consumer Nondurables	Australia	1.6	1.2
5	Lihir Gold	324	208	1.6	208	Industrial–Materials	Australia	1.6	1.4
BELGIUM, NETHERLANDS, LUXEMBOURG									
1	**Royal Dutch/Shell**	**214,667**	**105,366**	**2.0**	**10,213**	**Energy–oil**	**Netherlands**	**2.8**	**1.4**
2	**Philips Electronics**	**60,102**	**34,799**	**1.7**	**9,964**	**Consumer Durables**	**Netherlands**	**2.6**	**1.7**
3	Groupe Bruxelles Lambert	5,850	1,710	3.4	1,583	Financial Services	Belgium	5.6	1.9
4	Heineken	16,010	6,567	2.4	2,774	Consumer Nondurables	Netherlands	2.3	2.7
5	Royal Numico	6,119	3,061	2.0	2,293	Consumer Nondurables	Netherlands	3.5	2.2
6	United Pan-Europe Comm.	11,100	810	13.7	718	Media and Entertainment	Netherlands	1.8	1.9
7	Qiagen	5,630	144	39.1	129	Pharmac. and Medical Suppl.	Netherlands	1.2	3.7
8	VNU	11,373	2,992	3.8	1,876	Media and Entertainment	Netherlands	1.6	1.0
9	TNT Post	11,454	8,963	1.3	2,952	Transportation and Logistics	Netherlands	1.2	2.0
10	Carrier1 International	3,312	136	24.3	136	Telco Services	Luxembourg	1.0	2.5
11	Tractebel	11,580	12,075	1.0	5,117	Utilities	Belgium	1.0	1.2
CANADA									
1	**Nortel Networks**	**155,476**	**24,467**	**6.4**	**16,402**	**Communications products**	**Canada**	**1.9**	**1.5**
2	**Bombardier**	**18,004**	**9,170**	**2.0**	**6,229**	**Industrial–Diversified**	**Canada**	**3.2**	**2.2**
3	Barrick Gold	7,237	1,363	5.3	772	Industrial–Materials	Canada	1.4	3.7
4	Potash /Saskatchewan	3,039	2,102	1.4	1,885	Industrial–Materials	Canada	4.9	1.5
5	Abitibi + Donohue	5,487	4,398	1.2	2,913	Industrial–Materials	Canada	3.2	1.7
6	Alberta Energy	5,456	2,162	2.5	1,712	Utilities	Canada	2.1	2.0
7	Enbridge	3,595	1,819	2.0	1,582	Utilities	Canada	3.8	1.5
8	Toronto-Dominion Bank	15,562	10,491	1.5	6,286	Financial Services	Canada	1.5	1.2
9	Celestica	9,411	5,297	1.8	2,817	Technology–Other	Canada	2.7	1.1
10	PanCanadian Petr.	5,716	2,608	2.2	1,851	Energy–oil	Canada	2.0	1.7
11	Royal Bank of Canada	15,822	13,255	1.2	7,215	Financial Services	Canada	1.6	1.2
12	BCE Emergis	4,741	126	37.6	126	Software and I/T Services	Canada	1.0	2.5
13	Canadian Pacific	7,616	7,694	1.0	3,886	Transportation and Logistics	Canada	2.2	1.5
14	Biovail	3,378	190	17.8	178	Pharmac. and Medical Suppl.	Canada	1.5	2.1
15	Magna International	3,675	9,347	0.4	7,461	Automotive	Canada	3.0	1.1
16	Talisman Energy	4,427	1,337	3.3	1,138	Energy–oil	Canada	1.6	1.4
17	Loblaw Companies	8,029	12,648	0.6	6,738	Retail, Intermediaries	Canada	1.7	1.2
18	Canadian Natural Res.	3,362	741	4.5	642	Energy–oil	Canada	2.6	1.1
19	BioChem Pharma	2,402	206	11.7	188	Pharmac. and Medical Suppl.	Canada	2.4	1.4
20	C-MAC Industries	3,072	791	3.9	641	Technology–Other	Canada	1.6	1.4
21	Canadian Occidental Pet.	3,400	1,147	3.0	761	Energy–oil	Canada	2.1	1.2
22	Precision Drilling	1,812	466	3.9	418	Energy–oil	Canada	2.9	1.1
23	Creo Products	991	218	4.6	218	Industrial–Diversified	Canada	1.2	3.8
24	Research In Motion	2,675	85	31.5	85	Telco Services	Canada	1.0	1.3
25	Mackenzie Financial	1,913	499	3.8	384	Financial Services	Canada	1.5	1.1
26	Gildan Activewear	457	231	2.0	212	Consumer Nondurables	Canada	1.9	2.4
27	Dupont Canada	2,858	1,491	1.9	503	Industrial–Materials	Canada	1.2	1.5
28	Kinross Gold	321	318	1.0	289	Industrial–Materials	Canada	3.8	1.5
29	Descartes Systems	1,235	46	26.6	46	Software and I/T Services	Canada	1.0	1.1
30	Cameco	823	502	1.6	318	Industrial–Materials	Canada	1.1	1.6
31	Cinram	329	448	0.7	380	Consumer Durables	Canada	2.2	1.2
32	Cominco	1,216	1,137	1.1	522	Industrial–Materials	Canada	1.1	1.0
FRANCE									
1	**Vivendi**	**64,020**	**42,079**	**1.5**	**18,124**	**Business Services**	**France**	**2.6**	**2.8**
2	**L'Oreal**	**46,112**	**11,399**	**4.0**	**4,881**	**Consumer Nondurables**	**France**	**3.2**	**3.0**
3	Altran Technologies	6,709	719	9.3	624	Mngt. and Advisory Svcs.	France	1.3	5.9
4	Canal Plus	23,753	3,052	7.8	1,633	Media and Entertainment	France	1.4	2.1
5	Carrefour-Promodes	49,122	55,340	0.9	20,705	Retail, Intermediaries	France	1.5	1.0
6	Pinault-Printemps-Redoute	25,499	20,136	1.3	9,911	Retail, Intermediaries	France	1.2	1.7
7	LaFarge	8,082	11,145	0.7	6,216	Industrial–Materials	France	3.2	1.5
8	Dassault Systems	8,540	532	16.1	403	Software and I/T Services	France	1.0	3.1
9	Hermes International	4,950	988	5.0	525	Consumer Durables	France	1.2	6.2

The Non-U.S. Market Leaders (Part 2)

Rank by region	COMPANY (status as of May 2000)	Market value $M	Sales latest 12 mos. $M	Market value/ sales ratio	Six-year sales growth $M	Category	Country	Sales-change index	Market-value index
FRANCE (CONT'D)									
10	Business Objects S.A.	3,718	265	14.0	254	Software and I/T Services	France	1.4	3.0
11	Bouygues	20,008	16,892	1.2	1,141	Construction, public works	France	2.7	2.9
12	Havas + Snyder	5,497	1,954	2.8	1,242	Mngt. and Advisory Svcs.	France	1.7	1.2
13	Sidel	2,594	935	2.8	642	Industrial–Diversified	France	1.2	2.9
14	L'Air Liquide	11,567	6,921	1.7	1,991	Industrial–Materials	France	1.0	1.7
15	Valeo	4,217	8,169	0.5	4,886	Automotive	France	1.9	1.1
16	Coflexip	1,803	972	1.9	638	Industrial–Materials	France	1.1	2.6
GERMANY									
1	**SAP**	**48,102**	**5,166**	**9.3**	**4,571**	**Software and I/T Services**	**Germany**	**3.0**	**1.4**
2	**Allianz**	**89,018**	**70,305**	**1.3**	**28,754**	**Financial Services**	**Germany**	**2.5**	**1.0**
3	Aixtron	4,320	90	48.2	90	Technology–Other	Germany	1.1	9.8
4	BMW	20,231	36,370	0.6	20,416	Automotive	Germany	2.2	1.2
5	Munchener Ruckvers	51,859	33,444	1.6	17,048	Financial Services	Germany	1.2	1.1
6	Mobilcom	6,098	1,518	4.0	1,487	Telco Services	Germany	4.0	1.0
7	Heidelberger Druckmasch.	5,590	4,747	1.2	3,111	Industrial–Diversified	Germany	4.0	1.7
8	Bayer	28,041	28,920	1.0	6,745	Industrial–Materials	Germany	1.9	1.3
9	BASF	24,976	31,199	0.8	7,880	Industrial–Materials	Germany	2.2	1.1
10	Henkel KGAA	7,940	12,026	0.7	4,485	Industrial–Materials	Germany	2.8	1.3
11	Porsche	4,554	3,509	1.3	2,247	Automotive	Germany	1.2	2.7
12	Beiersdorf	6,466	3,678	1.8	1,102	Consumer Nondurables	Germany	1.3	2.0
13	Linde	4,779	6,262	0.8	2,361	Industrial–Diversified	Germany	1.4	1.2
14	PrimaCom	773	115	6.7	115	Media and Entertainment	Germany	1.1	1.5
IRELAND									
1	Elan	11,420	1,098	10.4	991	Pharmac. and Medical Suppl.	Ireland	3.3	1.8
2	CRH Public	6,753	6,239	1.1	4,308	Industrial–Materials	Ireland	3.1	1.1
3	Kerry	2,165	2,601	0.8	1,410	Consumer Nondurables	Ireland	1.7	1.1
ITALY									
1	Unicredito Italiano	22,130	12,978	1.7	7,547	Financial Services	Italy	2.2	1.7
2	Luxottica	5,188	1,684	3.1	1,388	Consumer Nondurables	Italy	2.8	2.2
3	Alleanza Assicuraz	8,927	3,356	2.7	2,151	Financial Services	Italy	1.5	1.9
4	Edison	5,673	1,564	3.6	1,116	Utilities	Italy	1.4	2.4
5	Industrie Natuzzi	708	556	1.3	347	Consumer Durables	Italy	1.5	1.3
JAPAN									
1	**NTT DoCoMo**	**247,200**	**33,381**	**7.4**	**23,182**	**Telco Services**	**Japan**	**2.3**	**2.2**
2	**Sony**	**80,800**	**60,053**	**1.3**	**26,514**	**Consumer Durables**	**Japan**	**6.8**	**1.3**
3	**Softbank**	**50,612**	**4,905**	**10.3**	**4,347**	**Software and I/T Services**	**Japan**	**3.3**	**2.1**
4	**Toyota Motor**	**170,214**	**115,671**	**1.5**	**30,300**	**Automotive**	**Japan**	**1.8**	**3.3**
5	**Murata Manufacturing**	**41,440**	**4,303**	**9.6**	**1,848**	**Technology–Other**	**Japan**	**1.4**	**5.1**
6	Trend Micro	9,678	121	80.0	120	Software and I/T Services	Japan	1.1	5.1
7	TDK	16,487	9,262	1.8	5,241	Technology–Other	Japan	5.1	1.1
8	Shin-Etsu Chemical	20,512	6,362	3.2	2,279	Industrial–Materials	Japan	1.1	3.4
9	Ryohin Keikaku	4,088	941	4.3	664	Consumer Nondurables	Japan	1.5	5.7
10	Denso	20,761	17,650	1.2	5,472	Automotive	Japan	1.0	3.2
11	Honda	32,126	54,774	0.6	20,070	Automotive	Japan	1.2	1.3
12	THK	5,538	915	6.1	423	Industrial–Diversified	Japan	1.1	6.3
13	Fuji Television Network	16,358	3,829	4.3	1,518	Media and Entertainment	Japan	1.1	1.7
14	Oji Paper	6,483	10,826	0.6	4,995	Industrial–Materials	Japan	2.9	1.2
15	Aiful	7,419	2,098	3.5	1,420	Financial Services	Japan	1.2	1.7
16	Yamato Transport	10,391	7,613	1.4	2,645	Transportation and Logistics	Japan	1.1	2.0
17	Konami	5,942	1,290	4.6	929	Software and I/T Services	Japan	1.3	1.3
18	ORIX	11,531	5,777	2.0	3,038	Financial Services	Japan	1.2	1.0
19	Sharp	20,297	17,381	1.2	4,282	Consumer Durables	Japan	1.1	1.2
20	Ito En	3,157	1,376	2.3	725	Consumer Nondurables	Japan	1.6	2.3
21	Kinki Nippon Railway	6,483	10,701	0.6	4,282	Transportation and Logistics	Japan	1.6	1.1
22	Matsushita Electric Works	8,303	10,504	0.8	1,794	Industrial–Materials	Japan	1.3	1.5
23	Sekisui House	6,956	11,769	0.6	618	Construction, public works	Japan	1.5	1.5
24	Daiwa House Industry	3,883	8,913	0.4	622	Construction, public works	Japan	1.5	1.1
MEXICO									
1	Wal-Mart de Mexico	9,346	6,456	1.4	4,965	Retail, Intermediaries	Mexico	1.4	3.4
2	Grupo Modelo	7,171	2,576	2.8	1,910	Consumer Nondurables	Mexico	1.7	3.7
3	CEMEX	6,120	4,808	1.3	3,862	Industrial–Materials	Mexico	3.2	1.9

The Non-U.S. Market Leaders (Part 3)

Rank by region	COMPANY (status as of May 2000)	Market value $M	Sales latest 12 mos. $M	Market value/ sales ratio	Six-year sales growth $M	Category	Country	Sales-change index	Market-value index
MEXICO (CONT'D)									
4	FEMSA	4,380	4,093	1.1	3,246	Consumer Nondurables	Mexico	3.2	1.2
5	Grupo Televisa, S.A.	9,841	1,884	5.2	1,550	Media and Entertainment	Mexico	1.3	1.3
6	Kimberly Clark de Mexico	3,974	1,435	2.8	1,097	Consumer Nondurables	Mexico	1.3	2.9
7	Coca-Cola FEMSA, S.A.	2,467	1,488	1.7	1,381	Consumer Nondurables	Mexico	2.5	1.5
8	Grupo Mexico	1,829	1,815	1.0	1,524	Industrial–Materials	Mexico	2.4	1.3
9	Panamerican Beverages	1,997	2,461	0.8	2,099	Consumer Nondurables	Mexico	1.9	1.2
10	Tubos de Acero de Mexico	955	617	1.5	538	Industrial–Materials	Mexico	1.5	1.9
11	Grupo Elektra, SA de CV	1,081	900	1.2	803	Retail, Intermediaries	Mexico	1.3	1.3
NORDIC REGION									
1	**Nokia**	**244,940**	**23,770**	**10.3**	**19,523**	**Communications products**	**Finland**	**2.2**	**2.4**
2	**LM Ericsson**	**159,282**	**32,018**	**5.0**	**24,381**	**Communications products**	**Sweden**	**2.8**	**1.2**
3	**Hennes & Mauritz**	**20,902**	**3,375**	**6.2**	**2,217**	**Retail, Intermediaries**	**Sweden**	**1.3**	**6.9**
4	**Skandia Forsakring**	**26,138**	**16,009**	**1.6**	**9,852**	**Financial Services**	**Sweden**	**2.8**	**1.9**
5	Assa Abloy	6,269	1,244	5.0	818	Industrial–Diversified	Sweden	1.8	3.0
6	Volvo	10,374	15,135	0.7	8,317	Automotive	Sweden	2.1	1.7
7	Netcom AB	7,317	989	7.4	989	Telco Services	Sweden	1.2	1.4
8	Europolitan	6,529	531	12.3	506	Telco Services	Sweden	1.2	1.6
9	Skanska	4,253	9,328	0.5	5,239	Construction, public works	Sweden	4.0	1.1
10	Novo-Nordisk A/S	12,416	3,128	4.0	1,600	Pharmac. and Medical Suppl.	Denmark	1.5	1.0
11	Scania (A + B)	4,993	5,553	0.9	3,132	Automotive	Sweden	1.3	1.8
12	Sandvik (A + B)	5,640	4,749	1.2	2,110	Industrial–Diversified	Sweden	1.2	1.6
13	Atlas Copco (A + B)	4,600	4,367	1.1	2,078	Industrial–Diversified	Sweden	1.2	1.5
14	Orkla	3,636	4,017	0.9	1,663	Consumer Nondurables	Norway	1.7	1.1
OTHER									
	Global Crossing	21,872	3,834	5.7	2,803	Telco Services	Bermuda	1.9	1.4
	Sonae, SGPS SA	3,206	4,366	0.7	3,155	Retail, Intermediaries	Portugal	3.4	1.0
	Teva Pharmaceutical Ind.	6,500	1,200	5.4	856	Pharmac. and Medical Suppl.	Israel	1.2	1.2
	RenaissanceRe Holdings	835	266	3.1	228	Financial Services	Bermuda	5.2	1.6
	Hellenic Bottling	2,259	1,395	1.6	1,001	Consumer Nondurables	Greece	1.7	1.6
	Nice Systems	738	124	6.0	120	Technology–Other	Israel	1.2	2.1
	Triton Energy	1,073	248	4.3	188	Energy–oil	Cayman Isl.	1.2	1.5
	Steiner Leisure	354	139	2.6	119	Consumer Nondurables	Bahamas	1.1	2.8
SOUTH AFRICA									
1	Anglogold	4,252	2,201	1.9	1,722	Industrial–Materials	South Africa	3.0	2.1
2	Anglo American Platinum	5,981	1,394	4.3	933	Industrial–Materials	South Africa	1.5	3.0
3	De Beers Consol. Mines	8,269	5,627	1.5	3,201	Industrial–Materials	South Africa	1.5	2.0
4	Nedcor	4,529	3,215	1.4	1,980	Financial Services	South Africa	1.0	1.2
5	Sasol	3,985	3,407	1.2	1,927	Energy–oil	South Africa	1.2	1.1
SOUTH AMERICA									
1	Petrobras	27,650	16,351	1.7	8,048	Energy–oil	Brazil	2.5	1.3
2	Vale do Rio Doce	10,056	3,787	2.7	2,133	Industrial–Materials	Brazil	1.4	3.6
3	Eletrobras	9,725	5,936	1.6	3,953	Utilities	Brazil	1.4	1.4
4	Embraer	2,159	1,772	1.2	1,695	Industrial–Diversified	Brazil	3.8	1.4
5	Comp. Cervej. Brahma	5,223	1,794	2.9	1,114	Consumer Nondurables	Brazil	1.2	2.0
6	Banco Itau	9,762	8,490	1.1	4,946	Financial Services	Brazil	1.4	1.1
7	Companhia Siderurgica	2,360	1,630	1.4	1,288	Industrial–Materials	Brazil	2.3	1.4
8	Copec	5,653	3,129	1.8	1,491	Energy–oil	Chile	1.1	1.7
9	Aracruz Celulose	1,803	474	3.8	303	Industrial–Materials	Brazil	1.0	3.6
10	Distribucion y Servicio	1,660	1,081	1.5	765	Retail, Intermediaries	Chile	1.1	2.0
11	Banco Rio de la Plata	2,378	1,366	1.7	953	Financial Services	Argentina	1.2	1.3
SOUTHEAST ASIA									
1	**Taiwan Semiconductor**	**50,034**	**2,862**	**17.5**	**2,472**	**Semiconductor**	**Taiwan**	**2.1**	**1.9**
2	**Infosys Technologies**	**11,202**	**203**	**55.1**	**197**	**Software and I/T Services**	**India**	**2.1**	**3.7**
3	**Flextronics International**	**9,527**	**5,740**	**1.7**	**5,495**	**Technology–Other**	**Singapore**	**8.7**	**1.0**
4	Reliance Industries	8,001	2,022	4.0	1,451	Industrial–Materials	India	2.3	4.0
5	Johnson Electric	6,888	465	14.8	271	Industrial–Diversified	Hong Kong	1.1	9.8
6	Nan Ya Plastic	10,440	4,231	2.5	2,135	Industrial–Materials	Taiwan	1.9	3.6
7	Tenaga Nasional Berhad	11,100	3,185	3.5	1,866	Utilities	Malaysia	1.7	2.4
8	Venture Manufacturing	2,399	512	4.7	450	Technology–Other	Singapore	3.3	3.0
9	Citic Pacific	10,600	3,405	3.1	1,916	Retail, Intermediaries	Hong Kong	1.1	3.1
10	DBS Holdings	13,711	2,727	5.0	1,606	Financial Services	Singapore	1.1	2.3

The Non-U.S. Market Leaders (Part 4)

Rank by region	COMPANY (status as of May 2000)	Market value $M	Sales latest 12 mos. $M	Market value/ sales ratio	Six-year sales growth $M	Category	Country	Sales-change index	Market-value index
SOUTHEAST ASIA (CONT'D)									
11	ASE Test	2,132	276	7.7	252	Technology–Other	Taiwan	2.1	2.9
12	Singapore Airlines	10,678	5,189	2.1	1,586	Transportation and Logistics	Singapore	1.1	3.3
13	Compeq Manuf.	3,322	541	6.1	410	Technology–Other	Taiwan	1.0	3.7
14	ST Assembly Test Serv.	3,383	237	14.3	237	Semiconductor	Singapore	2.0	1.1
15	Formosa Chemicals	4,535	1,450	3.1	651	Industrial–Materials	Taiwan	1.3	2.3
16	Overseas Union Bank	3,839	1,383	2.8	814	Financial Services	Singapore	1.2	2.0
17	Oil & Natural Gas Corp	4,075	4,609	0.9	2,591	Energy–oil	India	1.6	1.2
18	Keppel Corp	1,765	2,412	0.7	1,507	Industrial–Diversified	Singapore	2.2	1.3
19	Gudang Garam	2,823	1,701	1.7	1,182	Consumer Nondurables	Indonesia	1.2	1.4
SOUTH KOREA									
1	**SK Telecom**	**30,380**	**3,786**	**8.0**	**3,426**	**Telco Services**	**South Korea**	3.2	1.9
2	Pohang Iron & Steel	7,911	10,684	0.7	4,863	Industrial–Materials	South Korea	3.4	1.4
3	Samsung Electro-Mech.	4,867	2,136	2.3	1,520	Technology–Other	South Korea	1.3	1.3
SPAIN									
1	Banco Santander Central	39,980	24,275	1.6	15,281	Financial Services	Spain	2.4	1.1
2	Endesa	21,940	13,990	1.6	9,259	Utilities	Spain	2.0	1.9
3	Gas Natural SDG	7,902	3,205	2.5	1,906	Utilities	Spain	3.1	1.7
4	Acerinox S.A.	1,921	1,524	1.3	922	Industrial–Materials	Spain	1.8	1.1
SWITZERLAND									
1	Nestle	74,285	49,377	1.5	10,992	Consumer Nondurables	Switzerland	2.3	1.1
2	Adecco	13,858	12,145	1.1	7,704	Business Services	Switzerland	1.2	2.8
3	Richemont	12,935	7,842	1.6	2,114	Consumer Nondurables	Switzerland	1.4	1.3
4	Holderb. Finanicere Glaris	9,851	7,702	1.3	2,159	Industrial–Materials	Switzerland	1.0	1.7
UK									
1	**Vodafone AirTouch**	**280,126**	**37,065**	**7.6**	**15,471**	**Telco Services**	**UK**	1.3	2.2
2	**British Sky Broadcasting**	**34,809**	**2,687**	**13.0**	**1,797**	**Media and Entertainment**	**UK**	1.6	3.1
3	**Sage Group**	**12,375**	**616**	**20.1**	**540**	**Software and I/T Services**	**UK**	2.2	3.6
4	**Lloyds TSB**	**59,408**	**22,672**	**2.6**	**11,853**	**Financial Services**	**UK**	1.6	1.8
5	3i	11,272	531	21.2	354	Financial Services	UK	1.5	5.9
6	HSBC Holdings	93,703	39,348	2.4	12,233	Financial Services	UK	1.2	1.9
7	Hays	9,662	3,060	3.2	2,163	Transportation and Logistics	UK	2.0	4.3
8	TeleWest	11,982	1,624	7.4	1,499	Media and Entertainment	UK	3.4	1.3
9	Granada	16,565	6,887	2.4	4,257	Hospitality, Foodservice	UK	2.3	1.9
10	Scottish & Southern En.	6,887	4,815	1.4	3,533	Utilities	UK	5.5	1.6
11	Reuters	21,147	5,057	4.2	2,024	Mngt. and Advisory Svcs.	UK	2.8	1.8
12	Capita	4,850	529	9.2	462	Business Services	UK	1.1	9.2
13	Scottish Power	14,518	6,501	2.2	3,962	Utilities	UK	1.7	1.9
14	Logica	10,886	1,107	9.8	784	Software and I/T Services	UK	1.3	2.6
15	AMVESCAP	8,841	1,914	4.6	1,428	Financial Services	UK	1.7	2.3
16	Tesco	20,482	29,612	0.7	15,691	Retail, Intermediaries	UK	1.8	1.0
17	Compass	7,578	7,823	1.0	6,425	Business Services	UK	2.7	1.1
18	CMG	8,310	983	8.5	790	Software and I/T Services	UK	1.5	1.6
19	Abbey National .	18,905	17,072	1.1	8,267	Financial Services	UK	1.6	1.2
20	Marconi	32,124	13,546	2.4	3,276	Industrial–Diversified	UK	1.1	1.9
21	WPP	14,157	5,298	2.7	1,830	Mngt. and Advisory Svcs.	UK	2.6	1.2
22	Halifax	22,063	14,456	1.5	5,789	Financial Services	UK	1.2	1.6
23	Pearson	18,720	5,392	3.5	2,366	Media and Entertainment	UK	1.2	1.2
24	Smiths Industries	3,834	2,167	1.8	969	Industrial–Diversified	UK	1.5	3.7
25	Bank of Scotland	11,677	8,821	1.3	4,875	Financial Services	UK	1.2	1.2
26	Berisford	1,209	1,223	1.0	1,095	Consumer Nondurables	UK	6.2	1.2
27	Scottish & Newcastle	5,382	5,796	0.9	2,939	Consumer Nondurables	UK	2.8	1.0
28	Shire Pharmaceuticals	3,657	650	5.6	553	Pharmac. and Medical Suppl.	UK	1.6	1.3
29	Serco	2,933	1,082	2.7	779	Business Services	UK	1.4	2.0
30	Next	2,814	2,144	1.3	1,351	Retail, Intermediaries	UK	1.8	1.6
31	Schroders	4,738	3,208	1.5	1,990	Financial Services	UK	1.5	1.2
32	Great Universal Store	6,246	9,186	0.7	4,061	Retail, Intermediaries	UK	1.1	1.4
33	Trinity Mirror	2,665	986	2.7	768	Media and Entertainment	UK	1.7	1.1
34	British Land	3,111	805	3.9	478	Financial Services	UK	1.4	1.3
35	Wetherspoon (J.D.)	1,078	436	2.5	373	Hospitality, Foodservice	UK	1.4	1.9
36	Ocean	2,536	2,866	0.9	1,324	Transportation and Logistics	UK	1.0	1.2
37	Mayflower Corp	622	1,091	0.6	928	Automotive	UK	1.3	1.1

Appendix Two

The most recent ranking of the database follows. It shows the companies' status on March 16, 2001, when the stock market was at its lowest level in several years. And, as one can see, despite the market's drop, our new market leaders are sustaining themselves very well. I attribute this to the fact that we're comparing each company with its peers—that is, *every company* is affected, so only changes in position relative to the peer group will register. In sum, the leaders' intrinsic strengths help them weather the storm.

- 85 out of the top 100 market leaders continue as market leaders.

- Even companies whose stock prices tumbled precipitously continued to outperform their peers. For example:

- Cisco dropped from number 1 to number 3 in the context of a drop in its market value of 63 percent since my May 31, 2000, ranking.

- Yahoo and Amazon remained in the top 100, even though their stock prices were hammered.

- Nokia, which moved up to number 5 despite a stock price drop, benefited from the strategic setbacks of some of its peers.

- Among the companies that lost their market leadership role, Coca-Cola, HP, Toyota, and Lucent experienced strategic setbacks, not stock market woes; only two dropouts (Priceline.com and Softbank) tumbled because the stock market collapsed.

- The point is that the stock market alone is a good barometer neither of companies' competitive strengths nor of their influence in the marketplace. Viewing companies' performance relative to their peers yields far more robust and meaningful insights.

COMPANY	Rank in book May 31, 2000	Current rank March 16, 2001	Notes
Top 100 companies that continue to be market leaders (85 out of 100)			
Cisco Systems	1	3	
General Electric	2	1	
Microsoft	3	2	
Intel	4	8	
Yahoo!	5	86	
Home Depot	6	7	
Wal-Mart Stores	7	6	
Oracle	8	24	
Nokia	9	5	
AOL-Time Warner	10	9	
JDS Uniphase	11	12	
NTT DoCoMo	12	11	
Pfizer	13	10	
Dell Computer	14	22	
EMC	15	28	
Sprint PCS Group	16	18	
Amazon.com	17	80	
Citigroup	18	16	
QUALCOMM	19	13	
Nextel Communications	20	74	
Amgen	21	20	
Enron Corp.	22	19	
Broadcom	23	50	
American Int'l Group	24	15	
Sun Microsystems	25	54	
Medtronic	27	23	
Network Appliance	28	90	
Vodafone Group	29	4	

COMPANY	Rank in book May 31, 2000	Current rank March 16, 2001	Notes
Sony	30	47	
Nortel Networks	33	81	
United Parcel Service	35	25	
Palm	36	70	
i2 Technologies	38	97	
CIENA	39	34	
Paychex	41	64	
Siebel Systems	42	27	
Morgan Stanley	43	63	
Vivendi	44	21	Reclassified as media
McDonald's	45	94	
MedImmune	46	73	
L'Oreal	47	31	
Berkshire Hathaway	48	40	
SAP AG	49	67	
Gap	50	44	
Taiwan Semiconductor	51	30	
Charles Schwab	52	66	
Tyco Int'l.	53	43	
Viacom	54	39	Includes Infinity B/casting
Wells Fargo	56	61	
Gemstar-TV Guide	58	88	
IBM	59	100	
Murata Mfg.	60	75	
Hennes & Mauritz	61	59	
EchoStar Communications	62	37	
British Sky Broadcasting	63	92	
DuPont	64	139	
PMC-Sierra	65	159	
Solectron	66	35	
Agilent Technologies	67	191	
Ariba	68	210	
Eli Lilly	69	51	
Schlumberger	70	84	
Infinity Broadcasting	71	39	Now part of Viacom
Kohl's	72	38	
MBNA	73	79	
Genentech	75	82	
Comcast	76	55	
Sage Group	77	301	
Schering-Plough	79	76	
Fannie Mae	80	53	
Bombardier	81	68	
Royal Dutch-Shell	82	89	
Infosys Technologies	83	45	
Flextronics Int'l	84	48	
Marsh & McLennan	86	85	
Amdocs	88	46	
Bristol-Myers Squibb	90	93	
Philips Electronics	91	56	
E*TRADE Group	92	250	
Cox Communications	93	65	
Carnival	95	99	
Firstar	96	72	Part of U.S. Bancorp

COMPANY	Rank in book May 31, 2000	Current rank March 16, 2001	Notes
Walgreen	97	36	
At Home	98	268	
Omnicom	100	128	

Companies currently lagging their peers (15 out of 100)

LM Ericsson	26	lagging
Hewlett-Packard	31	lagging
Softbank Corp.	32	lagging
Toyota Motor	34	lagging
Lucent Technologies	37	lagging
Coca-Cola	40	lagging
SK Telecom	55	lagging
Bank of America	57	lagging
Applied Materials	74	lagging
priceline.com	78	lagging
Allianz	85	lagging
Walt Disney	87	lagging
Lloyds TSB Group	89	lagging
Skandia Forsakring	94	lagging
UnitedHealth	99	lagging

Newcomers to the current top 100

Elan	102	42	
BEA Systems	104	29	
Immunex	105	58	
Reliance Industries	117	98	
Duke Energy	127	52	
Concord EFS	129	33	
Nestle	144	41	
Vitesse Semiconductor	147	78	
Tellabs	152	62	
Fifth Third Bancorp	190	57	
Household Int'l	243	87	
U.S. Bancorp	256	72	Includes Firstar
Celestica	267	77	
Merck & Co.	lagging	14	
Juniper Networks	lagging	17	
Check Point Software	lagging	26	
Hutchinson Whampoa	lagging	32	
COLT Telecom	lagging	49	
ADP	lagging	60	
UBS	lagging	69	
Telefonica	lagging	71	
eBay	lagging	83	
SBC Communications	lagging	91	
Novartis	lagging	95	
TOTAL Fina Elf	lagging	96	

Acknowledgments

As was the case with my previous books, the single most important source of inspiration for this work has been my interactions with thousands of leading-edge business practitioners. They represented a highly diverse cross section of companies from around the world. Whether or not they were featured in the book, their action-flavored perspectives helped me separate what's real from what's speculative and to size up what's imminently practical and what's out of reach. I am extremely appreciative of their willingness to share their perspectives and experiences.

Unlike the prior works, this effort has benefited from the vast amount of information available on the Internet. My thanks go to the many companies whose Web sites helped to convert a Herculean research effort into a manageable and ultimately much richer investigation.

Also as with my previous books, my heartfelt thanks go to the writers, editors, and researchers at Wordworks, Inc.—among them Donna Carpenter, Maurice Coyle, Deborah Horvitz, Larry Martz, Toni Porcelli, Cindy Sammons, Robert W. Stock, and Ellen Wojahn. Deep gratitude also goes to my agent, Helen Rees, and to Fred Hills, my editor at Simon & Schuster, both of whom recognized this book's potential well before it was completed.

Finally, I want to acknowledge the steadfast support of the most precious people in my life—my wife and my daughter. It is to them that I dedicate this book.

Index

(Page numbers in *italic* refer to figures and exhibits.)

Index